Dear Reader:

The book you are about to rea[...] Martin's True Crime Library, t[...] "the leader in true crime!" Eac[...] you a fascinating account of the latest, most sensational crime that has captured the national attention. St. Martin's is the publisher of Tina Dirmann's VANISHED AT SEA, the story of a former child actor who posed as a yacht buyer in order to lure an older couple out to sea, then robbed them and threw them overboard to their deaths. John Glatt's riveting and horrifying SECRETS IN THE CELLAR shines a light on the man who shocked the world when it was revealed that he had kept his daughter locked in his hidden basement for 24 years. In the Edgar-nominated WRITTEN IN BLOOD, Diane Fanning looks at Michael Petersen, a Marine-turned-novelist found guilty of beating his wife to death and pushing her down the stairs of their home—only to reveal another similar death from his past. In the book you now hold, IN THE ARMS OF EVIL, acclaimed author Carlton Smith unveils a true story of fraud, deception, greed—and cold-case murder...

St. Martin's True Crime Library gives you the stories behind the headlines. Our authors take you right to the scene of the crime and into the minds of the most notorious murderers to show you what really makes them tick. St. Martin's True Crime Library paperbacks are better than the most terrifying thriller, because it's all true! The next time you want a crackling good read, make sure it's got the St. Martin's True Crime Library logo on the spine—you'll be up all night!

Charles E. Spicer, Jr.
Executive Editor, St. Martin's True Crime Library

Other True Crime Titles From

# CARLTON SMITH

Available from the True Crime Library of
St. Martin's Paperbacks

# IN THE ARMS OF EVIL

*Carlton Smith*

St. Martin's Paperbacks

IN THE ARMS OF EVIL

Copyright © 2010 by Carlton Smith.

Cover photograph courtesy Masterfile Royalty-Free.

For information address St. Martin's Press, 175 Fifth Avenue, New York, NY 10010.

EAN: 978-0-312-94802-3

Printed in the United States of America

St. Martin's Paperbacks edition / April 2010

St. Martin's Paperbacks are published by St. Martin's Press, 175 Fifth Avenue, New York, NY 10010.

10  9  8  7  6  5  4  3  2  1

**Grifter** *noun* A person given a concession with a circus or carnival to run a freak show or refreshment stand, or operate a game of chance, etc.
*Britannica World Language Dictionary*, 1956

**Grifter** *noun* A confidence trickster or fraud artist, thought to be an Irish-American slang amalgamation of the words "grafter" and "drifter" From ca. 1915—

# FOREWORD

It is often said that gambling is a disease, and so it is. Where many people believe that gambling is a moral vice—and it is—few perceive its truly pernicious effects for the truly consumed. Like alcohol or drugs for the most afflicted, the lure of chance is often something from which some people simply can't walk away. "Just say no" was a great slogan, but it doesn't begin to address the underlying compulsions that drive people to make bad, even fatal choices, whether for drugs, sex, alcohol or money. Who among us hasn't known someone who has succumbed to one or more of these?

Gambling can be particularly seductive. The exultation, the personal validation that winning brings—the high—can seize a soul as surely as the purest heroin. And the losing—in gambling, the house always has the edge, which means that sooner or later, even the luckiest winner has to lose—can drive a human being to the most desperate of choices.

Even murder.

This is the story of Nancy Jean Siegel, a beautiful woman who succumbed to the lures of the God or Goddess of Chance, certainly a Devilish illusion, if statistics have any validity. By the time Nancy was tapped out—morally, at least, if not yet financially—a man was dead, and Nancy was facing the prospect of dying of old age in a federal penitentiary, far away from those she held most dear. The road of Nancy's life was filled with many twists and turns—many choices—but at almost every critical juncture, she chose the wrong path. She cheated her husbands, her friends, her own children—but most of all, herself. And even as she sat in the dock, accused of murder, almost everyone who knew her said they loved her still.

Nancy Siegel wasn't "born evil," or "evil incarnate," as some people like to characterize others. The Devil didn't creep into her mother's bed one night to spawn her. She wasn't Rosemary's baby. Nancy just got herself in a jam, admittedly all of her own doing, and then things went from bad to their ultimate, dreadful worst. Evil wasn't thrust upon her, nor was it in her stars. She did it to herself, by her choices, as Shakespeare intuited, by her own free will, and it could have happened to anyone who lost sight of what was truly important.

Even you and me. So we should all put down our stones—and maybe think a little about where "evil" comes from. Does it come from outside? Or is it in ourselves, and if so, why? Ethical people want to know.

*Selah.*

# PART I
## THE LOVE GRIFTER

# 1
# AT THE RIVER

The late model black BMW had been on the road for more than an hour. Its driver had taken the turn-off from I-70 at Frederick, heading southwest on Route 340 toward West Virginia. It was dark, the traffic sparse for the time of night, around 10 P.M. The BMW crossed the bridge over the Potomac River just east of Harpers Ferry, on the way to the racetrack and slot machine emporium at Charles Town. There, where three different states had their borders within a minute-and-a-half, the BMW's driver decided to stop and do what she had come to do. Just over the bridge over the river, within eyesight of where John Brown and Stonewall Jackson had once made the name of Harpers Ferry known to everyone in America nearly a century-and-a-half before, she pulled off the highway into a deserted wayside. There she turned off her engine and lights, and got ready to undertake the biggest gamble of her life.

At length, she got out of the car, then opened the back door. The old packing trunk was heavy—it weighed almost as much as she did. Somehow, though, she got it out. It fell to the dirt with a heavy thud. Fortunately, it had wheels along one side of its bottom. She dragged it toward the edge of the wayside, where there was an enclosed trash container. The wheels of the trunk left clear tracks in the dirt. She left it next to the trash can.

It was now just another piece of the past, something that, once out of sight, would be out of mind. It was the way she thought about life in general—always think ahead. Dwelling on the old never did anyone any good. She got back into the BMW and drove away, old anxieties floating away to make room for new ones that would soon settle in. But at the time, they were little worries, not big ones, and they were easier to tolerate than those that had chafed her too long to be borne. Out with the old, in with the new—that was the way to survive. Like Scarlett O'Hara, for Nancy Jean Sweitzer, tomorrow was always another day.

But in reality, not fiction, time has a way of catching up with everyone.

# 2
# LITTLE NANCY

So here we are, many years later, in the wood-paneled courtroom of the Honorable Andre M. Davis, judge of the United States District Court For the District of Maryland. A jury of fifteen men and women—twelve tried and true, and three alternates—has just been selected from a panel of 133 citizens of the district, a middle ground agreed upon by both the United States government, which wants to put Nancy Jean Siegel in prison for the rest of her life, and her defense lawyers, who want to keep her out.

Nancy sits at the counsel table, still blond, but rather more plump than when she was first arrested in August of 2003. It's been over 5 years in stir for Nancy Jean. She who once weighed a petite 105 pounds is now tipping the scales at close to 150. Jail food, along with the lack of freedom to move around, will do that to you.

The United States government—actually, the United States Attorney's Office for the District of Maryland—wants to make sure that Nancy pays for her crimes. And they are many: theft of government property, bank fraud, mail fraud, wire fraud, identify theft and most important, disposing of—meaning murdering—a potential witness to her transgressions. Nancy has come a long way from her hardscrabble upbringing in East Baltimore, Fell's Point, once a working-class neighborhood hard-by the Baltimore shipyards. In Nancy's day, Fell's Point was a place that generated the bad as well as the good, from mobsters to the Speaker of the U.S. House of Representatives, another Nancy, Pelosi by married name. People in Baltimore like to boast about that other Nancy.

Now our Nancy—born as Sweitzer, known today as Siegel—sits demurely in the courtroom that will decide her fate. She has finally run out of choices: soon, twelve citizens of the state of Maryland will decide her future for her.

And there, in the gallery, among those arrayed on the hard wooden benches of the courtroom—as hard as any fundamentalist church pew—sits her older cousin, a man of great accomplishment in his own life, a man who made different choices. Larry Kaskel, who also grew up in Fell's Point, who had nothing more than an eighth-grade education, now watches as his younger cousin, someone who was, for all practical purposes, a little sister to him, faces the trial of her life. Larry has worked for more than twenty years for Peter Angelos, a fabulously successful personal injury lawyer and owner of the Baltimore Orioles baseball team, who also owns much of downtown Baltimore. But Larry, or his patron Angelos, can't do anything now to help Nancy.

"My sweet baby girl," Larry says, unable to fully grasp the reality of what's about to unfold. Larry simply can't believe that his sweet Nancy is about to be convicted of cold-blooded murder. Larry, who's seen so much, can't understand: how could Nancy Jean Sweitzer Kucharski Geisendaffer Siegel have gone so wrong? Where did it all start?

That "sweet baby girl" was born on March 30, 1948, in Baltimore, the daughter of James ("Jimmy") Sweitzer, also a Baltimore native, and once a sailor who had survived the U-boats that preyed on the convoys that kept Britain alive in the first years of World War II.

Jimmy was a small but feisty man, according to his nephew Larry, who knew him well. Born in 1912, the son of Joseph L. and Jennie Jacobs Sweitzer, Jimmy was the fourth of nine children. According to the federal census, by 1930, Jennie Sweitzer was the head of the family, suggesting that she was by that year a widow. As the second oldest of four sons, Jimmy bore some of the burden of supporting the large family during the bleak 1930s. At 17, Jimmy was employed as an "office boy," as the census taker enumerated him, while his older brother Joe, 24, worked as a chauffeur for an undertaker. Sister Adele, 22, worked as a clerk, while Jessie, 20, had a job as a telephone operator. Younger siblings Elizabeth, 15, Grace, 12, Jack, 10, Mary, 7, and—the census taker's handwriting faltered, but it appears to be Vaughn, 6, were in school. All nine children lived with their mother in a dwelling rented for $35 a month. The family owned no radio, another indication of deep poverty. In 1930, a radio was the television of the age. A family without a radio was very poor.

By 1937, Jimmy was working full time as an "oil burner" in the shipyards, dirty work, but at least it was a job. At 24, Jimmy had learned one lesson from the Great Depression: it didn't pay to back down, not from anyone or anything. Jimmy was ebullient, confident, quick; he loved the action, and he would as soon fight you as buy you a beer, as Larry would remember him years later. It was hard to think of him as anything other than Leo Gorcey, leader of the Dead End Kids of 1930s movie fame: lithe, very quick, and smart-mouthed.

Then the war came, and Jimmy was in the service, probably the Merchant Marine, since the records of Army and Navy enlistments during the war don't record his name. In many ways, the war liberated Jimmy, even as Jimmy was helping liberate Europe. While in England awaiting D-Day, Jimmy met and married a young Englishwoman, who soon became pregnant, and who then gave birth to a daughter, Nancy Jean's older half-sister. After the war, Jimmy's English bride and the baby came to the United States, but the marriage soon faltered; less than a year after she arrived in Baltimore, the English wife returned to the United Kingdom with her child, and her own kin. It isn't clear, but it appears that Jimmy was never divorced.

By 1947, Jimmy had become involved with a new woman, Nancy Jean's mother, Doris Leary. They never married. Nancy was born in early 1948, and a sister, little Doris, followed in 1950. Early that same decade, Jimmy and Nancy's mother separated permanently. Jimmy took Nancy with him, and soon moved in with his sister Elizabeth, Larry's mother, known in Fell's Point as "Lil." Little Doris went with her mother, big Doris. According to Larry, Nancy had almost no contact with her natural mother and sister after that.

"We had," Larry remembered, "a dysfunctional family."

Dysfunctional family or not, Nancy grew up in Fell's Point, a working-class neighborhood where Italians, Germans, Poles and Jews congregated, drawn by the work in the shipyards. Larry's mother "Lil" ran a tavern there—a place where bookies and loan sharks felt comfortable hanging out. Everyone knew each other—church was important—but everyone in Fell's Point in those days was on the bottom of the economic ladder, and the only way out was by your own bootstraps.

Jimmy liked to gamble—it was part of living in east Baltimore at the time, Larry remembered. Bet on the Colts, the Orioles, the horses at Pimlico. Not big bets—no one could afford it—but enough so that when you won, you had the rush, the exhilaration of being somebody. There was nothing sweeter than the bookie paying off at the bar—the danger of the risk, the release of victory. Good times when you won, just another slap in the face when you lost. But a lot of people in Fell's Point at the time were used to getting slapped in the face. It was almost worth it. At least you knew you were alive.

Then one night in 1964, Jimmy was walking home through an alley near the tavern. Two men jumped him and beat him senseless. A few days later, he was dead at the age of 52, the victim of a blood clot in the brain. Jimmy had always been feisty, ready for a fight. But now he was down for the last count.

Nancy Jean was sixteen—sweet sixteen.

By 1958, Elvis Presley had already had his Blue Suede Shoes stepped on, been to the Heartbreak Hotel, admitted to being a Hound Dog, and begged to be loved tenderly, if he wasn't rocking in the county jail. He was soon to be All Shook Up, as was the rest of the country.

Larry Kaskel had joined the U.S. Army in 1956, 101st Airborne, and by September of 1957 was in Little Rock, Arkansas—"the invasion of Little Rock," as Larry put it years later, irony completely intended. President Eisenhower had ordered the troops in to integrate the schools, while Orval Faubus figuratively stood in the doorway. Larry was issued an M-14—no bullets—and was scared to death.

"I was too young for Korea, and too old for Viet Nam," Larry said later. The crisis passed, the black students were admitted, and a few years later, Larry was out of the Army, and working as a member of the asbestos workers' union, later Peter Angelos' most lucrative client, the key to his fortune, what with multi-million-dollar settlements for asbestosis claims.

Nancy, meanwhile, was growing up quickly. In fact, the world seemed to be speeding up—changes were coming faster and faster: school integration, integration of the Hit Parade, Chubby Checker, the twist, beehive hairdos, Freedom Riders, a president assassinated, British boys with long hair, yeah yeah yeah. Tequila! Almost before Nancy was old enough to drive, the times they were a'changin'.

It all happened so fast, Larry thought later. It seemed like only a few years had gone by since Nancy had been a flat-chested little girl in saddle shoes, but now she was a young woman. Nancy wasn't so little anymore, and there was another world all around them. They had drifted apart. Larry had his own family to think about, and a job in Delaware. In his mind Larry knew that Nancy was almost an adult, but in his heart he still saw her as "Little Nancy." Then the word came from Fell's Point—Uncle Jimmy was dead, beaten to death in an alley. Larry returned to Baltimore, now the man in the extended if still dysfunctional family, and then, almost before Larry knew it, suddenly Nancy was somehow on television.

Yes, there was Nancy on the small screen, bright, sociable, beautiful, with her terrific smile, in solid with the Baltimore in-crowd: a regular on the *Buddy Deane Show*, Baltimore's answer to Dick Clark's *American Bandstand*, where teenagers danced in front of the cameras to the Top Forty. Those were the days: when American music was in transition from Elvis Presley to the Beatles. None of the arbiters of taste knew exactly what to do with the longhairs from the United Kingdom—certainly not Ed Sullivan. "A Hard Day's Night" of working like a dog rang chords with American teenagers, while The Animals sang about regrettable dissolution in "The House of the Rising Sun." The Beach Boys tried for uplift with "Fun, Fun, Fun" and Daddy's T-Bird, along with "I Get Around." Ricky Nelson had traveled the world and made a lot of stops, but was fading on the Hit Parade. Lurking on the horizon were the Zombies with "She's Not There," a harbinger of the psychedelia to come. In a sense, almost all of the popular groups of the age could have been singing about Nancy, in one way or another.

"No one told me about her, the way she lied," the Zombies sang, in a sort of weird syncopation. "Don't bother trying to find her, she's not there." Cue the calliope, the grifters' instrument of choice . . .

With her frequent dance partner and high school sweetheart, Ted Geisendaffer, Nancy was a member of "The Committee," as it was then called, the group of kids who helped Buddy

Deane decide which songs were hot, and who got to dance—a star, and the object of the virginal lust of just about every high school kid in the metropolitan Baltimore area. Five feet tall, blond, blue-eyed, barely 100 pounds, Nancy was a living Kewpie doll. She had also become more, much more than Larry's "Little Nancy."

In fact, she had become a very good actress, someone able to seem whatever anyone wanted to see in her—"She's Not There." Nancy's intuition allowed her to reach out and sense what someone else wanted to believe, and Nancy had learned to compartmentalize herself so well that no one could ever know how often it was all an act. As one of her later acquaintances put it, Nancy could con the "skin off an alligator." What had begun as a defense mechanism for a little girl abandoned by her mother had turned into a reflex, and then, finally, into a talent, a skill Nancy took satisfaction in, if not pride. Nancy was both smart and beautiful, and in time would learn how to use those talents with a ruthlessness that would shock those who persisted in seeing her as "Little Nancy," or as a loving wife, mother and friend. Beneath her charming exterior, Nancy would become a manipulator and a predator, and if she could put one over on you, well, too bad for you.

Life had given *her* no breaks—no loving mother, no house in the suburbs, no college education where she could learn a profession and meet the man of her dreams. No one was going to take care of Little Nancy but Nancy, so she wasn't about to give any slack to anyone else. That much Nancy had learned from her father, before he was beaten to death in an alley.

Three years later, Nancy, then 19 years old, married Charles Kucharski.

# 3
# NANCY, CHARLES
# AND TED

Charles was compact, well-built, handsome. Larry liked him from the start. He seemed very solid, down to earth, just what someone like Larry's cousin needed. He was obviously in love with "little Nancy," as Larry and the family still called her. Charles was also a hard worker—he would go on to establish a successful business renovating older homes, an artist of sorts. He would father two beautiful daughters with Nancy—Jennifer and Amanda—in the 1970s. Life throughout that decade was good for the Kucharskis, or so Charles thought.

Larry thought so, too. He thought his little cousin was on the right track, after a rough beginning with a mother who had abandoned her and a father who'd been murdered.

Then, in 1982, after almost two decades of marriage, it all came apart. Charles discovered that Nancy had been gambling—making secret trips to Atlantic City, New Jersey, where Nevada-style casinos had been legalized since 1976. With the girls in school and her husband at work, Nancy was free to make the two-hour trip to Jersey, where she soon became addicted to slot machine action—video poker, in fact. The news came from the federal Internal Revenue Service—the Kucharskis owed nearly $60,000 in back taxes on Nancy's gambling winnings, and another $40,000 or so on other debts, mostly credit card accounts that Nancy had opened in her husband's name, but without his knowledge.

Because Charles had given Nancy the responsibility for maintaining his business books, and paying all the bills, Nancy had been able to keep her husband in the dark about the true state of the family and business finances; Nancy was soon revealed as an adept and inveterate liar. Like most gambling addicts, she rationalized her deception and secrecy by convincing herself that she would win big, replenish the money she had diverted from her husband's accounts, would somehow make everything go back to zero, with no one the wiser. But it only illustrates the sort of delusional thinking that addictive gamblers develop.

The idea that sooner or later the Internal Revenue Service, or other creditors wouldn't somehow make Charles aware of his true financial situation never entered Nancy's mind; or if it did, it was quickly pushed out with the far more pleasant fantasy of the big score. Of course, Nancy kept no record of her gambling *losses*—those dwarfed the winnings, but without proof, the Kucharskis were still on the hook for the taxes on the sporadic payouts.

Nancy's addiction to video poker—a game based on five-card draw in which the player had a possibility of drawing ten total cards from a virtual electronic 52-card deck generated by a random number calculator inside the machine—was far more insidious than a habit someone might have succumbed to with an old-time "one-armed bandit." At least then you had to exert some muscles to pull the handle, and so had the potential relief of sheer arm fatigue.

But the new machines were fully automated, and much faster than their old mechanical ancestors: all a bettor had to do was put the money in a slot, then push a button. Again.

And again and again, on and on, until the money ran out. Whereupon you simply inserted another $20 bill. It was like feeding a robot money simply to watch it light itself up and spin its eyeballs—ace, trey, jack, six, two, hold 'em or draw, again and again and again. It was not unheard of for a mesmerized addict to churn through hundreds, even thousands of dollars in only a few hours.

Nancy dumped large sums from her husband's bank accounts into these electronic rat holes, then raced home to try to assemble dinner for her husband and daughters, telling herself that she surely was due for the royal flush and the big payout on the next trip north. Just why Nancy became addicted to these automated rip-off machines, with their odds so stacked in favor of their owners, was never made clear, later. But it seems possible, maybe even likely, that she wasn't happy in her marriage to Charles, and hoped desperately to win enough money to set herself free. Like the Zombies had sung years before, she wasn't there anymore, and maybe never had been.

But the big score never came, or at least not often enough, and the bills kept piling up, until the day Charles finally realized what was going on, thanks to the IRS.

Charles tried to pay off the tax people, and the rest of the bills, but then watched his marriage fall apart. How could Nancy have kept this problem from him? It wasn't the money so much as Nancy's secrecy that doomed the marriage; *that* was corrosive. If Nancy could lie about this, what else was she lying about? By early 1984, the marriage dissolved in bitter recriminations, leading to divorce.

That same year, Nancy renewed a relationship with her old high school sweetheart and one-time dance partner on the *Buddy Deane Show*, Ted. Like Larry Kaskel, Ted Geisendaffer had become an expert on removing toxic substances such as asbestos from buildings. After Ted suffered an injury on a job, Larry, who was at the time an official in the asbestos workers' union, went to visit him. Ted asked about Larry's niece little Nancy, and Larry told him that Nancy had recently separated from her husband. Soon Nancy visited Ted in the hospital, and once he was out of the hospital, almost before he knew what was happening, Ted and Nancy were dating, Ted's own marriage and children notwithstanding.

Soon Ted was divorcing his first wife to be with Nancy. The one-time high school sweethearts married in Columbia, Maryland, on February 8, 1985.

The relationship between Ted and Nancy was fraught with conflict almost from the beginning—as might be expected with a couple prone to seeing one another as they had seemed to be as teenagers, even though they were each by then pushing 40. In a way, Ted, at least, was caught up in a romantic illusion, an artifice that Nancy did all she could to foster—at least at first.

Beneath their rekindled teenaged attraction, Ted and Nancy were as different as possible. At five-eight and nearly 220 pounds, Ted towered over Nancy and outweighed her by more than 100 pounds. And where Nancy was impulsive and often volatile, Ted was methodical, organized, and tended to plan everything out far in advance. Unlike Nancy, Ted had an absolute horror of owing anybody any money.

Still, it is a measure of Nancy's persuasiveness that, as with Charles, Nancy had taken over Ted's personal finances. As an "industrial hygienist," or a "building engineer," as he was called, Ted often had to work at night as he and his crew cleaned a building of toxic substances like asbestos. That left Nancy free most days, and soon she was back at her old haunts in Atlantic City and Delaware, which had recently approved its own legalized gambling dives. Nancy soon opened credit accounts in Ted's name without his knowledge, and put the money she'd scammed down the poker machines' ever-hungry metal maws.

Nancy began staying away from home for days at a time. Ted never knew where she was. He began to suspect that Nancy was seeing other men. He was right.

Sometime in 1991, after Ted and Nancy had been married for a little over six years, Nancy was introduced to a Baltimore woman named Linda Mayberry. Linda operated an escort service that catered to wealthy Baltimore-area men. She kept a basement apartment beneath a health supplement store, and charged clients $150 an hour—$110 to the escort, $40 to Linda. Late in 1991, Linda said later, Nancy went to work for her as an escort. According to Linda, Nancy specialized in wealthy, middle-aged Jewish men. The extra money Nancy earned was apparently gobbled up by the poker machines.

Ted was at first oblivious. Then the day came when he discovered several plastic bags of unpaid bills stashed behind the washing machine in the utility room of the house they shared. It was as if Nancy had, in her own mind, "paid" the bills by hiding them from sight. And then Ted discovered that Nancy had been endorsing the mortgage checks over to herself, then cashing them. The couple's house was about to go into foreclosure.

How could Nancy be so stupid? Ted thundered. Didn't she realize that sooner or later he was going to find out she hadn't been paying the bills? That she was *cheating* him? And then Ted discovered that Nancy had gambled away all the money Ted had set aside to pay his daughter's school tuition. Ted went ballistic. There was a physical confrontation. Nancy broke her wrist trying to hit Ted. Ted put his fist through a picture on a wall. The arguments grew increasingly bitter and violent. On one occasion, in fact, Ted shut himself in a closet; he was so angry at Nancy that he felt like killing her, and came to the conclusion that the only way he could save her life—and his—was to keep away from her until he cooled off.

On February 22, 1992, after another argument, Nancy left the house she shared with Ted in Ellicott City, Maryland. She and her daughters moved to another place in Ellicott City, and Nancy took more referrals from Linda Mayberry's escort service. That spring, Nancy began seeing Eric Siegel, a wealthy Baltimore commercial loan broker, regularly. Linda later said that Eric was a client of her escort service when he was introduced to Nancy. Soon, according to Linda, Nancy was seeing Eric outside the escort service, which made Linda angry, since she no longer got her $40 cut.

Eric was coming off a terrible tragedy when he first met Nancy. In mid-1991, the 41-year-old Eric had been driving his car, drunk, in Baltimore County, when he crashed. His two children, daughter Courtney and son Josh, were in the car with him. Josh was injured and Courtney was killed. A few months later, in November of 1991, Eric was charged with manslaughter, vehicular homicide, drunken driving, speeding and several minor traffic offenses. Facing trial, Eric separated from his wife, Faye. While the case was unfolding in Circuit Court in the spring of 1992, Eric began seeing Nancy frequently.

Besides Linda Mayberry, Eric and Nancy had other things in common. As a condition of his release on bail, Eric began attending Alcoholics Anonymous meetings; Nancy had been attending Gamblers Anonymous meetings for some time. Both were frank with each other about their addictions. But while Eric was capable of stopping his drinking, Nancy's gambling was soon out of control again.

Then, in September, Ted Geisendaffer found out what Nancy had been up to during all those days when he didn't know where she was. Like Charles Kucharski before him, Ted got a bill from the IRS. The Kucharskis owed taxes on $38,000 of Nancy's winnings in Atlantic City in 1990. Again, there were no records of the losses. Ted refused to pay—he said the undeclared income was all Nancy's doing, not his, and the casinos' records showed only Nancy's Social Security number, which seemed to prove his assertion.

The following month, Nancy filed for divorce from Ted. In her complaint, Nancy's lawyer, Melvin Kodenski, charged Ted with "constructive desertion," in that Ted had forced Nancy out of the marriage "due to the constant and continued [sic] physical abuse directed against her by her husband, the defendant, causing her severe physical and mental anguish, causing the loss of her self-esteem and the placing of her safety in jeopardy, all without just cause or reason, and the defendant has a serious drinking problem as a result of which, he was constantly out of control causing damage to the parties' personal property and threatening the well-being of the plaintiff with on at least one occasion breaking her wrist which resulted in her having to leave the family home on the date aforesaid to protect her own health, safety, and well-being with the defendant causing said constructive desertion and said constructive desertion has been continuous and uninterrupted since February 22, 1992."

Nancy wanted the court to grant her a share in the Ellicott City house, any other property held jointly, as well as alimony. Not only that, Kodenski said in the complaint, Nancy wanted the court to "restore the maiden name of the plaintiff so she will now be known as Nancy J. Kucharski." From this, it appears that Nancy hadn't told Kodenski about her prior marriage to Charles, the father of her two children. Nancy's real maiden name was Sweitzer, of course.

Within a few months, Ted countersued, alleging that "plaintiff [Nancy] has committed adultery at various times during the course of the marriage of the parties, and defendant [Ted] has neither condoned nor forgiven said acts of adultery." Ted denied abusing Nancy.

Moreover, Ted asserted in his answer and countersuit that "plaintiff has a serious gambling problem and she has left defendant in great debt as a result of gambling debts and various loans and payments made to plaintiff during their marriage and prior to the abandonment of the marriage by the plaintiff."

Not only should Nancy get nothing from the real property, as well as no alimony, Nancy should have to pay his legal fees, Ted asserted.

The divorce suit puttered through the courts for a few months in late 1992 and early 1993 before both sides agreed to a settlement in February. Ted agreed to pay Nancy $5,000 for her interest in the family house, which Nancy thought was worth as much as $170,000, and Nancy agreed to sign over her interest in the property to Ted. That Nancy settled so cheaply was evidence of Nancy's desperation at the time, as well as Ted's evidence of Nancy's infidelities, not to mention Nancy's documented love for the casinos' poker machines.

"The parties expressly agree that wife has been assessed taxes by the IRS for her winnings from gambling in tax year 1990. Wife contests this assessment because she alleges that her losses exceeded her winnings. Wife expressly agrees to assume full responsibility for any tax liability stemming from her gambling." In fact, Nancy agreed to hold Ted harmless from any penalties sought by the IRS for the unpaid taxes. This was a complete win for Ted.

The Ted/Nancy marriage was formally terminated June 1, 1993. That ended Ted's dalliance with the blast from the past, but Nancy's troubles were only getting worse by the day.

# 4
# A ONE-WOMAN
# CRIME WAVE

Even as Ted and Nancy were finalizing their divorce, Nancy was getting a different kind of divorce from her one-time benefactor, Linda Mayberry. Not only was Linda sore at Nancy for seeing Eric Siegel on the side, but also because Nancy had defaulted on a car loan Nancy had convinced Linda and her husband John to co-sign for her shortly after departing from Ted. The Mayberrys had advanced a $3,000 down payment on a Toyota Camry for Nancy, in addition to guaranteeing the loan, since Nancy had no verifiable employment, and could hardly cite Ted as a credit reference. But by the spring of 1993, Nancy stopped making the payments on the car. Then Linda Mayberry discovered that Nancy had falsified another loan application, this one using John Mayberry's Social Security number and other personal identifiers to get the money. The Mayberrys got the default notice for a loan they didn't know they owed when Nancy didn't pay.

Other issues plagued Linda's relationship with Nancy. On one occasion, Linda said later, Nancy altered the $500 check a client had given her for the escort service so it read $5,000.

The client complained. Linda was furious with Nancy—Nancy was ruining the reputation of her escort business! Then, when Linda confronted Nancy about the car loan default and the falsified loan, Nancy threatened to expose Linda to the IRS—blackmail. Linda backed off, but that was the end of her friendship with Nancy.

Nancy had even worse problems to deal with than her troubles with Linda. By early 1993, even before her divorce from Ted was final, Nancy had embarked on a life of crime: she began stealing other women's wallets, and raiding their mailboxes. Soon she was cashing checks on strangers' bank accounts, making withdrawals from their savings accounts, and using their credit cards, at first unbeknownst to them.

In first two-timing, then separating from, then filing for the divorce from Ted, Nancy was making more bad choices, just as she might have done in leaving Charles Kucharski, assuming that whatever problems they had could possibly have been ameliorated. While Nancy later attempted to justify these decisions by claiming that her two husbands were abusive to her, there's no evidence of that, other than their frustration and anger at her deceptiveness and, to them, her unfathomable addiction to gambling.

What neither Charles nor Ted could quite grasp was that Nancy's impulsiveness and her volatility, so charming at first acquaintance, was actually what drove her into taking terrible chances, and making her almost impossible to live with. In a way, that was what the gambling was about—the impulsiveness, the seat-of-the-pants, emotion-based decision-making intermittently rewarded by a big payout *was* Nancy. And in another way, it was how she saw herself as finally getting free of all the compromises she'd made in her life to that point: among them, the two marriages, and the stint with the escort service. A really big score would set her free—or so Nancy kept telling herself; and every time the screen lit up with a new poker hand, potential manumission was in the video cards.

But in the meantime—back in the real world, not fantasyland—Nancy was in a very bad way. At 45, having walked away from two marriages to husbands who earned more than enough money to support her and her children; then having alienated her escape hatch, Linda Mayberry; having no higher education, no professional skills, no real work experience, a gnawing addiction, an increasingly volatile mental state, no income, and no prospects, Nancy was in big trouble. It was undoubtedly desperation and depression, admittedly the results of her own poor, impulsive decisions, that led to Nancy's first official crime—if one doesn't count the escort dating or the bamboozling of the Mayberrys.

Over the next year-and-a-half, Nancy would be arrested more than a dozen times for crimes ranging from shoplifting to grand theft, to writing bad checks, forgery, bank fraud and counterfeiting, all occurring in Baltimore or its surrounding counties. In none of the cases did Nancy ever serve more than a few days in jail, even though the aggregate of money she stole or diverted was nearly $25,000.

Based on court records, it appears that Nancy's crime wave had begun in early December 1992, even before her divorce from Ted was finalized. Nancy found herself in the linens section of a department store in a sprawling shopping mall in Columbia, Maryland. Feeling low amid all the pre-Christmas cheer, Nancy saw a chance to feel better, and took it. Observing a seemingly well-to-do woman who briefly left her purse unattended, Nancy snatched a wallet from the bag and went into the nearby ladies' room, where she quickly removed the woman's driver's license, Social Security card, bank card and several credit cards. Who would suspect her? She was white, well-dressed, obviously affluent herself, middle- or upper-middle-class. Then she returned to the linens department and unobtrusively returned the now-empty wallet to the handbag.

Nancy left the store, and a few minutes later, entered an up-scale specialty store in the mall. There she charged a $729 watch on the unsuspecting woman's American Express card and a second $315 watch on another credit card, as well as $94 in cosmetics. Within a few days, Nancy had pawned the two watches for a fraction of their retail value in Atlantic City.

Doubtless reasoning that she'd better move fast before the stripped-out wallet was reported to the police, over the next few days Nancy forged withdrawal slips totaling about $5,700 from the unsuspecting woman's savings account. Nancy perfected the drive-through heist—dressing soccer-mom casual, pulling her baseball cap low to conceal much of her face, Nancy breezed up to the drive-up window of the bank in her Mayberry-paid-for Camry, tossed over the sto-len driver's license and the withdrawal slip, and was soon on her way with the cash with no questions asked, other than if she wanted the money in hundreds or twenties.

This initial foray into the fruits of surreptitious wallet-snatching was soon accompanied by mail fraud. A week or so after the purse raid, Nancy received some unsolicited home equity checks in the mail. Unfortunately, they were intended for someone other than Nancy, and had been misdelivered. Undaunted, Nancy simply used the driver's license from the department store woman's stripped-out wallet to forge the checks to cash payable to the name on the driver's license she'd stolen from the wallet. Then back to the drive-up windows—a toss of the forged check and the license, and Nancy was on her way again with the green. This netted Nancy $2,400 be-fore the new year.

Soon Nancy was forging more of the mis-mailed checks at the local supermarket—$834 worth of groceries between December 22 and December 30. The holiday season indeed boasted a full larder at Nancy's apartment that year.

Nancy forged two more withdrawals from the first victim's savings account before deciding that things were getting a little too risky to continue using that identity. By that point, the first victim had reported the wallet raid to the police, and in fact had been notified that someone seemed to be using one of her credit cards. The police had begun to circulate the word to the bank's branches to be on the lookout for someone using the woman's stolen driver's license to make bogus withdrawals. Nancy decided to find a new victim.

She returned to the scene of the crime.

In fact, back to the very same department store that had netted her such rewarding results in December. On January 20, 1993, Nancy found another wallet to steal, and reasoning that she could use the same third-party cut-out procedure to get cash that she'd used before, stole bank statements from the mailbox of a second woman for the purpose of finding a name she could endorse bogus checks to. Then it was simply a matter of forging checks payable to the second woman, then cashing them at the drive-through window while posing as the second woman.

Nancy also learned something else: people often sent personal checks in the mail. Even before returning to the mall, Nancy had begun to randomly raid mailboxes, searching for anything she could turn into cash. In one, she found two personal checks payable to a woman, probably a landlady. Nancy soon posed as the payee, and cashed those checks—altogether, about $3,000. Then Nancy discovered that the landlady had a savings account. Bingo! Another $1,500 from forged withdrawal slips.

All of this was going on while Nancy and Ted were still squabbling over the terms of their divorce, and with Nancy denying under oath, for that case, that she had any sort of gambling problem. But what Ted didn't know—or maybe did—Nancy had run afoul of a loan shark in Atlantic City.

Later, the details of this incident were murky: Nancy claimed that the man had loaned her money to gamble, then threatened to expose her to the police if she didn't pay him back. That was one reason she was desperate, Nancy said later, and why she had resorted to raiding wallets and mail-boxes. Exactly what sort of extortionate hold the shark held over Nancy wasn't clear, but it may have had something to do with her escort career. By this point, Nancy and a friend had tried to go into the escort business for themselves, and Nancy might well have been anxious to keep Jennifer and Amanda from knowing what she was up to on at least some of her trips to Atlantic City.

In any event, in late February of 1993, just a week after signing the settlement agreement with Ted, while at a Columbia dance studio with her daughter, Nancy stole a woman's wallet. This turned out to be a real jackpot—not only were there credit cards, bank cards, a checkbook and a driver's license, but the victim was also rather well-off.

This time, though, the victim reported the theft almost as soon as she found the wallet missing. Nancy didn't know that, but was experienced enough by now to know that she had to move quickly. Three days after swiping the wallet, Nancy cashed a withdrawal slip for the victim's savings account for $1,500. A week later Nancy wrote two checks to Sears totaling about $3,500—for a computer and a fax machine—then returned the merchandise to another branch of the store for a cash refund.

Then, over the next ten days, Nancy cashed two more savings withdrawal slips for a total of $4,000. This wasn't the victim's fault—she'd reported the theft almost immediately. But for some reason, it took the bank time to put out the word to its employees.

By now, of course, the Howard County police were on the case—all of the cases, as a matter of fact. At first, though, detectives didn't realize they were dealing with a one-woman crime wave. Nevertheless, they'd put out the word to all the area banks to be on the look-out for women with baseball caps who were using forged checks and withdrawal slips at the drive-through windows, and disseminated the names and account numbers of the various victims. On March 29, 1993,

Nancy tried to cash another withdrawal slip for $2,000 from the dance studio woman's savings account, and this time the bank said no. Nancy drove off. All anyone could remember was that the would-be forger was driving a silver Toyota Camry.

Two days later, Nancy tried again, at a drive-through window at a bank branch in Baltimore County. This time the police got there in time. Nancy was arrested. At that point, the police, with help from the bank, realized that Nancy had been pulling all these forgery jobs in Howard County as well as Baltimore County. A detective from Howard County collected Nancy from the Baltimore authorities, and soon she was giving a confession.

Well, not exactly a full confession. Nancy quickly realized that the Howard County detective had only half the story. There were at least five or six other victims the Howard County detective didn't know about, because those cases were being handled by another Howard County detective— apparently the two investigators weren't communicating, at least at first. Or maybe these sorts of crimes were so common that the idea they were connected never surfaced. So Nancy confessed to some of her crimes, and Jennifer, then a little over 21 years old, came down to the jail to bail her out. Nancy went home for the night.

About two weeks later, the light finally dawned on the two Howard County detectives that they were probably dealing with the same perpetrator—someone whose *m.o.* of baseball cap and drive-up window forgeries was rather distinctive. The detectives met with other detectives from Anne Arundel County, south of Baltimore, and realized that the drive-up window forger had been busy there, too. On May 6, 1993, Nancy, accompanied by defense attorney Richard Berger, went to the Howard County police headquarters in Ellicott City, and confessed to her crime wave.

And here was the Nancy people would see repeatedly over the next decade every time she got into trouble. Nancy wept, was contrite, and said she was a compulsive gambler, that she couldn't help herself. She blamed the blackmailing loan shark for all her crimes, and claimed to be attending Gamblers Anonymous meetings, and praying that a Higher Power would help her through. She had two daughters in school, Nancy said, and she was their sole support. She couldn't go to jail. Bail was set at $25,000. Somehow, Nancy raised it.

Nancy was charged in two separate cases, fourteen counts of theft and forgery in the dance studio wallet theft, and seventy-seven counts of theft and forgery in the other Howard County crimes that had begun on December 8, 1992. Because of the multiple felonies involved, Nancy was held for trial in Howard County Circuit Court. On December 10, 1993, two days more than a year after her first wallet theft, Nancy pleaded guilty to seven felony counts of theft and eight felony counts of forgery on the dance studio case, and seventy-three counts of forgery on the other case. For some reason, four of the seventy-seven original counts were dismissed.

Still, Nancy's plea for leniency worked. (And, defense lawyer Berger was something of a magician.) It didn't hurt at all that Nancy was white, contrite, seemingly middle-class, and the mother of two. For both cases, she was given concurrent sentences of 15 days in jail, to be served on weekend work release, and 4 years, 11 months and 15 days in prison, all suspended, provided that she keep on attending Gamblers Anonymous meetings and get psychotherapy. She was ordered to pay $15,579 in restitution to the banks, which had been the ultimate victims of her drive-through forgeries, and another $3,581 in fees to the court, at a rate of $163 a month. She was also ordered to serve two consecutive 5-year terms of supervised probation by the state Division of Parole and Probation. That meant reporting to the probation people on a monthly basis as to where she was living and who she was working for, for the next decade. The probation people were also ordered to collect the monthly payments, including the court costs, for a total of $19,160 in restitution and various court fees.

Given the severity of the crimes, this was a remarkably light sentence. But at least some of its merciful quality might be attributed to a report provided to the judge by a licensed clinical social worker, Susan F. Darvas, who was contacted by another Gamblers Anonymous member to help Nancy. Darvas sent a report on Nancy to defense attorney Berger, and Berger forwarded it to the judge in support of his plea for a light sentence. Darvas wrote:

> *Mrs. Sweitzer has been in treatment with me for pathological gambling and major depression since 12/15/93. She has been referred to me by a member of Gamblers Anonymous, because of my long-standing association with the study and treatment of compulsive gambling.*

Darvas listed her qualifications: director of a local hospital's outpatient services for compulsive gambling, senior clinician for counseling of compulsive gamblers at Johns Hopkins University in Baltimore, and senior clinician for a private medical center in Columbia. She had also testified as an expert witness in both state and federal court on cases involving compulsive gambling. She continued:

> *Compulsive gambling, or pathological gambling, has been recognized as a serious and treatable psychiatric disorder by the American Psychiatric Association Diagnostic and Statistical Manual (DSM III) since 1980. The disorder is characterized by "chronic and progressive failure to resist the impulses to gamble," and gambling behavior that "compromises, disrupts and damages personal, family or vocational pursuits . . ." problems that arise as a result of gambling lead to an intensification of gambling behavior.*

People with compulsive gambling disorder often resort to illegal activities in order to feed the habit, Darvas said. As many as 2 to 3 percent of the adult U.S. population may be suffering from the disorder at any given moment. Then she went on to describe some of Nancy's background:

*Mrs. Sweitzer is a 46 year old woman, who grew up in a dysfunctional family and experienced repeated trauma and abuse throughout her life. Her mother, who had a history of apparent mental illness and irrational behavior, had abandoned her since infancy. She lived with her father and later, her aunt, who was an alcoholic, until 1967. Mrs. Sweitzer's father was the victim of a mugging and was, reportedly, beaten to death in 1964 in Baltimore. She was 16 years old at the time.*

*In 1967 she married her first husband, Charles. She had two daughters by him, now aged 16 and 20. The marriage lasted for 16 years and during this time Mrs. Sweitzer led a stable, responsible and productive life. She married her second husband, Ted, in 1985. This relationship turned out to be extremely troubled. He was reportedly abusive both emotionally and physically, to the extent that Mrs. Sweitzer had to call the police repeatedly.*

*Mrs. Sweitzer first began to gamble in February, 1989, at local gambling parlors and later in Atlantic City casinos. Her gambling behavior escalated and eventually became uncontrollable, and she began to borrow money from questionable sources to finance her gambling addiction. She joined Gamblers Anonymous and with their help stopped gambling in August, 1991. As she was struggling to overcome her addiction to gambling, pressure and threats mounted for her to repay her debts. She became frightened and desperate as she had neither adequate financial resources nor adequate emotional support. Her depression worsened and she became increasingly more irrational and confused. She began to use illegal means to satisfy demands for money from her creditors. She was arrested in March of 1993 as a result of this.*

After her arrest, Darvas continued, Nancy sought professional help for her addiction, as well as support from Gamblers Anonymous. She was able to abstain from gambling, and found a job, Darvas reported. Still, Darvas added, Nancy continued to suffer when she first came to see her a few days after pleading guilty.

*At the time of her first consultation with me, she was clearly suffering from a major depressive episode, possibly due to bipolar disorder, in addition to pathological gambling. Her presenting symptoms were anxiety, sleeplessness, guilt, confusion and low self-esteem.*

But during the month-and-a-half she'd been seeing Nancy, Darvas added, Nancy had shown great progress in getting more stability in her life. In fact, her gambling was "in remission."

*She has been abstinent for over two years, and under acute stress showed motivation, strength and courage, as well as remarkable capacity for recovery and rehabilitation. Her prognosis is good, if she is allowed to follow her treatment regimen.*

Darvas recommended that Nancy be approved for probation.

There are some interesting aspects of Darvas' assessment of Nancy's situation, as Darvas herself seemed to recognize.

For one thing, there is evidence of dissembling on Nancy's part, at least in her "presentation" to Darvas. As a professional, Darvas was careful to qualify critical parts of

Nancy's story with the word "reportedly." It seems fairly clear that the reporter in this case was Nancy herself, and as someone intent on convincing the clinical social worker that she shouldn't go to prison, Nancy had an obvious interest in bending the facts to her advantage. There's no evidence in Darvas' account of her sessions with Nancy to indicate that she attempted to verify Nancy's claims. Particularly suspect is the assertion that Nancy's relationship with Ted was marked by emotional and physical abuse. This was likely Nancy's way of trying to win Darvas' sympathy. Then there's the assertion that Nancy began gambling in 1989, when the facts show this problem actually began while she was married to Charles Kucharski, at least seven years earlier. Also suspect is Nancy's assertion that she was "abstinent" from gambling.

Then, too, there's the reference to the "questionable sources" of the financing of Nancy's gambling—cue the shadowy loan shark, who was behind all the criminality. In other words, according to Nancy, the Devil made her do it.

But in other areas, Darvas' assessment had validity. There is the reference to possible "bipolar disorder," which fairly describes Nancy's mercurial mood swings, and which, as most professionals would attest, tends to become progressively worse with age if left untreated. "Pathological gambling," to use the DSM's terminology, is often associated with bipolar disorder, as the DSM notes.

Then there's the reference to a "major depressive episode"—who wouldn't be depressed after being arrested, charged with nearly 100 counts of theft and forgery, and facing the prospect of up to 10 years in prison?

But in another way, Darvas' evaluation sheds light on perhaps the root cause of all of Nancy's troubles: mental illness, possibly organic at inception, as bipolar disorder often is. There's the reference to the "reported" mental instability of Nancy's mother, possibly also via bipolar disorder, which is likely genetic in origin, according to many experts. As with many types of mental illness, organic pathologies like bipolar disorder, or attention deficit disorder, both of which may have been symptomatic in Nancy's behavior, are often exacerbated by environmental coping mechanisms adopted by the sufferer, which soon manifest themselves in personality disorders that are reactive to the way the rest of the world treats the person with organic brain dysfunctions.

One such personality disorder, which Nancy had begun to manifest with her one-woman crime wave, is often anti-social personality disorder, marked by inveterate lying and victimization of others—in other words, the absence of conscience. By all accounts, anti-social personality disorder isn't born, it's made.

So the chances are, Nancy was mentally ill, and had been since birth, and her organic brain problems, which caused people to react to her in certain ways as she grew up, in turn made her own reactive personality the way it was, in terms of coping with problems. But being mentally ill is not the same thing as being insane, as we shall see. It's just that some people have the resources to deal with their organic brain dysfunction better than others.

As for coping: there is evidence that the counseling and even Gamblers Anonymous were seen by Nancy, not as a true path back to mental health, but rather as something necessary merely to avoid a substantial term in prison. In fact, by April of 1994, Nancy was already in violation of her probation—she'd failed to make any payments on the hefty restitution bill. Nancy's probation officer, Sandra Whye, filed papers with the court to revoke the probation. Nancy responded by writing the judge, saying that Whye had made her quit two jobs because the work required her to handle money. She'd found another job, as a reservation clerk, paying $5 an hour. She pleaded with the judge to give her a chance to get caught up with the payments. The judge apparently agreed, and Nancy stayed out of jail.

Meanwhile, in the summer of 1994, Nancy was brought to trial in district court on a Baltimore County shoplifting case from October of 1993, another incident from her crime spree. This time, the judge lowered the boom on Nancy, finding her guilty and sentencing her to 18 months in prison. Nancy appealed to the Circuit Court, and eventually, in February of 1995, the state agreed to reduce the charge to misdemeanor theft. Nancy was found guilty, but the judge suspended the sentence once more, and referred her to probation.

By then, Nancy had met Jack Watkins.

# 5
# JASPER

There's no fool like an old fool, or so goes the cliché, but like most overused expressions, there's more than a grain of truth in it. As all of us get older, we may get wiser, but that only makes our dearest illusions even more potent. All Jack Watkins ever wanted was to be loved, and it was his fate that his fondest wish was also his greatest vulnerability. Nancy Jean Sweitzer saw right through him, almost from the instant they met, and by the time it was over, she'd stripped him of everything he had, even his dignity.

According to Jack's step-daughters, and later the police, Nancy met Jack in November of 1994. Nancy by then was working as a salesperson for Evergreen Memorial Gardens, a cemetery in Finksburg, Maryland, a small town just northwest of Reisterstown, itself a suburb northwest of Baltimore. According to the story, Nancy met Jack while she was peddling gravesites door-to-door.

The tale is likely apocryphal. Jack was almost universally described as a simple soul, a rather happy-go-lucky type, who tended to get enthusiastic about various goods and services he saw advertised on television, be they Veg-O-Matics or Ginsu knives. The chances are, Jack saw an ad for Evergreen Memorial Gardens on television, and being 74 years old and a year removed from major heart surgery, thought to make arrangements for his final resting place before it was too late. As it happened, Jack had a mortal dread of being buried underground. He wanted an above-ground crypt. He called the cemetery, and Nancy soon came calling. Still, if it wasn't actually a cold call, it was close.

Jasper Watkins, known all his life as Jack, was a native of Virginia. Born March 21, 1920, Jack grew up in Richmond. Later, details of Jack's early life were sketchy, but some who knew him would come to believe that he was the son of a fairly well-to-do family. At least, this was what Jack himself would hint over the years, along with a vague notion that somehow his father had lost everything in the Great Depression.

However, the details of the 1930 federal census seem to tell a different story. The only Jack Watkins listed in that census is Jack F. Watkins, then 9 years old, the son of 27-year-old Edythe Watkins, of Richmond, Virginia. Rather oddly, the same census lists Doris Watkins, apparently a daughter of Edythe, and a sister of Jack, as being 8 years and 5 months old, thus raising the possibility that one or the other or both of the Watkins children were adopted. There was no adult male Watkins listed in the census. Edythe Watkins was listed as the daughter of Richard L. Mays, 62, a candy salesman, and his wife, Idaline, 58. There was also a Mays son, Richard, 24, listed as a building architect. The three Mayses and the three Watkinses lived in the same dwelling, along with four lodgers, in a house renting for $75 a month. The Mays family owned a radio set. While not as poor as the Sweitzers, the Watkinses were hardly well-to-do, at least in the 1930s while Jack was growing up.

The 1920 census, ten years earlier, sheds a little more light on Jack's past. That enumeration lists Jasper F. Watkins, then 26, an automobile salesman, residing with his wife, "Edith," in the home of Richard L. Mays and his wife, Idaline, along with the Mays' son Richard, then 14, and one servant, Elizabeth Brown, 28, a cook. The elder Richard Mays was listed as a supervisor of candy salesmen.

It appears from other records that Jack's apparent father, Jasper (also Jack's given name), married Edith while she was very young, either 15 or 16. In a World War I draft registration card, filled out by Jasper Frederick Watkins on June 5, 1917, Jack's father listed his age as 25, and his job as a "chauffeur" for a business in Richmond, Virginia, the McGraw-Yarbrough Company. He asked for a draft exemption on the grounds that he was the sole support of his wife. The draft registration listed Jack's father as "tall," with a "medium" build, with blue eyes and light-colored hair. Jack himself was darkly complected, with dark eyes and dark hair, even at the time of his death.

It appears from still other records that Jasper and his child bride, Edith, separated sometime between 1920 and 1930. By 1942, when Jack's father registered again for the draft, this time for World War II, he listed a "Myrtle Lee Watkins" of Richmond as the person who would always know his address. Myrtle was likely the 49-year-old Jasper's wife at the time.

As for Jack himself, more details of his early life can be found in his January 1, 1946, discharge from the United States Army. Jack listed his father's Richmond address as his permanent mailing address, rather than his mother's residence. (Jack would later say his birth mother, Edith or Edythe, died of tuberculosis in 1941). From this document, it appears that Jack worked as a grocery clerk in Richmond prior to his enlistment in the Army on November 4, 1941. The record of Jack's enlistment shows he had two years of high school prior to his joining the Army.

Once enlisted, Jack was assigned to the 358th Air Service Squadron of the Army Air Force. He qualified as Marksman with the M-1 carbine, and was trained as a teletype operator.

On November 2, 1943, he and his squadron shipped out to an airfield in India, where Jack "operated a teletype machine using perforated tape for transmissions and reception," kept a log of all messages, and "transmitted 30 words per minute," which qualified him as a telegrapher, if not a typist. Jack doubtless assisted in scheduling air shipments over the Himalayan "hump" to China, along with air support missions in Burma.

At the end of the war, Jack was awarded the American Defense Service Medal, the American Theater Ribbon, the Asiatic-Pacific Theater Ribbon, and the World War II Victory Ribbon. He was demobilized at Fort Meade, Maryland, on January 1, 1946.

It also appears that Jack was briefly married during the war while stationed in Louisiana. The marriage, in October 1942, to Louise Gentry ended in divorce in July 1946. It isn't clear whether Jack and his wife ever lived together after Jack was shipped overseas.

In any event, Jack came home from the war, and eventually took a job as a supply clerk for Western Auto Supply. At some point in the 1950s he moved to Reisterstown, where, in the early 1960s, he encountered Mary Triplett, a divorcee then in her early 40s.

By all accounts, Mary was an unusual woman—rather ahead of her time, at least in terms of gender liberation. She would eventually have four children by two different men. For the most part, her children were raised by her parents, who lived in the Baltimore vicinity, except for one daughter Mary put up for adoption. She rose to a responsible position with a leading electronics manufacturer, while working part-time managing the Fifteen Mile House Tavern in Reisterstown. In a strange twist, Mary's three daughters, Cheryl, Anita and Carol—like Nancy—felt abandoned by their mother, at least during their childhood, and in an even stranger coincidence, the father of Anita and Carol, Roland Triplett, a gambler like Jimmy Sweitzer, was murdered in the early 1960s. Like Jimmy, he had been attacked in an alley and left to bleed to death.

It was while working at the tavern that Mary Triplett first met Jack Watkins. According to Mary's daughters, Jack at the time had something of a drinking problem. Jack wasn't a mean drunk, they recalled, but rather a jolly one. He loved to sing and tell stories and jokes, and the social atmosphere of the tavern animated him. But after Roland, Mary made it clear to Jack: if he wanted a serious relationship with her, he had to put down the bottle.

By the time Jack took up with Mary, Anita, Cheryl and Carol were grown up, as was their younger brother, Darrel, who eventually moved to Texas.

"It was a marriage of convenience," Anita said later, and Cheryl and Carol agreed. The marriage took place in 1964, and from that point forward, Jack was on the straight and narrow, as far as alcohol was concerned. To Mary's daughters, Jack seemed almost pathetically eager to please Mary, at least at first. It seemed to them that their mother completely dominated Jack, telling him what to do and where and when to do it. To the three sisters, Jack seemed extraordinarily naïve for a man in his 40s.

"The best way I can describe Jack," Cheryl said later, "is to use the word 'child-like.' It was like he never matured. He always saw the best in everyone," even when it was hardly in his own interest. While Mary was intellectually acute, Jack almost seemed simple-minded, at times. "He was not the sharpest crayon in the box," his step-granddaughter Connie said later.

With an inheritance from her father, Mary eventually bought a small house in Reisterstown, at 613 Sungold Road. There she and Jack settled in, with Mary directing Jack on the upkeep of the yard. Jack kept the lawn mowed, and tended to the flowers that Mary loved. The three daughters, by now adults, married, moved away, and had children of their own. Mary helped Jack get a job at Litton Electronics, where she also worked, and the couple prepared to live out their remaining years in peace and tranquility.

But then, sometime in the 1980s, Mary developed multiple sclerosis. At first, the disease's symptoms came and went, but as the 1980s progressed, Mary became increasingly incapacitated, eventually being confined to a wheelchair. At first, Jack tried to take care of her, quitting his job to stay home with his wife, and began to draw monthly Social Security payments, along with an annuity from his work at Western Auto. With the house completely paid for, and with Mary insured, the couple's expenses were minimal. But as the task of caregiving became ever more onerous, Jack found excuses to get out of the house, according to Mary's three daughters. Jack found release not so much in the bottle as in the bowling alley, and at social events at the Reisterstown Senior Center, or bingo games at the Sons of Italy. Jack loved to socialize, and particularly to sing, especially with the karaoke machine he'd bought after seeing it advertised on television. He learned to play a simple electronic organ—not well, but enough to keep a tune.

Then, in 1989, Mary died, and Jack was left alone in the house at 613 Sungold Road. His neighbors knew him as a quiet if friendly person who was dedicated to his flower garden and lawn, who enjoyed greeting everyone as they came home from work. After Mary died, Jack began a relationship with an older woman, a widow he'd met at the Senior Center, Vera. Jack had hopes of marrying Vera; he liked to boast of her cooking skills. But Vera had other ideas, and the relationship dwindled away. Vera eventually married someone else.

Jack was left alone.

Then, in June of 1993, Jack was diagnosed with congestive heart disease—one of his heart valves was malfunctioning. He went into the hospital for an operation, and the valve was replaced with an implant, which involved a Dacron ring. The operation was a success, and Jack soon returned to Sungold Road. His step-daughters and their children dropped by frequently to help care for him. Eventually Jack recovered, and returned to his favorite pursuits, bingo, bowling and singing at the senior center. And Jack found himself enjoying weekly breakfast get-togethers of other seniors at the local Woolworths, which had a restaurant in its basement. "The Five and Dime Breakfast Club," as it became known informally, was a place to socialize for those of similar ages and life experiences.

One of Jack's closest friends, at both the senior center and the "breakfast club," was Ralph Hodge. A professional musician by trade, by then retired, Ralph still enjoyed playing various clubs and halls in the area, such as the Sons of Italy. Jack often went with him. Jack became very close to Ralph and his wife during the early 1990s, after Mary died.

"Jack was an easy-going guy," Ralph later recalled. "He loved plants, flowers of all kinds. He had a hot bed, and grew herbs." But Jack tended to get confused from time to time. "He wasn't very mechanically inclined," Ralph remembered. Once, after a long winter, Jack wasn't able to get his lawn mower started. He was going to give it away, to Connie, because it didn't work anymore. Ralph took a look at it. The battery was worn down from Jack's futile attempts to start it. Ralph looked inside and discovered a dead mouse in the flywheel. He removed the defunct rodent, charged the battery, and started the machine. Jack was both grateful and impressed.

Ralph had grown up on the streets of Detroit back in the 1930s and 1940s, and had done time in juvenile institutions there and in another state. It was while he was serving a sentence as an incorrigible youth that he learned to play the clarinet. He'd wanted to learn the trumpet, but the clarinet was the only instrument available. Later, Ralph became proficient with the saxophone, and soon became a professional musician, playing gigs throughout the Midwest. So Ralph had been around, and knew a con when he saw one. Jack, Ralph knew, was far too naïve and trusting for his own good.

"You could almost talk him into anything," Ralph remembered.

Then, one day—Ralph thought it might have been late in 1994—Jack came to the "breakfast club" grinning from ear-to-ear.

"I found a gal," Jack told Ralph.

The records seem to indicate that Nancy first came to the Sungold Road house on November 10, 1994, peddling the reservation for the crypt Jack wanted. As Ralph recalled, Jack was adamant about not wanting to be buried.

"I said, 'What difference does it make? When you're dead, you're dead. You won't care where you are,'" Ralph remembered. But Jack said the idea of being below the surface of the earth gave him the willies.

"I don't want dirt thrown over my face," Jack told Ralph. He had to have an above-ground vault, and Evergreen Memorial Gardens had just the spot for him in their mausoleum. Just $328 down, another $1,900 or so, and he could rest in peace for all eternity, above the depredations of worms and other creepy crawlers.

So Nancy sat down in Jack's living room, and took down all his financial information: his Social Security number, his credit card account numbers, the names of his soon-to-be surviving relatives, the fact that he owned the Sungold Road house free and clear of any mortgage, and that he had a spotless credit record, as a quick check showed. And his age—74 years young, going on 75. She got Jack to sign on the dotted line.

Whether anything else transpired between Jack and Nancy that day, or in the next two weeks, isn't clear, but on November 26, Nancy pawned an expensive Gruen watch, an 18-karat gold ring, and a 14-karat pin at a Baltimore pawn shop. This was while she was awaiting trial on the Baltimore shoplifting charge, in which she potentially faced up to 18 months in prison, and while she was on probation in Howard

County. One thing was clear—the pawned items did not belong to Nancy. Otherwise, she would have pawned them long before that date. Police later came to believe that the items were Jack's. Whether Nancy pilfered them while visiting Jack, or Jack gave them to her in response to some tale of Nancy's isn't clear. But as Ralph had said, "You could almost talk him into anything."

In any event, by December of 1994, Jack was speaking in glowing terms of his "new gal." And when Ralph pressed him for details of this new-found love, Jack told him all about Nancy—or some about Nancy. That she was in her late 40s, blond, smart, gainfully employed at Evergreen Memorial Gardens, and beautiful. That she was a divorcee with two grown daughters. That she was genuinely interested in Jack and impressed by him. And hey—did I mention she was beautiful?

"Jack, that doesn't sound like too good of a relationship to me," Ralph told Jack. "She's too young for you." Ralph was sure that this "new gal" was just after Jack's money.

But Jack didn't want to hear this from Ralph. After all, Ralph didn't have to live by himself—his wife Rosalie was still alive.

That winter, Jack talked a lot about Nancy—mostly, how she was in love with him. At least one thing about the relationship was true—Jack seemed happier than he had been in some time.

What Jack didn't know was that that winter, Nancy had already used his financial information to open seven new credit accounts in his name. Eventually Nancy would open twenty-one more accounts in the name of Jack Watkins, including two after he was dead—and by the end, almost all of them would be in arrears, Nancy's supply of free money.

# 6
# TRIPLE-TIMING

Nancy, meanwhile, had ended her relationship with Eric Siegel. Or rather, Rick had ended his relationship with Nancy. After having separated from his wife in the aftermath of the car wreck and trial, Rick tried to reconcile with Faye throughout the years 1993, 1994 and the early part of 1995, while Nancy was measuring Jack for his crypt. Interestingly, the post office box in Ellicott City that Nancy had rented in September of 1993 was in her name, the names of her daughters, and also, Eric Siegel. This was likely unknown to Eric—already, according to government, much later, Nancy was planning to open credit accounts in Eric's name, and have the bills sent to the bogus post office box, where, of course, they would remain unpaid and unknown to Rick.

At one point during this period, Nancy told Rick that she had begun a relationship with a doctor at Johns Hopkins, "Gershon Lewis," although this was a fiction: no such doctor existed, and it seems likely that Nancy was trying to win Rick back by making him jealous. It didn't work—Rick was anxious to repair his severely damaged marriage, and seemed to want to put Nancy into his past.

So it seems likely that Nancy, having struck out in trying

to induce Rick to permanently leave his wife and take up
with her, was eyeing Jack as a potential new cash cow. In
early 1995, someone obtained a new driver's license and a
new Social Security card for Jack. Later, experts would say
the signatures on the applications seemed "suspect," as if
Jack hadn't actually signed them. These identity documents
would've been very useful for anyone intending to open still
more accounts in Jack's name, without his knowledge, and
indeed, according to the police, later, that's exactly what happened. Eventually Jack's name was also on the post office
box in Ellicott City.

Meanwhile, Ralph Hodge and his wife Rosalie were becoming increasingly suspicious of Nancy, whom they had
never actually met. They had, however, spoken to her on the
telephone. This happened on several occasions when Nancy
dropped by the Sungold Road house to visit Jack, only to find
him gone. Nancy immediately called Ralph and his wife,
demanding to know if Jack was there. When told that Jack
wasn't, that he was probably off bowling or singing or playing bingo, Nancy grew angry and short with them. And
Jack's neighbors occasionally saw Nancy drive up in her sil-
ver Toyota to check Jack's mailbox. She was probably "weed-
ing" the mailbox to intercept the bills from the bogus credit
cards before Jack could see them. But Nancy exchanged almost no words with Jack's neighbors.

That's how it was with Jack's step-daughters, too. Cheryl
and Anita occasionally called Jack to see how he was, and
when Nancy answered the phone, the conversation was short
and not particularly sweet. They left messages on the an-
swering machine, but Jack never returned their calls. Mary's
daughters soon got the impression that Jack wasn't interested in seeing them, and their relationship with their late-
in-life stepfather slowly withered away.

Then, in late May of 1995, Jack and Nancy showed up at
a Baltimore-area BMW dealership, where Jack signed to
lease a brand-new 1995 BMW for a total price of a little over

$44,000. Jack, who had a total monthly income of around $1,300 from Social Security and his annuity from New York Life, had just agreed to make monthly payments of $680. There must have been a balloon payment in the deal at lease end to make the payments that low, although the records weren't that clear, later. He gave the new car to Nancy.

A few weeks later, as Nancy was whizzing back and forth in the new BMW to casinos in New Jersey, Delaware and West Virginia, plunging away with cash she'd obtained from new credit accounts she'd opened in Jack's unwitting name, Nancy and Rick Siegel resumed their relationship. Rick's marriage with Faye had finally, irretrievably collapsed.

Now that Nancy had Rick back, she decided to do something about Jack, or more exactly, all the debts she'd run up in Jack's name. Likely, Nancy had decided to clear the decks of all Jack's debts, on the off-chance that one of the creditor banks decided to track Jack down and let him know just what was going on, which would have inevitably led to her, and fouled up her rekindled relationship with Rick.

On August 10, 1995, Jack and Nancy appeared at the offices of a Maryland mortgage broker, where Jack signed the papers for a $44,600 mortgage on the Sungold Road house. Almost all the money went to pay off bank loans and credit card debts in Jack's name, although until Nancy had come into his life, Jack owed nothing, and in fact, didn't even have any of the nineteen accounts that were opened after November of 1994.

Jack willingly signed the papers, even though none of the debts were actually his. None of the money went to pay off the BMW lease finance arm, which was already trying to collect on past-due payments.

This loan transaction on Jack's Sungold house remains one of the enduring mysteries of the Jack/Nancy entanglement of 1994–1996. Why would Jack agree to pay off all these banks? Surely he knew, however dull a crayon he was, that he didn't owe anything like these amounts, to banks he'd never heard of. Why didn't Jack simply walk away from the mortgage company, claiming, truthfully, ignorance as to this indebtedness? Why didn't he cry foul, demand that the police come and rescue him from Nancy? After all, it wasn't as if Nancy wasn't a known commodity to Baltimore-area law enforcement types in the summer of 1995—she was on ten years' probation from three years of unrelenting credit card fraud and forgery. Of course, Jack probably knew nothing of Nancy's past. But still—signing over $44,600 to creditors he'd never known about—what was going through Jack's mind?

One likely explanation is that Nancy somehow sweet-talked Jack into signing off on "his" debts, with some sort of story about the Devil in Atlantic City, who was supposedly squeezing her relentlessly. Jack, the Galahad, had to save her from a fate worse than white slavery. Or maybe Jack signed over his house and his life, not understanding that this wasn't some sort of legalistic formality needed to clear the decks so he could go off in wedded bliss with his "new gal." Whatever, Jack signed, and was therefore on the hook for mortgage payments for a house that Mary had bought years before, then left to him, free and clear, for his old age. There's no fool like an old fool, especially one in love.

By now, Nancy was two-timing Jack with Rick Siegel, and maybe even the fictitious Johns Hopkins doctor, "Gershon Lewis," whom Rick knew about, even if Jack didn't. The BMW finance people were becoming insistent—where was Jack? When was he going to make his lease payments? They kept calling Nancy—she'd given them her telephone number, not Jack's. Nancy was evasive—the check was either in the mail, or had been misplaced by the finance people. What was wrong with them?

Over the next few years, Nancy made excuse after excuse for Jack every time they called, usually after expending considerable effort to track down either Jack or Nancy. Sometimes

Nancy was Jack's girlfriend, sometimes his wife, sometimes his daughter. Sometimes Nancy didn't know where Jack was, sometimes he was sick, sometimes he was visiting relatives in Virginia. He'd had a stroke, he was dying, he was in the hospital. He had a gambling problem, he was seeing his mother in Pennsylvania. She hadn't seen him, didn't know where he was. The BMW finance people grew exasperated; eventually the account was assigned to a collection agency, which repeatedly struck out in trying to locate the elusive will 'o the wisp, Jack Watkins.

Meanwhile, the BMW was parked in the driveway of Nancy's condo in Ellicott City. Probably any repo man worth his hot wires could have found it, if only someone had looked. Just why the BMW people didn't drop by the Sungold Road house to look for Jack is an enduring mystery. Maybe, if they had, they could have saved his life.

In November of 1995, Nancy returned for another bite at the apple that was Jack. This time she convinced him to refinance the Sungold house. The original $44,600 mortgage was paid off with a new loan, this one for $77,000. After bank fees, late fees, appraisal fees, title insurance and other expenses, there was $20,341 left over. This was made payable to Nancy, or at least, Nancy somehow got the money. Nancy told Jack she'd use the cash for a down payment on the Ellicott City condo she lived in with Amanda. With Amanda in college in Virginia, Nancy told Jack, he could soon move in with her! Soon! She'd take care of him, she promised.

# 7
# GASLIGHTED

By early 1996, Jack was becoming anxious about his supposedly imminent wedding to Nancy. Nancy kept insisting that it would happen, just as soon as all the arrangements could be made. First among those arrangements was: what to do with the Sungold house? Based on the refinancing of November, Jack was on the hook for payments of $829.65 a month, about 60 percent of his total income. And this didn't include the unpaid BMW lease—that brought the total of Jack's monthly payments, at least on paper, to about $1,510, or approximately 110 percent of his total income. And those payments didn't include the credit card accounts Nancy had opened in Jack's name, apparently without his knowledge. For all practical purposes, Jack was not only insolvent, on paper he was below water—he was drowning.

All of this seemed to go over Jack's head. There is no evidence, from his conversations with Ralph Hodge, or his neighbors, that Jack had any idea that he'd been wiped out. All he knew was that he was soon to marry and move in with Nancy, his "new gal," who had promised to take care of him. And hey—didn't I say she was beautiful?

On February 2, 1996, Nancy called a real estate agent who

specialized in distressed property. She offered to sell the Sungold Road house. Nancy claimed that she had Jack's power of attorney. The sale would pay off the refinanced mortgage of $77,000. What with other expenses, the sale price of about $90,000 (the property was worth a minimum of $110,000, and was soon resold for that amount) would net Jack around $4,000. The deal was to go through in early April 1996.

On March 15, 1996, Nancy called Jack's long-time doctor, Craig Haber. Haber had treated Jack for more than two decades. He had first been Mary's doctor, then had diagnosed Jack's heart trouble in early 1991. As far as Haber could tell, Jack was a very healthy, happy 76-year-old man, whose appearance made him seem even younger than his actual age. But Nancy—Haber had never met her face-to-face—told him that Jack was acting strangely. Jack was falling down, occasionally belligerent, drinking to excess, complaining about money. Nancy identified herself as Jack's "girlfriend." She was worried, she added—Jack had a rifle in the house, and Nancy was concerned that he might use it.

This alarmed Haber. He wrote a note for his file:

*March 15th, 1996. Telephone call from Nancy Sweitzer, girlfriend of Jack Watkins. For weeks now Mr. Watkins is acting in a bizarre fashion, leaving cigarettes burning on his TV set, acting belligerent at times, urinating in bed, urinating into his drinking cups, becoming confused at times, forgetting things. Trying to drive off in somebody else's car, thinking it is his. Patient has not been physically abusive nor threatening. There is a gun, unclear if it is loaded, found in his apartment. It is a rifle. Never threatened, but the patient's girlfriend notes that it is there. Patient denies anything wrong.*

*We have tried contacting him but the phones are call forwarded to the girlfriend's house. The patient had an appointment today. He refused to come in. The patient is manifesting bizarre behavior, calling the bank daily. It is not clear to me why. There is no head trauma history per the girlfriend. Patient scheduled to move into the girlfriend's apartment April 1st and has been in the process of moving out of his apartment.*

*Physically, he seems to be fine. No falls or weakness. Can maintain his bowling. His relationship with the girlfriend is even-keeled otherwise. Last known medications are Lanoxin, .25 milligrams only, and he is not taking any narcotics or mind altering drugs. He continues to smoke. Patient was confronted by girlfriend and he denies any problems. No fever, sweats.*

*My concern is several, as follows: Of course, the bizarre mental status changes of a rather rapid onset probably speaks of either a toxic encephalopathy or, more likely, a space occupying lesion of the brain. I cannot rule out thyrotoxicosis or digitoxosis, either, but that would be unusual.*

*My concern with the patient is, of course, is, number one, his bizarre behavior and risk of life and limb with that rifle. The patient's girlfriend promised me she will move the rifle from the premises today but since he is not belligerent to her or threatening to her or anybody else in a physical sense, it would be hard-pressed to force a commission. The girlfriend promises that we can get him to have some testing done. And I have made arrangements to get a CAT scan or brain scan Monday and blood tests, including thyroid, general chemistry, CBC, and Digoxin level.*

*Do not know what else to do except again severely warn the girlfriend that should there be any violent tendencies or if she cannot get that rifle out of the house, that somebody will have to call the police. My intention is to call the police on Monday if she cannot removal the rifle today.*

Eventually Nancy told Haber that she'd gotten rid of the rifle, and that Jack had calmed down. Jack was just drinking too much, Nancy told Haber over the telephone. He was probably stressed out because he was soon to move in with her, to her condo in Ellicott City.

But first Jack wanted to show off his "new gal" to his old friends at the "breakfast club." Just before the house closed escrow, Jack and Nancy arrived at the club's weekly gathering. Ralph Hodge was there, along with his wife Rosalie.

"He came down there," Ralph recalled, of the encounter at the Woolworths. "He was pretty well set on going." Ralph remembered that Jack had introduced Nancy to all his friends. Ralph saw a much younger woman, pretty, blond, assertive. Nancy sounded very sure of herself, Ralph thought. She was saying that she and Jack were moving into her condo, that Jack wouldn't be coming back.

"I was listening to her," Ralph recalled, "and I didn't like what I was hearing. I got Jack aside. I was leaning up against my van."

"Jack, this romance is no good for you," Ralph told Jack. "Stay away from her."

But Jack wouldn't listen.

"He kept saying she was going to take care of him," Ralph recalled. And Nancy assured the breakfast clubbers that Jack would be happy with her.

Ralph didn't believe her, and neither did Rosalie. Nancy was a gold-digger, Ralph's wife said, after Jack and Nancy had driven away in the BMW. Anyone could see that.

Except Jack.

The sale of the house cleared on April 9, 1996. What happened next would remain murky for years. According to one of Nancy's stories about the events, told much later to investigating authorities, she and Jack took the remnant from the sale, around $4,000, and went to Atlantic City, to celebrate.

But this wasn't what Nancy said at the time, back in April

of 1996. In fact, at that point it wasn't even clear whether Nancy herself had ever actually gone to Atlantic City, at least in her version of the events. She seemed to suggest that Jack had gone there on his own, in the grip of some sort of delusion that they were going to be married. Much later, some suggested it was possible that Nancy had lied about this to hospital personnel at the time, in April of 1996, and had actually taken Jack to Atlantic City and dumped him there, but not before pumping him full of booze. Then, in this scenario, somehow the abandoned Jack had found his way to a bus terminal and had returned to Ellicott City on his own, like an unwanted penny. Then, in this scenario, Nancy had tried to get him committed for dementia.

In any event, the next thing anyone knew, Nancy was checking Jack into Howard County General Hospital on the afternoon of April 11, 1996, complaining of dizziness and slurred words. Over the next few hours, Jack told of going to Atlantic City to celebrate his forthcoming marriage to his "fiancée," Nancy. For her part, Nancy said she was just Jack's landlady, and that any ideas of marriage between her and Jack were wholly a figment of his imagination.

Jack, Nancy said, had been falling down, not making any sense. He'd been wandering off, without supervision. He'd gone all the way to Atlantic City by himself, she seemed to say, and somehow had made his way back on a bus. She thought he might have had a stroke. But most assuredly, there had never been any plans for them to marry. Jack was making the whole thing up.

Is there anything more frightening than the idea of being checked into a hospital for a mental ailment you don't think you have, and being told, repeatedly, calmly and profession-ally, that you're crazy? You can insist all you want that you're perfectly fine, and people only nod sympathetically, and tell you, in the most polite and solicitous of phrases . . . you're nuts. The more you insist that there's nothing wrong with you, the more everyone else insists that, sorry, you really are mentally ill, and they're going to help you. After a while, with so many of *them*, all claiming to be experts, and only one of *you*, when do you start to doubt yourself?

That's what happened to Jack Watkins between April 11 and April 18, 1996. He kept insisting he was perfectly normal, mentally speaking. The people at the hospital insisted he was not, and Jack couldn't convince them otherwise. Nancy was going to marry him, he insisted. She'd promised him. They were engaged. They'd gone to Atlantic City to celebrate. True, he'd had a bit too much to drink there—but once he'd sobered up, he felt fine.

The hospital people, doctors, nurses, social workers—come whom they may—merely nodded and agreed among themselves that, yes, poor Jack was making things up. They knew for sure, because Nancy had told them so.

Within a few hours of his admission to the hospital, Jack had been slotted by the diagnosticians: he was an alcoholic, possibly suffering from the "DTs," or delirium tremens, a consequence of years of battling the bottle, they decided, in part based on Nancy's information, and Jack's own sheepish admission of his troubles with booze in the past. Jack's weight, normally around 137, was down to 118, a sure sign of malnutrition endemic to excessive alcohol abuse, the doctors decreed. He was "confabulating," making up stories, such as his forthcoming marriage to a much younger woman, a sure sign of "Korsakoff's syndrome," an alcohol-abuse–precipitated form of vitamin deficiency, and a form of dementia that caused people to imagine things, and forget reality, very common to severe alcoholics. Left untreated, Korsakoff's syndrome would only get worse. The only hope for Jack was an adult-care facility—a nursing home, according to the hospital's consulting psychiatrist, Dr. Alix Rey.

This was all in contradistinction to a leading expert on

Korsakoff's syndrome, Dr. William Alwyn Lishman, a widely recognized expert in neuropsychiatry—the relationship between brain diseases and injuries, and behavior. Dr. Lishman, in *Organic Psychiatry*, one of the leading survey texts in the field, had opined that "Korsakoff's syndrome" was over-diagnosed by harried clinicians working under pressure. It is possibly significant that Jack's hospital records, lodged with the court trying Nancy Siegel for his murder years later, reflect no brain-imaging tests such as a CAT scan to see if Jack had the sort of organic brain damage usually associated with Korsakoff's syndrome. Nor is there any record that the doctors at the hospital attempted to consult with Jack's previous doctor, Craig Haber, about the brain scan he had conducted on Jack only a month before—the one that showed his brain seemed to be completely normal. Had they done so, the outcome—for both Jack and Nancy—might have been very different.

The hospital enlisted Nancy—or, perhaps, Nancy enlisted the hospital—to look for a place to stash Jack. Thus, the semi-witting plan for the care and concomitant disposal of Jack Watkins was off and running, and there was no one to slow it down, let alone stop it. Beliefs led to assumptions, assumptions led to conclusions, conclusions led to decisions, and from that moment forward, Jack Watkins was doomed.

After being stabilized in the medical portion of the hospital, a day or so later, Julia Lubis, a social worker, and Nancy met with Jack. As far as can be determined, this was the only time that anyone from the hospital met with Nancy and Jack in the same room. It appears that Nancy had enlisted Lubis in an effort to convince Jack that he was sick, to prepare him for the bad news. Lubis explained that she and Nancy were trying to find a place for him in a group home. Jack became very agitated, "upset," as Lubis recalled later. He insisted that he wasn't moving to any group home, that he and Nancy were going to be married. Nancy told Lubis, apparently privately, perhaps before this three-way discussion, that Jack was delusional. The medical records that Lubis had from Jack's hospital treatment so far seemed to agree: years of alcohol abuse, possible DTs, and the likelihood of Korsakoff's syndrome. So Jack was already on the road to supposed madness even before Lubis talked to him. At that point, Jack could have said Nancy was cheating him of everything he owned, and it's possible Lubis would have put it down to Jack's "Korsakoff's syndrome." But Jack, according to Lubis' notes of the encounter, said nothing of the sort. Apparently, he still believed in Nancy. But likely, also, Jack had begun to wonder, by that point: *Is there really something wrong with me? Do I really have dementia?* That would only be human, for anyone, given the way Jack was being treated at the hospital.

By the night of April 16, Jack was transferred to the hospital's psychiatric ward. He still kept insisting that he and Nancy were going to be married. By the morning of April 16, Jack was participating in a group therapy session with other psychiatric patients. He was cheerful and helpful to the nurses and other patients—it was almost a scene out of *One Flew Over the Cuckoo's Nest*, only Jack wasn't Randle McMurphy, he wasn't crazy or even pretending. If they'd had a sing-along, Jack would have led it. But he still insisted: he was perfectly fine, and that he and Nancy were going to be married. They'd gone to Atlantic City to celebrate, after his house was sold. He was convinced he still had all his marbles.

True, Jack admitted, he'd had a bit too much to drink there in Atlantic City, but he was fine now. Now he just wanted to go home, so he and Nancy could get married.

*It's a pity*, all the doctors and nurses said to each other. *Such a nice man. Too bad he's crazy.*

Well, it just wasn't so, Nancy kept insisting to all the doctors, nurses, psychiatrists and social workers at the hospital. There was nothing between them, and they certainly weren't about to get *married*. She was just Jack's landlady, that was all. He'd been acting a little goofy for some time, she said. He kept falling down, or wandering off. Honestly, she didn't know what to do with him. He was a danger to himself, especially with all his drinking. He'd gone off to Atlantic City, she said, and no one had known where he was. She'd been worried about him—who wouldn't be?

Nancy had returned to her condo after checking Jack into the hospital, and as the next few days passed, Nancy cooperated with Julia Lubis in an effort to find a place for Jack to stay. Obviously, Nancy told people at the hospital, she couldn't have Jack back at her house, not with his strange ideas. He was just too much for her to take care of. Lubis began making calls to adult care facilities specializing in patients with dementia. Meanwhile, psychiatrist Dr. Alix Rey had seen Jack a few times. Jack was undoubtedly suffering from "Korsakoff's syndrome," Rey noted on Jack's chart. His continued "confabulation" about the supposed marriage to Nancy proved that much. The best place for Jack, Rey said, was a long-term, adult care facility, if not a group home, then maybe a nursing home.

Then came the question: who was going to pay for Jack's treatment at the long-term care facility? Jack was essentially broke, Nancy told the hospital. Certainly *she* couldn't afford to pay for it. And why should she? She was just Jack's landlady. It wasn't as if they were related.

It appears that no one at the hospital asked about Jack's Social Security or his annuity from Western Auto, not to mention his Medicare entitlement, which might have addressed some of these questions. This was one of the saddest omissions of the hospital's treatment of Jack. Finding those answers would almost certainly have led to Dr. Haber and Jack's step-daughters, and very soon thereafter, Nancy's exposure. But for some reason, no one pursued those questions—to the hospital, it appears, Jack was just another drunk, someone to be processed, not treated. To be fair, the hospital did ask Jack if he have any relatives in the area. Jack said he did—he had step-daughters. But Jack didn't give their names, and it appears from the hospital records that the hospital didn't ask. He'd once had a sister in Virginia, but she was dead. Whether this was something Jack had told the hospital people, or something Nancy told them, wasn't clear in the hospital's records. In fact, this was wrong: his sister Doris was still alive, living in Richmond, which suggests that this information actually was provided by Nancy. The provenance of the information isn't clear in the hospital records. But of course, hospital officials aren't trained to ferret out the agendas of those who lie to them about their patients.

And in any event, Jack balked: why should he go into a nursing home? He and Nancy were going to be married. Although the hospital records aren't very clear on this point, it seems that Nancy somehow managed to assuage Jack, perhaps reassure him that she would in fact take care of him until his dying day. If this was the case, the next question—probably a critical question—is why Nancy would have done this one-eighty. On April 11, she was trying to get him committed as a dementia patient. A week later, she was taking him home with her, despite her earlier protests that she couldn't take care of him. One possible conclusion is that Nancy realized that once her plan to gaslight Jack wasn't going to work, she realized that she had to get Jack out of the hospital before Lubis or Rey or anyone else realized what had actually happened to him.

In the end, the hospital decided it had no place to send Jack. On April 18, they released him—to the custody of Nancy Jean Sweitzer, his "landlady."

But this six-day stay in the hospital was in fact the last, best hope of saving the life of Jack Watkins, that regular, happy-go-lucky guy, even if he wasn't "the sharpest crayon in the box." Howard County General Hospital had it within their grasp to find out important, salient facts about their patient: for instance, who had treated him before he arrived on their doorstep as Nancy Sweitzer's "tenant"? Doubtless Dr. Haber could have told them a lot. What about Jack's step-daughters? Or Ralph Hodge? Or Jack's old neighbors on Sungold Road, or in the "breakfast club"?

And what about Nancy herself? Did the hospital do anything to validate her ability to take care of her "tenant" before releasing him to her care?

It wasn't as if Jack Watkins was nobody. He owned—or had owned—property in Reisterstown. He had friends and neighbors who cared for him, as well as family. He had, at the very least, nearly a decade of Medicare records to check, including a complicated surgical operation. In hindsight, there was no reason for the hospital to believe Nancy instead of her victim, Jack. And while it is true that hospitals aren't required to check the criminal history of those who bring them patients, even the slightest skepticism as to Nancy's qualifications as Jack's caregiver, or even "landlady," might have unearthed her unsavory past, including the fact that she was on probation for theft, forgery and fraud in at least three counties. But Nancy always did have a good patter—that's the way grifters are.

Still, that the hospital failed to do any of this—that they essentially processed Jack as a supposed drunk—should stand as an embarrassment, if not condemnation.

Nancy took Jack back to her condo in Ellicott City. There, the police said later, she literally tried to starve him to death, while keeping him overdosed on over-the-counter tranquilizers. In his drug-induced haze, Jack kept wondering when they were going to be married. Nancy kept wondering what to do with him, now that he'd served his purpose.

# PART II
## THE JACK-IN-THE-BOX CASE

# 8
# MERCHANT

So now, almost thirteen years later, in the paneled federal courtroom of the Honorable Andre M. Davis, Judge of the United States District Court For the District of Maryland, the witnesses come forth: the first, a Loudoun County, Virginia, sheriff's deputy, Clark Jackson. Clark is burly, wearing a tan uniform. His eyeglasses give him a mien of seriousness, of sobriety: this is a man who can be trusted. He has worked for the Loudoun County Sheriff's office three decades.

Jackson tells his story: in the early morning hours of May 14, 1996, he was patrolling the northwest corner of Loudoun County, the area closest to where the Appalachian Trail slices through the county, not far from where the Shenandoah River joins the Potomac near Harpers Ferry. Jackson tells the jury how he turned his cruiser onto U.S. Route 340, where a small, mile-long ribbon of 340 runs through Loudoun County, before crossing the West Virginia state line. The stretch of four-lane blacktop lay wholly within Harpers Ferry National Historical Park, where it overlooks the Potomac River.

A convenience store along the highway just before the state line was a frequent target for hold-ups by robbers who usually quickly crossed over into West Virginia. Just after he passed the convenience store, Clark pulled into a turnout overlooking the river to turn around to go back to check the store again. But then Jackson saw something odd.

"I came across a box," Clark tells Nancy Jean's jurors in March of 2009, years later, "in the parking area."

As far as he could make out, the box looked like a trunk of some sort. The trunk was underneath a chain that prevented people from walking further into a steep, wooded, hilly area overlooking the river. Jackson says he got out of his patrol car to take a closer look.

"It was kind of unusual," he says, "so I got out, to check it out. I opened it. I saw a duffle bag. I saw another duffle bag. And then I saw the body."

What Clark Jackson saw in the early morning hours of May 14, 1996, was the corpse of a rather small, elderly man, naked from the waist down, with a pillowcase over his head, stuffed inside two duffle bags and folded into a trunk perhaps eighteen inches wide and a little over two feet long. The trunk had been sealed with some sort of tape, he realized.

Clark called his supervisor, Sergeant Dave Kerr, who soon arrived at the scene. Kerr in turn called Loudoun County Sheriff's crime-scene analyst Brian Harpster, and Detective Jay Merchant. It was obvious to Kerr that this was a probable murder case. It wasn't likely that the dead man had put himself inside the trunk, sealed it shut with tape, then put the trunk at the wayside for Jackson to discover. Harpster and Merchant, both awakened at their homes, drove separately to the wayside, arriving there a little after 2 A.M.

Seeing the body in the trunk, folded over, eyes glaring, mouth grimacing, Merchant couldn't help but be reminded of a children's toy—the one where a grinning joker comes springing out.

*Like a jack-in-the-box*, Merchant thought. He knew Deputy Jackson was in an impromptu contest with another sheriff's deputy involving the salvage of items abandoned along the roadside. *I'll bet this was a shock to Grant,* Merchant thought. *Boinnng! And this time, the prize is—a corpse!* Then he had another thought. *Why is this trunk here? Why didn't whoever left it here take the time to push it over the side of the hill toward the river?* The bank beyond the wayside was quite steep. It would have been simple to open the trunk, tip it over, drag the body to the steep hillside, and roll it down into the trees on the side of the cliff. That way, the person who left the body at the wayside could have taken the trunk with them, instead of leaving it as evidence for people like him to examine. He could see the tracks in the dirt of the wayside, from the wheels—the trunk had small wheels along the bottom. Clearly the person who'd left it had pulled it out of a vehicle, then dragged it to its position next to the trash can.

Then it hit Merchant. *The person who did this wanted this body to be found. That means it's probably a caregiver.* Someone who wanted the man dead maybe, but didn't want to be associated with his death. Someone who still cared enough about the victim to want him found. It couldn't be a professional hit—no one who knew what they were doing would have done it like that. It had to be someone who knew the victim, Merchant realized.

Within a few hours, the trunk and the body of the unknown man were on their way to Leesburg, Virginia, the Loudoun County seat. By 6 A.M. on the morning of May 14, 1996, the body had been removed from the trunk, placed on a table, unfolded, photographed and fingerprinted. The duffle bags and pillowcases were examined, as was the trunk. There wasn't one single, solitary, obvious clue as to the identity of the dead man. There was, however, some evidence as to how he had died: from the dried blood on the back of his head, it appeared that someone had clobbered him with a hard object. And there on the neck were several abrasions that looked as though someone had tried to strangle him.

*Well,* thought Merchant, *someone might have cared enough about old Jack-in-the-box to leave him where we*

*could find him, but they didn't care so much about him that
they left him with his Social Security card.*

That was how the man in the trunk became the first mystery of what became known in Loudoun County as the Jack-in-the-box Case: who was the dead man? And until he had an answer to the first mystery, Merchant couldn't begin to go to work on the second one: who left Jack-in-the-box in a trunk by the side of the road in the middle of the night?

Merchant was an experienced detective. He'd had almost two decades as a criminal investigator in Fairfax County, Virginia, before relocating to the place where he'd grown up, Loudoun County, to the west of Washington, D.C. In the old days, Loudoun had been a mostly rural county, with rolling green hills carpeted with dense green forests, interspersed with pastures and a few crops. Loudoun was horse country, farming country. But with the construction of Dulles International Airport on the east side of the county, and the explosion of housing in the D.C. metro area, Loudoun was changing. Nowadays, it wasn't unusual for Loudoun to get ten or fifteen murder cases a year. Most of them, though, were dump cases like Jack-in-the-box—where the crime took place elsewhere, but the body became Loudoun's headache. Which again meant figuring out who the corpse had been before he'd become a corpse.

The body on the table at the hospital in Leesburg was that of an elderly man. The dead man measured a little over five feet six inches in length, and weighed exactly 111 pounds. There was evidence of significant malnutrition, along with the clear injuries to the head and neck. The hair was dark, and while it was obvious that the man was of older years, he still seemed vital in some vague way. Merchant was quite sure that the man hadn't died of natural causes. In that case, who would have taken the trouble to stuff him in a small trunk, and leave him by the side of the road?

The best lead was the man's fingerprints. The first doctor

to examine the corpse guessed that the man hadn't been dead much more than forty-eight hours, if that. Rigor mortis was just leaving, and decomposition of the remains hadn't really begun. That meant that Merchant could expect to get some good, clear fingerprints. With any luck, the prints would pop up in some record, somewhere, and the first half of the mystery would be solved.

Two days later, during an autopsy at the hospital in Leesburg, Dr. Frances Field, the assistant chief medical examiner for the Commonwealth of Virginia, examined the head and neck injuries more closely. The amount of hemorrhaging inside the neck and rear of the mouth seemed to prove that the man had died of strangulation—"cervical compression," as Field put it. Although there was no distinct ligature marking on the neck, such as from a rope or a cord, the bruising there seemed to show that some force had been applied to shut off the man's air supply. The head injury was to the top right rear of the skull, and was accompanied by substantial bleeding under the left side of the brain. This suggested a contra-coup injury, which often accompanies the whipping back-and-forth of the brain when the skull is struck by a hard object, or has taken an un-braced fall. There was also evidence of an earlier operation, a ten-inch scar down the middle of the chest, and when Field examined the heart, she found a small plastic-like ring in the dead man's mitral heart valve, which she identified as an implant used by heart surgeons to improve the pumping capacity of a damaged heart. The Dacron ring, she told Merchant, who attended the autopsy, might prove useful in identifying the dead man. At least it would narrow the field of possible victims rather considerably.

Field took tissue and blood samples and packed them off to the state's Department of Forensic Science in Fairfax. Over the next week, a forensic toxicologist, Anh Huynh, tested the samples for alcohol and drugs. The victim's blood contained .01 percent of ethyl alcohol—about half a glass of beer, perhaps. Huynh also discovered a fairly significant

amount of diphenhydramine, an over-the-counter cold medicine like Benadryl—5.28 milligrams per liter, along with
1.10 milligram per liter of doxylamine, a cough medicine
like NyQuil, and a trace amount of methorphan, contained
in a product like Robitussin, along with acetaminophen,
a painkiller found in products like Anacin or Tylenol. In
larger dosages, the first three substances would make a person woozy, while very large does of acetaminophen might
cause confusion or hallucinations, and in extreme cases,
liver shutdown, especially when the substance was combined with excessive alcohol use. Huynh found that the dead
man's liver contained 103.8 milligrams per kilogram of the
Benadryl-like substance, along with a very small amount of
the same stuff in the stomach contents. That indicated that
the dosage had accumulated in the dead man's system over
some substantial period of time, days at least, if not weeks.

A closer look at the trunk also provided some leads: upon
inspection with a magnifying glass, Lee County experts
found traces of what appeared to be nail polish on the lid.
Samples of this were taken for further identification. Also
present were samples of coarse hair, which proved to be from
a dog, along with tape used to seal the trunk, acrylic fibers
associated with blankets and sweaters, and a facial tissue
containing DNA that did not come from the victim—not that
these helped, without some idea of who the dead man was.
The pajama top, pillowcase and duffle bags would also prove
to be a dead end—there were no identifying marks, and they
could have come from any store, anywhere in America.

So, as May of 1996 turned into June, Merchant's thoughts
turned more and more to how the dead man had come to arrive in Loudoun County. If the dumper had only driven
another half-mile or so, he or she would have been in West
Virginia, and Jack-in-the-box would have been someone
else's problem. What nagged at Merchant was the sense that
someone, somewhere had to know who the dead man was,

and at some point, would have to realize that he was missing. Merchant had an artist prepare a sketch of the dead man's face—it was a lot less gruesome than the real thing—and put out the drawing and the circumstances of the body's discovery to the news media in the hope that someone might recognize him. No one did.

The toxicology results reinforced Merchant's initial thoughts about a caretaker. The report indicated that the dead man had been taking over-the-counter medications, which could mean a nurse or a relative who procured them and provided them. He knew it wasn't likely that such a person would provide a missing persons report, because whoever had dumped the body certainly wasn't going to file such a report, and the chances were, only *that* person knew, at least for the present, that the man was dead. Still, Merchant thought it couldn't hurt to make inquiries at area nursing homes. Perhaps the dead man had been a patient at one of the nursing homes, had been removed by a relative, then later killed for some reason. There had to be some sort of connection between the dumper and the dead man, Merchant was sure. He had already decided the dumper and the killer was the same person.

"I felt the killer had some feeling for this person," he recalled. "There's a little bit of decency they had. They wanted to see him get a decent burial. Whoever it was, had enough sympathy for him that they wanted him found." An unfeeling, unrelated killer, Merchant reasoned, would never have left the body where it could be so easily discovered.

One idea that bore no fruit was to canvass for possible witnesses. From a park ranger, Merchant discovered that the trunk hadn't been at the wayside when the ranger checked the area at 8:30 P.M. on May 13, but that it had been there at 10:30. Because the roadway was a short strip of less than a mile from the bridge over the Potomac to the West Virginia line, and virtually all the traffic over the highway had to cross the bridge at some point, the sheriff's department closed off the roadway one night between 8:30 and 10:30 to ask all the drivers whether they had driven on Route 340 on the night of May 13, and if they had, if they had noticed anyone parked at the wayside. The road check turned up nothing useful.

"It's like fishing," Merchant said later. "You never know when you're going to get a bite." And it didn't make any real difference that nothing was turning up. "You never think you're not getting anywhere. You've eliminated one piece of the junkpile, and you think, *I'm one step closer to finding out who did it*," Merchant said later. A very large part of being a detective, he knew, was engaging in the process of elimination.

Merchant sent the dead man's fingerprints off to the FBI in the hope that the bureau might have some match among all the millions of prints it had collected over the years, from criminals to federal job applicants. The bureau had recently automated some of its fingerprint analysis procedure, at least those for known criminals. Merchant waited with neither hope nor discouragement. Eventually, the results came back: there was no match for the dead man's fingerprints in the FBI's criminal fingerprint database.

Merchant had one more idea: Field had given him the heart ring, and Merchant consulted a cardiac surgeon, who identified it as a Duran ring, manufactured in France and distributed in the United States by Medtronic, Inc. of Minnesota. Duran Ring Model 601 came in sizes ranging from 25 to 35 millimeters. Merchant discovered that Medtronic kept records of the identities of people who had received the heart ring during surgery. Merchant called Medtronic, only to be told by lawyers for the company that the list of recipients was confidential, that it wouldn't turn the names of the recipients over without a court order.

On June 24, 1996, Mechant, relying on the police officers' informal "old boy" network, enlisted a colleague in Minnesota to help him get a search warrant for the Medtronic records. Officers with the Anoka County criminal investigations division swooped down on the offices of Medtronic that same morning and seized 209 pages of Medtronic records showing the names, addresses, ages, dates of birth and Social Security numbers of thousands of recipients of the Duran ring.

Once he got the pages, Merchant was aghast—there were so many recipients, it was virtually impossible to narrow down the field. Even when the list was limited by sex, age and state of residence, there were still thousands—it would take years to run them all down. Regrettably, there was no unique identifier on the ring to tie it to any individual patient.

Merchant had one more idea—if there were thousands of patients, there were only hundreds of doctors. Maybe one of them might recognize the dead man. He took photographs of the face, and engaged an expert, Dr. Eileen Bowers of Louisiana State University, to put some life back into it, which was accomplished mostly by using a computer program to "normalize" a swollen right eye and close his gaping mouth. Merchant got a list of heart surgeons in seven states, and sent out a letter to all of them, along with a copy of the altered photograph, as well as a narrow slip of paper for the surgeon to check: "I ____ Do / ____ Do Not Recognize the Person." Of the several hundred heart surgeons who got the letter, Merchant received replies from around 30 to 40 percent. While that was a very high return rate for an unsolicited mailing, that still left a whole lot of heart surgeons who might have treated the dead man.

By the end of the summer, Merchant had run out of ideas. He circulated the circumstances of the finding of the corpse in a regional violent crime newsletter shared by police agencies in the hope that someone in some other jurisdiction might recognize the dead man, or even a similar *m.o.*, although that was highly unlikely. Nothing came back. The world was as silent about the body in the trunk as the corpse itself was on the night Grant Jackson had lifted the lid on his macabre discovery.

Loudoun County's investigators, like Merchant, were

generalists, not homicide specialists. That meant they had to take all kinds of cases—rapes, burglaries, assaults, frauds, the whole gamut of human misbehavior. There simply wasn't time to concentrate on one case—there was always something else bad to handle. Eventually Merchant had to move on to other matters. He had done as much with the corpse in the trunk as he could, given the little he'd had to work with from the start. Another two years would go by, and then Merchant retired after thirty-five years in law enforcement. But he never forgot Jack-in-the-box, and he remained convinced that someone out there knew who he was, and why he'd been left that way.

# 9
# THE POSTMAN ALWAYS COMES TWICE

Despite her on-again, off-again relationship with Rick, Nancy continued to have money problems as the rest of 1996 unfolded. In September, Nancy filed for bankruptcy under Chapter 7, listing debts of a little over $21,000 to a variety of doctors, banks and credit card companies, as well as the IRS. This was Nancy's second bankruptcy in a dozen years, the first having occurred after the end of her marriage to Charles. The BMW people were still hunting for Jack Watkins, and the car insurance people cancelled the policy on the car when the elusive Jack failed to pay the premiums. Neither made any difference to Nancy—it was Jack's name on the dotted lines, not hers, even if the car was in her driveway.

That same month, Social Security was notified to stop making automatic payments to Jack's bank account. Instead, future payments should be made by check, and mailed to Nancy's condo in Ellicott City. After one glitch when the next check didn't arrive, the Social Security money resumed, this time by check payable to Jack F. Watkins. Nancy wrote the name "Jack F. Watkins" on the back of each check, and deposited them in her own account, or cashed them, with her own co-endorsement. Eventually, Nancy would use her own daughters' names for co-endorsements, without their knowledge. In February 1997, after her second bankruptcy was finalized, Nancy opened a new post office box in Ellicott City, and had the Social Security checks sent there.

On March 18, 1997, Rick and Faye Siegel were divorced.

Even with Rick's new freedom to marry, he was apparently holding Nancy at arm's length, at least for a while, and it appears that Nancy's money problems continued. That same month, someone who identified herself as Jack's step-daughter Anita called New York Life, which paid Jack's modest, $171 monthly annuity from his work at Western Auto. "Anita" asked if it was possible to convert the annuity to cash. The insurance company said it would check and get back to her. A week later, the insurance company sent a letter to "Anita" at Nancy's condo, saying sorry, it wasn't possible.

A few more months passed. Rick finally relented, and soon he and Nancy resumed their relationship. In August, Nancy was added as a signatory to a bank account that Rick had ostensibly opened the previous month. Whether Rick himself knew that he had opened this account isn't entirely clear. Given Nancy's history and her forgery skills, along with the fact that Rick was later to claim that Nancy had scammed nearly $300,000 from him between 1997 and 2003, it's likely that Rick never knew.

Then, in late 1997, Nancy was up to one of her old tricks, raiding mailboxes.

This time, Nancy found an unsolicited, "pre-approved" credit offer mailed to a neighbor woman by AT&T. This, of course, was back in the era of loose money—well before the crash of 2008—when banks were making huge profits packaging consumer credit lines to investors. In those days, the idea was to rope in the consumer with a "guaranteed" credit line, often with a low interest rate, then package the hooked debtor into a "basket" of similar loans to insurance companies, other banks and wealthy people. These initial credit extenders didn't much care whether the loans would ever be paid back—once they were "packaged" in the "basket," the loans would be off the lender's books, minus the handling fee, which was generating the only sure profit in the whole deal. Some banks and credit card companies were making so much money peddling this scheme of monetary musical chairs that soon all sorts of businesses were getting in on the act, even communications companies like AT&T.

Nancy took one look at the AT&T solicitation and couldn't resist: here it was, more free money. All she had to do was call and provide a telephone number, and the credit would be on its way. She only had to keep an eye out for the mailman so she could intercept the credit authorization and any future bills, keeping the neighbor in the dark about the account she'd never opened. Soon AT&T sent Nancy's neighbor a credit account, along with "pre-approved" checks. Nancy got them before the neighbor even knew they were there. Eventually Nancy obtained a supply of blank checks and credit cards in the neighbor's name from three banks and several department stores.

It appears that Nancy missed the mailman's delivery at one point, because in late November or early December of 1997, AT&T got a complaint from Nancy's neighbor about charges on a credit account she didn't have. After a little further checking, someone at AT&T called the Howard County Sheriff's Department and was connected to a fraud detective, William Block. Block looked at a copy of the "pre-approved" application and noticed that the telephone number of the applicant was different from that of the complainant, Nancy's neighbor. He tried to find out who had the number, only to be told that it was unlisted. So Block got a subpoena for the telephone company and obtained the name and address of the telephone subscriber: Nancy Jean

Sweitzer. Block ran Nancy through the Maryland arrest records, and up popped Nancy's long history with credit card fraud and mailbox raiding.

Block rounded up documentation on all the bogus charges made on the AT&T credit account and soon had enough for a search warrant for Nancy's condo. On January 20, 1998, Block and a number of police officers arrived at the house Nancy now shared with Rick in Laurel, Maryland, and began a thorough search. Nancy was there with her daughters. A photograph taken at the time by police shows Nancy sitting on a couch, and Jennifer and Amanda at a dining table. Jennifer and Amanda were soon allowed to leave. But in the confusion of the search, Nancy somehow was permitted to wander unescorted into the kitchen, where she obtained a sharp knife. Returning to the living room, Nancy sat down on the sofa and concealed the knife between the cushions. She later said she was getting ready to kill herself.

Block's search of the condo turned up nothing—not a shred of paper to connect Nancy to the AT&T fraud, let alone the knife. This was his first fraud case, and he couldn't help thinking that somehow he had messed up, that he had it all wrong—this attractive, well-dressed, articulate, middle-aged woman couldn't possibly be a professional grifter, no matter what the records said. Nancy was polite, although not very communicative under the circumstances. In fact, Block thought she was very confident and calm. She demanded to see a copy of the warrant.

After an hour's search turned up nothing, Block prepared to leave. On the way out he noticed a newer black BMW parked in the driveway. Obtaining the keys from Nancy, he went through the car, too. There he found blank "pre-approved" checks in the name of Nancy's victimized neighbor.

Block asked Nancy if the BMW belonged to her. Nancy said it did not—it belonged to Jack Watkins. Jack let her use the car sometimes, she said.

Block seized the blank "pre-approved" checks as evidence of a crime. But whose crime? The car was registered in the name of someone named Jack Watkins. Block couldn't be legally sure that Watkins, whoever he was, wasn't actually the fraud artist. Maybe he'd used Nancy's telephone number without her knowledge. Maybe Jack Watkins had stolen the checks. These were other possibilities that might mean Nancy wasn't responsible. He left.

Block had only been gone a short time before Nancy called a Baltimore lawyer she knew, Robert Feinberg. "Bobby," as Nancy knew him, had been introduced to Nancy by other members of Gamblers Anonymous. Feinberg could tell the search had freaked Nancy out. He thought she was so depressed as to be nearly suicidal.

Feinberg, who was experienced in dealing with compulsive gamblers and their legal problems, calmed Nancy down. It wasn't so bad, he said. The authorities were usually willing to negotiate these things, provided that restitution to the injured parties was made. Could Nancy manage that? Nancy thought she might be able to convince her boyfriend, Rick Siegel, to help out. Good, Feinberg told her.

Within a week or so, he talked to the assistant state's attorney who was overseeing Block's investigation. The prosecutor seemed willing to make a deal—if there was an agreement on restitution, Nancy might avoid jail time, or so Feinberg thought. He talked to Rick, who seemed willing to pay the restitution on Nancy's behalf. The state's attorney told Feinberg that it depended on how many frauds Nancy had committed, and what the total dollar amount was; Block was still working on that.

Then, on February 18, 1998, Nancy got another collection call from the BMW finance people, again in search of Jack. This appears to have alarmed Nancy—she had to consider the possibility that Block might learn of BMW's two-year effort to find Jack and the car. The car, she knew, might well lead to an investigation of Jack's presumed disappearance—after all, BMW hadn't been able to find Jack despite two years of trying. Four days later, the car turned up on the lot of the BMW dealer who had sold the car to Jack two years earlier. With the car out of her driveway, Nancy could always claim that Jack had come back for it, and that he was the one who had returned it to the dealer. That might be construed by Block as an indication that Jack was alive and well somewhere, on the remote chance that Block suspected Nancy of having done something to Jack. The art of a grifter is to always have a plausible story ready to hand. Nancy told Feinberg none of this, however.

Almost two months went by, with Feinberg attempting to cajole the state's attorney into agreeing to a plea for Nancy. The main thing, Feinberg kept saying, was to get the money back to those who had been harmed—mostly banks, lenders and department stores, which had already absolved the neighbors of their unwarranted debts. Feinberg got the idea that the state attorney was willing to listen, if Nancy—or Rick, on Nancy's behalf—provided restitution. Feinberg explained this all to Nancy, who was contrite and self-deprecating, almost demeaning. As far as he could tell, Nancy had fallen into a pit as a result of her addiction to the poker machines. Nancy seemed willing to plead guilty, as long as she could stay out of jail. Feinberg told he'd see what he could arrange.

A little over a month later, with Nancy ready to offer a plea, Block sat down with Nancy and Feinberg to sort things out. Feinberg still hadn't gotten assurances from the state attorneys that they wouldn't try to put Nancy in prison, but he had the idea that they might be lenient with her if she cooperated with the police investigation. He wanted Block to use his influence with the prosecutors to keep Nancy out of jail. That meant Nancy had to cooperate with the detective, Feinberg told her. Rick was still willing to pay the restitution—write checks to the various banks and department stores covering the frauds. But Rick wasn't going to write the checks unless the prosecutors agreed that Nancy *could* get probation, not jail. Feinberg was essentially acting as the middleman between the prosecutors and Rick, with Rick's conditional willingness to make the restitution as his leverage. Feinberg was eager to enlist Block as an ally in favor of this resolution.

The discussion between Block, Nancy and Feinberg took place in late April 1998, at the Howard County police station. Block tape-recorded it.

Block began by saying that he was new to fraud investigation, that Nancy was his first case.

"You're obviously very good at what you were doing," Block told Nancy. "I'd, uh, kind of like to pick your brain a little bit. That's going to be a huge help not only to me, but to the citizens of Howard County." In short, Block wanted Nancy to give him a primer on how she'd run her credit scam.

But first: did Feinberg or Nancy have any questions for him?

Feinberg jumped in, wanting to know if the state's attorney would agree to a no-jail-time plea. Feinberg could tell from Block's expression that it was too soon to talk deal. "But, I suspect that would be as a result of her rendering assistance to you," he conceded, mostly for Nancy's benefit.

Block now said he'd heard that the assistant state's attorney was willing to dicker, but the supervising state's attorney might be a little more hard-nosed. The main thing, Block said, was whether the victims were going to get their money back.

Nancy wanted to know what Block meant by "victims."

"He meant the people that had money taken from them," Feinberg said.

"Victims, yeah," Block agreed. "Things like AT and T."

"Oh," Nancy said. "Okay."

Yeah, Block said. Credit card companies. "They're the victims."

In retrospect, it seems fairly likely that when Nancy

wanted to know what Block meant by "victims," she was thinking of one victim in particular. How much did Block know about Jack?

Block didn't pick up on Nancy's subtle probe. "Because they're banks," he went on, "people think you can't think of them as victims."

"No," Nancy said, "I know."

# 10
# "I HAVE A TENDENCY
# TO SCHEME"

Block went through all the fraudulent charges Nancy had made on the AT&T account, and a number of other credit lines she had obtained using the neighbor's information. The total came to $22,776, Block said. Block offered to show Nancy and Feinberg how he'd come up with that figure, but Nancy and Feinberg both agreed that the total sounded about right. Feinberg wanted to press on with the restitution issue. If Block was done, he could begin calling people to make arrangements for Rick to repay them. The sooner that was done, the more ammunition he'd have with the state's attorney. But Feinberg's use of the word "arrangements" alarmed Nancy— she thought Feinberg meant that she'd have to agree to repay everyone on some sort of schedule. That wasn't what Rick had agreed to, she thought.

"Why are you saying, 'make arrangements' when it's going to be paid?" Nancy asked her attorney. "Do you know what I mean? Not payments."

Feinberg tried to assure her. "First of all, you're not paying it. He is."

"Correct," Nancy agreed.

"So until I really sit down with Rick and say, 'Rick, this one here is for this, and that one's for—' "

"Okay," Nancy said. She was clearly worried that Feinberg had new information from Rick, that Rick was backing away from paying the restitution. All Feinberg meant was that Rick would have to make separate checks payable to the "victims."

After another detailed discussion of who was owed what, Block returned to his original question. He wanted to know how Nancy had decided to fill out the neighbor's unsolicited AT&T credit card application in the first place. "How did you go about determining that this would be a good card hit?"

Nancy dithered for a few seconds, fumbling for an answer. Then she said all her troubles had begun years earlier, when she'd first started gambling compulsively.

"A long time ago," she said. "When I had my problem years ago. Four years ago. And— I'm so nervous, I'm sorry. I had gotten, how that began, I had gotten someone else's mail in my mail. And that grew from that. Uh, gambling. And when you gamble— It's hard to explain, the reason."

Block encouraged her to go on.

"I have a tendency to scheme," Nancy said. "Out of, whatever. Desperation."

But Block wanted to know Nancy's *m.o.*, not her rationalization.

"So you started driving around and you just picked [out] a mailbox?"

"Correct," Nancy said.

She'd looked through several mailboxes, searching for what she knew would be unsolicited, "pre-approved" credit applications. It was in the fall, with the holiday season approaching. Nancy knew the creditors liked to send out a ton of "pre-approved" credit offers as the holiday season arrived.

"Okay. So you filled it out?"

"No. Never filled anything out. Never. I just called."

"You called them on the phone, okay."

"I never wrote anything in writing."

"Okay. So, is that something you learned from a long time ago, not to do anything in writing?"

"I did."

Block asked where the credit cards were right then.

"I have no idea."

"Did you throw them away?"

"I might have."

Nancy was leaving open the possibility of claiming that Jack might have taken the cards when he'd supposedly reclaimed the car. It was another fallback position for her in case things got dicey later. If Jack had the car and the credit cards, he had to be alive, right?

Block relaxed a bit, and told Nancy that he'd rather enjoyed investigating the case. Once he'd gotten rolling, he said, things had just fallen in to place. But at time of the search warrant, he confessed, he hadn't been so sure he was right.

"My first impression of you," Block told Nancy, "was, well, maybe you didn't do this. You're very, very good. You buffaloed me. Especially after I went through the house. I didn't find anything . . . At which point I asked you if I could look in the car. You must have forgotten that the checkbook was there."

Nancy: "Mmm." She definitely did not want to discuss the BMW.

At this point, Nancy began to get a little choked up. Block offered to get her a cup of water. He left the interview room.

"He's okay," Feinberg told Nancy, after Block had left. "I don't think he wants to hurt you now. But you have to go through this, you know?"

"I know," Nancy said. "Fine. I'm fine. I'm just nervous."

Block returned with the water, which Nancy took with thanks.

"What did you mean when you said, you came to her house and, she had you 'buffaloed'?" Feinberg asked Block. "She never said anything to you when you were at the house." Nancy had told Feinberg she'd kept her mouth shut during the January search. Feinberg didn't want the state's attorney to think that Nancy had done anything to lead Block astray.

"Just that I was 'confident,'" Nancy explained.

It was just that Nancy had seemed so sure of herself at the time, Block said.

"Oh, I was not confident," Nancy said. "You mistook confidence for—"

"Actually, the first time I saw you shook was—"

"No," Nancy said.

"Was when I found the car," Block finished. "The checkbook in the car. At that point I knew I had you. Just by your expression."

She hadn't been confident at all when the police showed up, Nancy said, diverting Block from the car. She was just tired.

"The really weird part was, before you came, the day before . . . I had gambled, and it was very bad. And I was just giving up. It was bad, just bad. What to do? And I knew I was going to be caught. And it wasn't five minutes before you got there, I was like, 'Oh, Lord, just help me to do the right thing. What's going to happen?' And then there was a knock on my door, so . . ."

"Not that it's making light of this or anything," Block said again, "but I really enjoyed this investigation. It was something that, you know, I started with a really good suspect, but then, it was somebody who was intelligent and somebody who had a game plan, knew what she was doing . . ."

"Yeah," Nancy agreed.

Nancy thanked Block for not arresting her that day in front of Jennifer and Amanda.

"That's probably why my demeanor, too, was somewhat calm. But I was going to kill myself. So you mistook confidence, it wasn't confidence. It was like, *This is it. It's over.*"

Block was sympathetic. "You seem like you want to just get this behind you and pay it all off and go on with your life and hopefully get some help with your addiction to gambling."

Feinberg got behind this notion and shoved hard. "She's getting, you know, she's getting [help] since this thing happened. She's been seeing a psychiatrist, and— Who's the other person you've been seeing?"

Someone affiliated with Gamblers Anonymous, Nancy said.

Block wanted to go through the credit card charges— Nancy had been buying merchandise, then returning it to the store for cash refunds. Nancy said she couldn't remember all of them.

"All I remembered was what I did," Nancy said. "Because, see, what I thought was, if I could win the gambling, I would just pay them off. Do you know what I mean?"

Block expressed amazement that credit card companies would give out cards with only telephone acceptance.

"Oh, it's terrible," Nancy agreed.

"How easy it is to get started to do."

"What I think Nancy's trying to tell you," Feinberg said. "Just for what it's worth, and I don't know how far its worth on the criminal investigation, but in her mind at the time, at least the way I perceive it and the way it was explained to me, she's driven by this gambling thing, and I don't think there were any real focuses. I don't think there often is, at the time you're doing this stuff. But there's no great plot, no deviance here."

Nancy said she felt terrible, doing what she'd done. The worst of it was, there seemed to be no way out. That's why she'd thought about killing herself that day.

Block said that he'd interviewed people at the department stores where Nancy had charged things on the ill-gotten credit cards, and one salesclerk particularly, at Macy's. "She said you knew what you were looking for. 'She had great taste, excellent taste. A very nice lady.' Everybody said that."

"I *am* a nice lady," Nancy said. "It's just that I'm a nice lady with a mental problem."

When she'd first seen the neighbor's "pre-approved" credit offer, Nancy said, her first thought was that she could get enough money from it to gamble. And more.

"To be able to pay off my debts. To be able to take the pressure away." But with blank checks for "pre-approved" credit coming back to the neighbor's mailbox, Nancy knew she had to be there to intercept them. "And what happened, when I did go back, maybe a week later . . . I called to see if they sent it, and it just so happened, when I went back, it was meant to be . . . there was another pre-approved." Nancy meant there was another "free money" credit solicitation in the mailbox. So she called that one, too. And later, there was another one. It was easy.

# 11
# JACK'S GHOST

Sitting in on the Howard County police interview that day in April 1998, knowing things that Block or even her lawyer Feinberg did not, Nancy had great reason to be nervous, as she said she was. She must have been thinking: that surely someone must have known about her scam with Jack Watkins by then. How could they not? And what did Block really know? Was he simply toying with her, lulling her into making some incriminating remark? When would Block spring the trap, confront her with her darkest secret? He'd seen the BMW. It must have been excruciating for Nancy, waiting for the other shoe to drop.

What did Block know? Or did he know anything? Nancy herself knew enough from her years of experience with the police to understand that she should be as vague as possible. But Block continued to meander all around the credit frauds, trying to make all the numbers add up. The car and Jack Watkins seemed to have slipped his mind.

Block wanted to know where Nancy was gambling when she'd concocted her credit scam.

Delaware, Nancy said.

"At the slot machines?"

"Yes, uh-huh. In Delaware."

"I've only been to Delaware one time and I put two hundred dollars in the slot machines and—"

"Walked away with nothing," Feinberg finished for him.

"Walked away with absolutely nothing," Block agreed. "And I thought, *I'm never gonna come back to this place.*"

"Right," Nancy said. "Because you're normal."

Block was still curious about Nancy's *m.o.* He wanted to know if he'd missed anything during his search of her house.

"Did you have anything?"

"What?"

"Was there for me to find?"

"No."

"Have something hidden?"

"Oh no," Nancy said. "No. No. No. Nothing, I have— You— When you said, 'Did you have,' it was . . . I don't know if I can say that or not."

"You can say it," Feinberg told her.

"Do you know what I'm talking about?" Nancy asked.

"I think so," Block said.

"What?" Now it was Nancy who was asking the questions.

"Talking about the gun," Feinberg offered.

"Gun?" Nancy asked, dumbfounded.

"That I thought you had," Feinberg said, recalling Nancy's talk about suicide immediately after the search.

"A kni— A knife," Nancy said, stammering.

This unnerved Block—the idea that a suspect during a search had had a deadly weapon in her possession without anyone knowing about it at the time. He wanted to know all about this. Nancy said she'd gotten it from the kitchen during the search when no one was looking. But she'd never intended to use it on any of the police officers, Nancy said. She was going to try to kill herself instead.

It was amazing, Feinberg said—all the work that had been done to collect all the fraudulent accounts, down to the penny, and yet no one thought to search Nancy for a weapon, a cardinal violation of police procedure.

"It goes to show you, they talk about tunnel vision at the police academy," Block said. "You've got your eyes focused on this, and you see a nice-looking, uh—"

"Clean-cut white lady," Feinberg offered.

"A small lady, clean lady that you wouldn't expect anything [from], and . . . you start taking things for granted at that point," Block said.

"That's when trouble can happen," Feinberg agreed.

They were nearing the end of the interview. Ironically, it was Nancy's lawyer, Feinberg, who opened the subject of Jack Watkins. Feinberg, unwitting as to who Jack Watkins was, was intent on demonstrating to Block that Nancy was doing her best to cooperate. He asked Block if he had any questions about the BMW.

"That's actually at the bottom of my list here," Block said. "Uh, the name Jack Frederick Watkins keeps popping up."

"Uh huh," Nancy said.

"Who is Mr. Watkins?"

"He's a friend. And . . . But I haven't seen him in—"

"I understand he's in a great deal of indebtedness, too," Block said.

"Yeah. I met him at a, a GA conference."

"Gamblers Anonymous?"

"Uh huh. From years ago."

"Why— Why is it you're driving his car?"

"I'm not. Any longer. And it wasn't—who I worked for. They had— I couldn't get a car. In my name. So he signed for the car. For the car." The fact that Nancy's answers didn't seem to make any sense about this sensitive subject seemed to elude Block.

"So you were actually paying for the car? Or . . . ?"

"Right. At one point in time."

"Okay."

"And then he said that it was paid for. In total. He said he was, when I first met him, that he was like, very wealthy. He knew of my problem. But I haven't seen him in, maybe two years."

"You also admitted that you had a post office box with him," Block pointed out. And Amanda and Jennifer's names were on the post office box, too, he added.

"Right."

"What's that all about? Why would you all have a post office box together?"

"Just from when we moved."

"Wait," Block said. "Did you used to live with this guy?"

"No. No. Briefly, when I wasn't seeing . . . uh, Rick had gone back to his wife. And that's when we met."

"Okay. Is there any other kind of fraudulent activity going on with him?" Block meant Jack.

"None," Nancy said.

"Was he also in the frauds? Or is he just—"

"Was he into frauds? No."

"No. Did he do anything like this?"

"Never. No."

"We haven't been able to show anything along those lines," Block admitted.

"Well, she'd tell you," Feinberg assured him.

"No," Nancy said. "He's wonderful. I would tell you . . ."

"It just looks kind of suspicious when I see his credit cards are maxed out, too."

"He had the same," Nancy said, trying to say that Jack Watkins had shared her compulsion for gambling. "And an alcohol problem as well."

Nancy definitely wanted to head Block off from delving further into the subject of Jack Watkins. "He's not like— He's a wonderful person," she said.

"If I could talk to him, he— Would he say that you maxed out his credit cards?"

"No."

"Okay."

"No."

"Uh, would you mind if I talked to him? Would you give me his number so I can talk to him?"

"I have no idea where he is. Other than Virginia."

"Is there any way to contact him? He's living in Virginia?"

"Somewhere," Nancy said. "I think, uh, he went to live with— He had a stroke. A mini-stroke."

"I notice he was an older gentleman," Block said.

"That's correct," Nancy said. "That's correct."

"Uh, which kind of makes us think that, you know, you might have been playing him."

"I wasn't."

"And the thought did cross our mind when we saw that, that this is obviously an elderly man."

"I understand," Nancy said. "But that's not the case."

"Okay."

"I have to tell you, it's not the case."

"And you were driving his car?"

"That's correct."

Feinberg wasn't sure where Block was going with this, but if Nancy had taken advantage of Jack's credit, he knew it was better to get it out now—he didn't want to be sandbagged later by the state's attorney with a whole raft of new allegations.

"It's a reasonable inference," he assured Nancy.

Nancy said nothing.

"I guess what I'd really like," Block said, "what I'd like to do here, is [talk to Jack], and I'm sure you can get ahold of him."

"To confirm what she's telling you," Feinberg said, for Nancy's benefit.

"I'll try my best," Nancy said. "Absolutely."

Feinberg said he'd check with Nancy the following week to see if she could get a telephone number for Jack. Then he'd call Block.

"Okay," Block said. "Obviously, we'll just talk to him and make sure everything's okay."

"Uh-huh," Nancy said.

Despite all his best efforts, Feinberg was unable to convince the state's attorney to accept a plea from Nancy that would not encompass jail time. At one point, in fact, Rick withdrew $15,000 from one of his accounts, possibly to pay some of the restitution. But with Nancy's track record, the proposed deal fizzled. The case was sent to district court. That court, noticing that the charges involved ninety-one separate counts—signing a check fraudulently was "uttering a false document," and signing someone else's name was forgery, different acts, so Nancy got two bangs for every buck—decided that the case should go to the felony Circuit Court for trial. There were just too many crimes for the soft hand treatment. The state's attorney decided to convene a grand jury to probe Nancy's misdeeds. All this took time.

While the case was meandering through the Howard County court system, Nancy and Rick took out a marriage license in December of 1998. Based on assertions later made by prosecutors, it appears that Nancy opened accounts in Rick's name without his knowledge, even after the marriage. The trash can in the post office box in Ellicott City became the final destination for dunning notices to Jack Watkins, Eric Siegel, Nancy Sweitzer, and Amanda Kucharski. As the bills came in, Nancy pitched them out. The items she saved—for deposit or cashing—were Social Security and New York Life annuity checks payable to Jack Watkins.

Finally, the Circuit Court got its oars straightened out, and on February 17, 2000, Nancy was indicted by a Howard County grand jury on three counts of a felony theft "scheme" involving "a continuing course of conduct." The use of the words "scheme" and "continuing course of conduct" made the crimes more serious than simple theft. Based on Nancy's history, if convicted, she faced the possibility of going to prison for 4 years. Bail was set at $150,000. Someone, presumably Rick, put up $15,000 to secure Nancy's release on bond. The three counts involved banks that Nancy had scammed with her "pre-approved" foray into mailboxes.

With his new wife facing the definite prospect of serious prison time, Rick engaged another lawyer. This was Harold Glaser, a well-known member of the Maryland bar, famous for, among other cases, having once represented Vice-President Spiro Agnew, a former governor of Maryland. Glaser was getting on in years, but still relished giving prosecutors a good fight. He had a preference for large cigars. Like any tenacious defense lawyer, he was prodigious in turning out reams of defense motions—a paper blizzard calculated to make prosecutors work their tails off to respond. Glaser drew most of his motions from his previously prepared stock of similar efforts, almost like form letters. All he had to do was use a word processor to paste in the defendant's name and a sentence or two of the circumstances. That way, he could throw up a curtain of demands; sometimes prosecutors can be induced to dicker out of sheer paper fatigue. And who knew? Maybe something might tumble out of the responses that could lead to a chink in the case, and thence to a prosecutor's decision to drop the matter as too troublesome to pursue.

Within the first week of taking the case, Glaser filed a motion to compel the state to produce the identities of any informants who had provided information about Nancy; a motion to inspect the transcript of testimony before the grand jury; a motion to suppress evidence in the case because of allegedly faulty search procedure; a motion to suppress any statements Nancy might have made to Block or anyone else; a motion to force the state to disclose Nancy's criminal history; a motion to inspect and copy grand juror qualification forms; a motion to compel the state to disclose any promises of immunity to any witness; and an omnibus motion to suppress any evidence seized as a result of wire-taps, Block's afterthought search of the car, any mention of Nancy's prior record, any identification of Nancy made by eyewitnesses, and finally, asking that Nancy be given separate trials on each count, and separate from any other defendant. Most of these were for form's sake; Glaser had no way of knowing if the police had ever used wiretaps on Nancy, or if there were any other defendants. Glaser identified his client as "Nancy Jean Schweitzer," not Siegel or even Sweitzer, which seems to show that he wasn't on close acquaintance with Rick Siegel before the indictment.

In the end, whether because of Harold Glaser's snow-storm of motions, or Rick's agreement to pay the restitution on Nancy's behalf, the case was settled with a guilty plea to the first count, and the state's agreement to withhold prosecution on the other two. Rick wrote checks to pay off the banks. Nancy was given 5 more years of probation, to run concurrent with the 10 she was already doing.

Block never did talk to Jack Watkins.

# 12
# UNCLE SAM

Jack may have been gone, maybe even forgotten by Nancy after her narrow escape with Block, but some people in the Loudoun County Sheriff's Office weren't ready to give up on the case of the old man in the trunk.

True, after Jay Merchant's retirement, the Jack-in-the-box case lost its main sponsor. But Merchant had a colleague, a woman named Bobbie Ochsman, who knew that the inability to identify the man in the trunk had eaten away at Merchant—the case of the murderer who had gotten away with it. Ochsman decided to take over the case herself, as much out of loyalty to Merchant as to the dead man. Like Merchant, she couldn't help thinking of the dead man's family. Someone, somewhere, had to wonder what had become of him. Ochsman, in her imagination, could envision a family that could never come to grips with the mystery of their loved one who had simply disappeared, vanished off the face of the earth. There had to be someone—a son, a daughter, a brother, even an ex-wife, who would always wonder whatever had happen to the man the Loudoun County sheriff's deputies couldn't identify. Was there, Ochsman wondered, a grandchild out there who, in the middle of the night, still wished he or she knew why Grampa had left home without a word? Who would have left him dead, half-naked, folded up in a small trunk, with a pillowcase over his head and covered with two duffle bags?

But Ochsman was stuck in the same swamp as Merchant—until she could learn the dead man's name, there was no place to go.

In early 1999, Ochsman asked her supervisor, Sergeant Steve Craven, if she could work on Jack-in-the-box. Sure, she was told—as long as she kept up with her assigned cases. The dead man's remains had long before been cremated, there were no new leads, and meanwhile, there were plenty of other crimes to investigate. But Ochsman felt a pull—not only for Merchant, who had taught her a lot, but also for the man everyone else seemed to have forgotten.

Ochsman had a somewhat unusual background for a detective. She'd come a bit later in life to law enforcement. She'd grown up in Loudoun County, and had been educated as a teacher. Her first job had been teaching high school English and history to at-risk kids. Getting hormonally infused teenagers with histories of acting-out to pay attention to participles and the past was hard work. After a year or so, Ochsman knew it wasn't for her. She married her boyfriend, an expert in designing control systems, and moved with him to Arkansas. There she had two children, a farm, horses, and a life of involvement with the community, including work at a local hospital.

Then, Ochsman found herself caught up in a search for the car used in a fatal hit-and-run accident. Working with a local news reporter, Ochsman and the journalist scoured area wrecking yards for the suspect vehicle. One day, they hit paydirt: the car was in the wrecking yard, which in turn led to the driver, and the solution to the crime. Ochsman was hooked on detection—she knew it was something she had a talent for.

After some years, Ochsman and her husband returned to Loudoun County. Noticing a recruiting advertisement for the sheriff's department in a local newspaper, Ochsman decided to apply. By then she was in her thirties, rather late for a cop to be starting out. But she knew she could do it. She'd had enough experience in the real world to be wise, along with the sense of humor that every cop needs to survive. She was a natural.

After a year or so working in the jail—the best way to get familiar with the criminal element in any local jurisdiction—Ochsman went out on the road as a patrol deputy. She wasn't very big—maybe five-four on a good day, and weighing not much more than 130. But she whipped herself into top shape, and even nearing 40 years old, she looked like she could do some serious damage to someone twice her size if she had to. And then there was the 9-millimeter Glock on her hip. She knew how to use that, too. Then she was assigned to the department's Criminal Investigations Division. Merchant took her under his wing, and taught her how to be a detective. A real cop never gave up, Merchant told her—that's what came with the badge, at least for the good ones. Ochsman kept a gruesome copy of the photograph of Jack-in-the-box's face on her desk as a daily reminder of what it was all about.

After getting the bemused okay from Craven to work on the case, Ochsman decided to put the dead man's fingerprints through the FBI database once more. Again the word came back—no match. Ochsman wasn't sure whether anyone at the FBI really looked, beyond noticing that the prints had been checked once before with no results.

Ochsman still believed that someone would recognize the dead man if only they were made aware that he had been found, where, and how. By then a thorough canvass of all the local nursing homes had been conducted, and the mystery had been publicized in the local news. Ochsman was very sure, as Merchant had been before her, that the man in the trunk was not a local resident. Someone would have recognized his face, however distorted by death, long before. That meant the dumper, almost certainly the killer, had to be from outside the area; so did the victim.

Ochsman made contact with the producers of *America's Most Wanted*, John Walsh's weekly televised effort to engage the public in the search for predators. The trunk case was featured on an episode, then placed in the program's printed bulletin. Ochsman hoped that someone might call in with a tip—*Gramps disappeared, no one's seen him since.* She contacted producers for *Unsolved Mysteries*, which aired segments on the man in the trunk three different times. The local NBC affiliate also ran a segment. But nothing emerged.

Like Merchant, Ochsman was sure that the person who left the body in the trunk had also killed him. Like her predecessor, Ochsman had an idea that the killer was someone who was ripping off the dead man's Social Security benefits. That possibly meant a family member, or at least someone in a position to pose as the dead man. Such scams, while rare in the universe of all the Social Security payments made every month in the United States—over 160 million or so today—were hardly unknown.

There was, for instance, a notorious case in Sacramento, California, in the late 1980s, in which a landlady, Dorothea Puente, was arrested in connection with the deaths or disappearances of nine elderly or mentally disabled residents of her boarding house. Puente was suspected of killing the nine, burying some of the bodies in the back yard of the boarding house, and then collecting their Social Security or disability checks as if they were still alive. She was eventually convicted of three of the murders.

Social Security fraud—not just people illegally claiming others' benefits, but also people claiming their own benefits improperly—is a hardy perennial for the federal government's lawyers. Between the fall of 2001 and the spring of 2003, according to the Social Security Administration, the government received over 51,000 allegations of Social Security fraud. In that period, the government was able to open only 9,170 investigations, and these allegations brought charges against only 2,677 people. Of those, the government was able to win convictions against only 1,008. The small minority of system abusers made it harder for those legitimately qualified for the benefits, in that the system developed a skeptical attitude toward *all* claims, according to the government.

"The SSA [Social Security Administration] statistics suggest an alarming increase in fraudulent claims that threaten the integrity of the Social Security Trust Funds and block access by needy applicants with legitimate claims for benefits," the *United States Attorney's Bulletin* reported in November of 2004. "In many cases, benefits paid to needy applicants serve as a lifeline that means the difference between survival and death. As disturbing as the statistics are, they represent only the identified instances of overpayments in the SSA programs." That meant that for every reported instance of fraud, many, many more went undetected.

Having guessed that the motive for the trunk victim's murder was a Social Security scam, Ochsman developed contacts with the Social Security Administration. Ochsman's contacts agreed that the Jack-in-the-box Case appeared to be a murder for Social Security benefits. But without an identification of the victim, there was no way to tell who was getting the money instead of the dead man. The illicit recipient was highly likely to be the killer—who else would know he wasn't going to turn up claiming his benefits? But with more than 150 million recipients at the time of the discovery of the man in the trunk, there was simply no way to identify the murderous scammer.

Then, in one of the universe's happy accidents, Ochsman encountered another investigator at a seminar in late 2002, who told her of another fingerprint database she hadn't heard of—this one run by the Immigration and Naturalization

Service at the Biometric Support Center in Virginia. It turned out that the INS fingerprint database had been organized by a retired FBI fingerprint expert, Danny Greathouse. Ochsman contacted Greathouse and explained her problem: she had the corpse of an elderly man, found stashed in a trunk, and no way to identify him. Greathouse agreed to help. He took the fingerprint samples of the dead man that Merchant had collected years before, and said he would run them against the INS automated fingerprint files. He also forwarded copies of the prints to San Diego, where a second automated database of eight Western states' fingerprints was located. If there was still no match, Greathouse told Ochsman, she might try the FBI again, this time asking them to check the civil and applicant files of the bureau. The civil and applicant files also contained prints of military officers, Greathouse told her. Up until then, only the criminal files had been checked at the FBI.

While the bureau had also had access to enlisted military fingerprints for many years, checking those prints wasn't automated: without a name to go with the prints, a manual check of tens of millions of prints was difficult, maybe impossible. It wasn't clear to Ochsman if a manual check of the bureau's enlisted military fingerprint files had ever been conducted, but given the dead man's apparent age, it was possible, maybe even likely, that he had served in the military during World War II. Still, if he'd been an officer, his prints might be in the bureau's civil and applicant files, which *were* automated.

On December 16, 2002, Greathouse reported back to Ochsman: none of the four INS databases produced a match to the prints of the dead man. Neither did a check of the Western states' Automated Fingerprint Identification System, or AFIS.

Ochsman was only slightly discouraged. At least Greathouse had given her a suggestion of where to go next—back to the FBI for a check of the automated civil and applicant databases. These were prints accumulated by the bureau in the course of vetting people for government jobs, including military officers and would-be FBI agents, not criminals. Ochsman called the man in charge of the FBI's fingerprint operation, which had recently been moved to Clarksburg, West Virginia. That was when she learned that the man in charge, Billy Martin, was on the verge of retirement. Martin suggested that Ochsman talk to Debbie McMillen, who was to be his replacement. Unable to reach McMillen by telephone, Ochsman sent her a letter on December 23, 2002. Then she prepared to take the holidays off.

Unbeknownst to Ochsman, the FBI had upgraded its fingerprint database since the previous attempts to identify the dead man's prints. Now *all* the military prints were in the computer system, not just the officers'.

McMillen ran the prints through the expanded system. Shortly after the first of the year, the bureau's computers got a hit from the enlisted military database: The man in the trunk was Jack Frederick Watkins, born March 21, 1920, Private First Class, Army Air Corps, a veteran of World War II.

Ochsman returned to work on January 6, 2003, to find a message waiting for her from McMillen. Ochsman called back, and got the word that the dead man in the trunk back in 1996 was a 76-year-old Army veteran named Jasper Frederick Watkins, Jr. McMillen gave Ochsman Jack's Social Security number, which was part of his fingerprint record.

Ochsman immediately called her contact at the Social Security Administration. The contact ran Jack's number through the Social Security database. Jack F. Watkins, the contact reported, was still receiving Social Security payments in the form of checks mailed to a post office box in Ellicott City, Maryland.

Now the question for Ochsman was: who had the post office box? Who was collecting the Social Security payments that Jack Watkins had no need of since the night he'd been found stuffed in a trunk at a wayside overlooking the Potomac River, almost seven years earlier?

Ochsman's next call was to Jay Merchant.

The man in the trunk finally had a name, she told Merchant. "And you won't believe this, Jay," she said, "but his name really *was* Jack."

After this, things moved very swiftly. The Social Security Administration assigned an investigator, Sean Stephenson, to the case, as did the U.S. Postal Service, Mark Carr. The FBI came in, too, along with representatives from the Virginia State Attorneys' office. Federal prosecutors in Virginia and Maryland were notified. Another Loudoun County investigator, Greg Locke, was assigned to the case as well.

One of Postal Inspector Carr's first moves was to check with the Post Office in Ellicott City.

P.O. Box 1910 was rented by one Nancy Jean Sweitzer, a resident of Pikesville, Maryland, in Baltimore County, the wife of Eric Siegel, a Baltimore mortgage banking expert employed by one of the state's pre-eminent financial services companies. Just why the wife of someone who was apparently so well-to-do would be collecting a dead man's Social Security checks was anyone's guess, but it probably wasn't for an innocent reason. All Ochsman had to do was look at Jack-in-the-box's picture on her desk to know that.

# 13
# "TEAM WATKINS"

It took very little time for those assigned to the Watkins case to dig up Nancy Jean Sweitzer Kucharski Geisendaffer Siegel's checkered history of credit card and bank fraud. A credit check on Jack Watkins showed that he had twenty-six credit accounts, all but five of them opened after October of 1994. Two of the accounts, in fact, had been opened after Jack's body had been found in the trunk on May 14, 1996. Most of the accounts had large unpaid balances, or had been closed as uncollectible. One account, for a gasoline credit card, had Nancy Jean Sweitzer listed as a co-account holder with Jack. The credit application, from June of 1995, shortly after Jack leased the BMW, showed that Nancy Jean Sweitzer had identified herself as Jack's "fi-ancé."

Very shortly afterward, members of "Team Watkins," as the investigators began to call themselves, unearthed the audio tapes of Howard County Detective William Block's interview with Nancy back in April of 1998. One part of the interview, on the whereabouts of Jack Watkins, leapt out at the listeners:

Block: *"Uh, would you mind if I talked to him? Would you give me his number so I can talk to him?"*

Nancy: *"I have no idea where he is. Other than Virginia."*

Well, that was true, as far as it went. Jack *had* been in Virginia when he was found, jammed inside the trunk. Nancy's reference to Virginia, however coy, seemed to suggest that she might be the one who had left him there in the trunk. Who else might know that Jack was possibly in Virginia, even if dead?

Someone made an attempt to find out what the BMW finance people knew about Nancy and Jack. This inquiry was initially met with stiff resistance. Investigators formed the impression that someone had previously called them and threatened them with legal action or maybe even violence if they persisted in their efforts to locate Jack Watkins. The investigators couldn't convince the BMW finance people that they really were cops. Later the file from the BMW finance arm showed a notation: no one at the company was ever to talk about Jack Watkins or the car, ever again.

On February 4, 2003, members of "Team Watkins" went to the post office in Ellicott City, and placed it under surveillance. It was the time of the month for delivery of Jack's monthly Social Security check. Sure enough, along came Nancy. As she drove into the parking lot of the post office in Ellicott City that day, Nancy didn't know she was on candid camera. From an unmarked van in the parking lot, a federal agent videotaped Nancy driving in, parking, alighting from her Infiniti, and striding toward the post office, pulling her baseball cap down low over her forehead. Nancy seemed oblivious to being watched. She marched up to the glass doors and went inside, going directly to Post Office Box 1910. There she removed the contents and sorted through the bills and junk mail, pitching the culls into the trash as she looked for Jack's Social Security check. Finding it, she removed the check and tossed the empty envelope, too, into the trash.

The surveillance team trailed Nancy to a nearby First Union National Bank branch, and watched as Nancy rolled through the drive-up teller's window. Nancy, driving her white Infiniti, idled at the window for more than ten minutes while the teller tried to deposit the check. In the end, the teller refused to accept the Jack Watkins Social Security money for deposit, "due to suspicious activity on the account," according to Agent Stephenson's later report. This may have been a result of investigators' earlier inquiries as to signatories and balances on the account. Nancy drove off.

Four days later, a woman claiming to be Jack's daughter called the Social Security service center to report that his check was missing. The call-back number was for a telephone subscriber named Nancy Jean Siegel at an address she shared with her husband Eric, in Pikesville, Maryland. The court records in Howard County showed that Nancy had married Eric Siegel before she was sentenced to probation on her most recent mailbox-raiding case in 2000.

Over the next few weeks Stephenson tracked down all the Social Security checks that had been sent to Jack Watkins at Nancy's addresses over the years. Altogether, there were seventy-two of them, at least half of them co-endorsed by Nancy Sweitzer or Nancy Siegel. About half had been deposited in four different accounts at two different banks; about half had been passed for cash. For the month of February, there were two checks—the one that the bank had first refused to deposit, then the replacement check. Both were later cashed, according to investigators. The checks averaged almost $1,000 each, nearly $90,000 in total over the years since Jack's emaciated body had been found in the trunk. Stephenson ran a credit check on Jack, and discovered the numerous accounts that had been opened in Jack's name since November of 1994. He discovered that Nancy had been depositing Jack's New York Life annuity checks, too, about $10,000 worth over the years since Jack had been found dead, sometimes co-endorsing them as Nancy Sweitzer, sometimes Nancy Siegel, or occasionally with the names of her two daughters.

The endorsement and deposits of the checks provided grounds to suspect Nancy of federal crimes, including theft of government property (the Social Security checks), mail fraud, and bank fraud. The February 8, 2003, telephone call to Social Security asking for a replacement check, when Nancy claimed to be Jack's daughter, and in which she also claimed that Jack had misplaced the February Social Security check, was grounds for an allegation of wire fraud—use of the telephone. And the killing of Jack Watkins might be the most serious crime of all: not murder, since there was no federal statute to cover it (murder, except under certain circumstances, is usually a state crime), but tampering with a witness by way of murder. That one alone could net Nancy the death penalty, if the authorities could prove she'd been the person who strangled Jack Watkins, under the theory that Nancy had killed Jack in order to prevent him from reporting her frauds to law enforcement, and if she had planned to do it.

Surveillance was maintained on Nancy early every month when the retirement checks were delivered to her post office box. The drill was always the same: Nancy would drive to the post office from Pikesville, often wearing her baseball cap, pick up the mail from the box, throw away the credit card bills and junk mail, pluck out the checks, dump the envelopes, then head off to the drive-up teller's window. These checks were usually cashed by the banks with no questions from the tellers about "suspicious activity on the account." "Team Watkins" didn't want to tip Nancy off that she was being investigated until the case was ready.

In late March of 2003, the investigators obtained a federal court order for the installation of a pin register on Nancy's telephone line at the house she shared with Rick in Pikesville. The register, essentially a sophisticated caller identification system, allowed investigators to determine who was calling Nancy, and who Nancy was calling, for a period of sixty days. The telephone company was served with the court order, and the register was installed to record the pulses emitted by incoming and outgoing dialing beeps. The idea was to find out if anyone else was involved with Nancy in the overall scam.

Already, based on the bank records that seemed to show Nancy making deposits of some of the Social Security or annuity checks into accounts with Rick's name on them, some members of "Team Watkins" were of the opinion that Rick was also involved. True, it didn't make a lot of sense: Rick was wealthy, and had no need of the relatively small deposits Nancy was making into an account that had his name, no need to rip off Jack Watkins' relatively meager Social Security money. But this suspicion couldn't be allayed until investigators sat down with Rick to find out what he knew.

Before going further, a plan was hatched to mildly confront Nancy, just to see how she might react. On May 5, 2003, Postal Agent Mark Carr, posing as a post office employee, asked Nancy to update her rental box application. Carr asked Nancy to list the names of people authorized to pick up mail from the box, and Nancy listed herself, as Nancy Siegel, her husband Rick Siegel, her daughter Amanda Kucharski—and Jack F. Watkins. Carr asked Nancy who Jack F. Watkins was. Nancy told him that Jack was her father. Carr took Nancy's new post office box application, in which she admitted receiving mail for a dead man, and this went into the evidence pile.

That month, too, Jack's Social Security check was not delivered, as part of a plan to see what Nancy would do. For some reason, it took almost a month, but Nancy finally called the Social Security service center in early June, and asked that a duplicate check be sent to Jack at the post office box.

That check was sent, and Nancy cashed it a short while later. Now the agents had Nancy on *two* counts of possible wire fraud.

By late July of 2003, most of the pieces were in place. Stephenson prepared an affidavit in support of a request for a federal search warrant of the Siegel house in Pikesville, just outside the city of Baltimore. The warrant was approved by a federal magistrate on August 4, 2003. Team members made lists of people to interview, and divided them up. The idea was to drop in on a number of people associated with Nancy or Jack and confront them at approximately the same time, so that no one would have the opportunity to call any of the others, in case Nancy was involved in some sort of conspiracy.

By August 1, Jack's monthly Social Security check had arrived, but postal authorities withheld it from the mail box. Nancy returned on August 4, and again the check was withheld. The idea was to make Nancy anxious for the money, willing to engage officials and answer any questions.

The next day, August 5, 2003, all the investigators prepared to confront Nancy and her closest associates to see how far the scam extended.

# 14
# "HE IS PHYSICALLY
# IN FINE SHAPE"

A little after 11 A.M., Nancy rolled up to the Ellicott City
Post Office in her white Infiniti, her third trip in five days.
Ochsman, Greg Locke and FBI Special Agent Jon Moeller
had been waiting for her for almost four hours. A note had
been placed in the box, asking Nancy to see the postal inspector. Carr, still posing as a post office employee, greeted
her. He asked if she had time "to speak to a couple of people."
He ushered her into the postmaster's office just off the lobby.
There Nancy was handed an envelope marked "Department
of the Treasury" and addressed to Jack F. Watkins. Carr
then left Nancy alone with Moeller and Locke. Ochsman
was listening in from an adjacent room. Nancy could see
that Moeller had possession of the Social Security check.

This initial encounter with Nancy had been the subject of
previous discussion among the investigators. At first, the idea
had been to put Nancy with Ochsman—after all, as she was
the investigator who had persisted with the case, and was
therefore the primary detective, Nancy should be her "collar."

But team members had by now listened to Nancy's discussion with Howard County Detective Block, from April of 1998, and the consensus was, Nancy would probably try to soft-shoe two male detectives with her mien of compulsive victimhood, as she had done with Block. That was good, it was decided—Nancy would probably try to talk her way out of trouble, playing on the men's anticipated sympathy, and the more she said, the more she would enmesh herself. If Ochsman conducted the interview, there was a chance that Nancy might clam up, get her back up, not wanting to give another woman the satisfaction of doubting her tale. Of course, the difference between Block in 1998 and the two male investigators in 2003 was that Locke and Moeller knew the whole story. It would be difficult, probably impossible, for Nancy to lie her way out of trouble, but she would probably still try, relying as she always did on her feminine charm when dealing with men. The investigators wanted to let Nancy talk as much as she wanted.

Locke introduced Moeller and himself, but didn't identify either of them as criminal investigators. Nancy probably thought at first that the two might be postal officials like Carr was supposed to be.

Locke told Nancy that he and Moeller had been assigned to look into "concerns" about Jack Watkins' Social Security checks. With this, Nancy might next guess that if the two weren't postal officials, they might be from Social Security, responding to her earlier calls about the missing Jack Watkins checks. Or so the investigators' scenario contemplated. Either way, they wanted Nancy to commit herself as the person who collected Jack's checks.

"Do you normally pick up Mr. Watkins' checks?" she was asked. Nancy said she did.

Maintaining their ruse, still implying they were possibly with the U.S. Postal Service or Social Security without actually saying so, the agents asked Nancy if she was satisfied with the issuance of the duplicate checks for February and May. Nancy said she was, except that there seemed to be a recurring problem with the delivery of the Watkins checks to her post office box. Moeller said the first problem, the re-issued February check, seemed to be because Jack had misplaced the first check. Was that true?

Nancy agreed—she said Jack had lost the original check. This was confirmation of a sort that it had been Nancy who had called Social Security back on February 8—who else would know that? Hardly Jack.

"So you think that the problem is with the post office?" Moeller asked.

Yes, Nancy concurred, it was probably the post office's fault.

Nancy was asked if the duplicate checks had arrived, and Nancy agreed that they had been delivered. Locke then asked her if she had been the person who called Social Security to report the lost check.

"I called to say the check wasn't there," Nancy confirmed. This was a criminal admission of possible wire fraud on Nancy's part—use of the telephone to collect money that didn't belong to her.

Actually, Locke now told Nancy, the records seemed to show there had been *two* checks for Jack Watkins that had been "cashed" in February. Nancy shrugged this off. Sometime after she'd called on Jack's behalf, Jack must have found the original check and "cashed it," she said.

There was a way of getting around the post office problem, Moeller now told Nancy. All Jack had to do was set up a direct deposit option with Social Security. Nancy shook her head. That wasn't possible, she said. Jack had "financial problems, and he couldn't have a bank account."

By this point, Nancy must have been growing wary, even suspicious of the two men who were asking her these questions, but still she plunged ahead. When asked if Jack was senile, or if he had any other health problems, Nancy shook her head. "He's not senile," she said. "He's fine."

She'd only been helping Jack, calling Social Security on his behalf, Nancy said. Jack, she added, had a lot of financial problems due to his compulsive gambling. (Of course, the investigators already knew Jack had rarely bet on anything while he was alive, unless one counted a few dollars playing bingo at the Sons of Italy, and even that had been almost more than ten years before Nancy made this statement—a dead and cremated Jack hadn't even pitched pennies since the night his corpse had been found jammed into the trunk.)

Moeller and Locke asked Nancy if it was possible that Jack hadn't been receiving all of his Social Security payments. No, Nancy said. There'd only been one problem, the prior February, when Jack "accidentally threw the check away."

Moeller asked if Nancy had any identification. Nancy showed him her Maryland driver's license and then provided her telephone numbers. Moeller wrote these down, then asked Nancy where Jack was then residing.

"He lives with— He lives in Pennsylvania," Nancy said. "He's staying in Pennsylvania."

The investigators asked where. Nancy said she didn't know exactly, but that he'd been in Pennsylvania for about six years.

Well, was Jack in a nursing home? Did he have some sort of condition that might prevent him from collecting his Social Security checks himself?

"No," Nancy said. "He's living with a woman named Ruth."

What was Ruth's last name? Nancy said she didn't know. But if anyone thought Jack had any health problems, Nancy added, they were wrong.

"He's doing very well," she said.

Moeller asked Nancy who usually cashed Jack's Social Security check. Nancy said she usually did. What about

"Ruth"? Did she ever cash any checks for Jack? Nancy said she didn't think so. Well, did Nancy ever drive to Pennsylvania to give any checks to Jack or Ruth? No, Nancy said.

Moeller asked Nancy if Jack was still capable of driving a car. Nancy said no. How long had it been since Jack drove a motor vehicle?

"About eight years," Nancy said.

The investigators pressed Nancy for more details about "Ruth." They had already noted to themselves that Rick's mother's name was Ruth, and guessed that Nancy had come up with this name on the spur of the moment. "Ruth," she said, was an old friend of Jack's, not a girlfriend, just an acquaintance from the past.

Moeller and Locke now told Nancy that they'd been assigned to locate Jack. Did Nancy know where Jack and Ruth were living? Did she have a telephone number for them?

No, Nancy said.

Well, how did Nancy contact Jack and Ruth when it was time for him to get his money?

Nancy said she'd arrange to meet Jack and Ruth at a rest stop along a highway, and give them the cash. She didn't explain how Jack and Ruth knew when to meet her.

Moeller and Locke now backed up a bit, and began to ask Nancy questions about her relationship with Jack. At this point, if she hadn't realized it before, Nancy had to know that this wasn't some routine Social Security inquiry. Still Nancy plunged on, saying she'd first met Jack back in 1991 or 1992 at a meeting of some organization she identified as "Children of Alcoholics and Addicts." The investigators asked Nancy where Jack had been living when they'd met, and Nancy said she couldn't recall the street, but thought it might be "Sungold." With that, Locke produced a photograph of the Sungold Road house. Nancy admitted that Jack had lived there. Now Nancy had to know for sure something was up—why would the Social Security people or even the

Post Office take the time and effort to photograph a house Jack hadn't lived in for six years?

Moeller and Locke now gave Nancy a little slack—a breather of sorts marked by questions that would be easier for Nancy to answer. This, too, was an interrogation technique—feeling relieved to be back on safer ground, the interrogation subject often provides confirming details, but unwittingly opens up new areas of inquiry.

The investigators asked if it was true that Jack had been having financial problems, and Nancy said it was—that was why she'd had to cash his Social Security checks for him. She added that Jack had begun to miss depositing his Social Security checks around 1996, which was when she'd taken over. But already Nancy had enmeshed herself in several apparent contradictions, if not lies—according to what she'd told Block in 1998, Jack was wealthy, but in 2003, he'd had financial problems so severe he couldn't keep a bank account; Jack was "fine," not senile, but unable to drive a car, and had lost the ability to manage his Social Security income; she didn't know how to contact Jack and "Ruth," but she met them at a rest stop on a highway.

Moeller and Locke asked Nancy if she knew of any other places where Jack had lived since 1996, and Nancy claimed that Jack had lived with her in her condo off and on for eight months while he still owned the Sungold Road house. After that house was sold, Nancy said, he'd moved to Pennsylvania to stay with "Ruth."

Locke pressed Nancy again on Jack's health.

Jack was in good health, Nancy insisted. "When I met him, he drank. Now he is physically in fine shape."

Moeller and Locke asked Nancy if it was possible that postal employees might be stealing Jack's checks, or if "Ruth" was ripping him off. "Oh no," she said, "Jack is getting all his money."

Moeller asked Nancy when she had taken over Jack's finances. Nancy denied that she'd ever taken over his finances. It was true, she said, that Jack had once refinanced his house to pay his gambling debts. After that, she said, Jack had stayed at her condo for eight months. "He was drinking then," she said. "Now he is mentally fine. When he drinks, he's not."

Nancy claimed that Jack had filed for bankruptcy in 1995 or so. She said he knew he owed money to various banks and credit card companies. To both investigators, it sounded as though Nancy were describing herself, only substituting Jack for her part in the tale. They knew full well that it had been Nancy, not Jack, who had filed for bankruptcy in September of 1996—more than four months after Jack had been found dead.

By this point, the interview had lasted a little less than an hour. Nancy told Moeller and Locke that she had to leave— Amanda was waiting for her to take over babysitting duties for Jennifer's toddler back at the house in Pikesville. Moeller continued to press her, asking if Jack had any credit accounts. Nancy said that he did, but that he couldn't use them anymore, which was why no bank would open an account for him. Moeller asked about the BMW.

This was a difficult problem for Nancy. How could she explain why Jack had given her a $44,000 car, and then had seemingly disappeared? She launched into another one of her round-about, non-sequitur–laced circumlocutions. After a few false starts, Nancy got a grip on her story. When she'd first met Jack, she said, "he told me that he was wealthy." Jack had obtained the car for her, she said, leasing it. Nancy said she'd turned the car back in to the dealer in "1996 or 1997." (Actually, as the dealer's records showed, it was 1998.)

Nancy was anxious to get home to relieve Amanda on babysitting duty. She told Moeller and Locke she really did have to leave. Then Nancy did something strange: she invited the two investigators to come to her house if they wanted to know more about Jack.

Why Nancy did this wasn't entirely clear. By that point

she had to know that the investigators had strong suspicions about Jack and his Social Security money. Inviting them to her home for still more discussion was an invitation to disaster—for her, anyway. Berger would have told her not to do it, Feinberg would have told her not to do it, and so would Harold Glaser—their advice would have been: *Shut up, don't give up anything more.* That's usually good advice from a criminal defense attorney—after all, their job is to protect their clients' rights, if not their innocence. That's what they're paid to do.

But Nancy might have believed she could somehow put the investigators' minds at ease, as she had with Block five years before. It was, in a way, like gambling—Nancy betting her life that she could somehow outwit the two investigators, a push of the poker machine's button, hoping for the some sort of flush. If she got away clean, if they went away empty-handed, there would be a terrific high, a huge risk met with an enormous psychic payoff. It would be, for Nancy, like drawing four electronic aces, along with a wild card deuce in the video machine—five aces! As Robert Feinberg put it, years later, as well as others who knew Nancy, it wasn't winning or losing that animated a compulsive gambler, it was the risk. Nowhere else did life offer such a sharp definition, some way of saying that one was really *alive*. Taking a chance was what it was really all about.

But there's also another possibility: that Nancy knew in her heart and mind that this was finally, really "it"—that she was about to be arrested, and that she was going to go down, permanently. In agreeing to talk to Moeller and Locke in her own house, she may only been trying to make sure that Jennifer's child was taken care of, before being led away in handcuffs. She'd promised Amanda she'd be back to take care of the child after a short trip to the post office, and so far the trip had taken more than an hour. This was the contradiction of Nancy—the murky boundary line where the heart met the grifter. Who can really say?

Nancy asked the investigators to wait for an hour before coming to the condo she shared with Rick—she didn't want Amanda to be there when they came. This seems to suggest that Nancy didn't want her daughter around when the investigators asked her more questions—perhaps she didn't want Amanda to see her under the law enforcement microscope. It also seems to show that Nancy knew in her heart that her grifting was over, that her last hand had been dealt: nothing but deuces and treys, most of them not of the same suit.

Moeller and Locke were genial, very accommodating. Sure, they said, they'd be happy to come to Nancy and Rick's condo in Pikesville to continue the discussion in an hour. With that, Nancy departed. Of course, Nancy was followed all the way home.

# 15
# "I'LL TELL YOU WHAT HAPPENED"

Moeller and Locke waited for a while, then called the Siegel house. There was no answer. They knew Nancy was there, but she didn't seem to be taking calls. Probably she was making them—maybe to a lawyer. The surveillance team reported that Amanda left the house shortly before 1 P.M. At that point, Moeller and Locke approached the condo on foot after parking some distance away. Nancy was outside with the toddler and her dog, Joshie. Nancy invited them inside. "Team Watkins" had checked—the four-year-old condo was worth a bit over $300,000. Rick had paid $215,000 for it in 1999. Nancy had come a long way from her mailbox-raiding days.

They went into the kitchen and sat down at the table. Nancy held her grandson on her lap and gave him graham crackers and juice. Moeller and Locke asked Nancy again about Jack's Social Security, and this time, about the New York Life annuity checks. Nancy reiterated: she only cashed the checks for Jack, then gave him the money, and that only because Jack's credit was so bad he couldn't have a bank account.

The investigators still wanted to know how Nancy arranged to give the cash to Jack. Nancy had by now apparently thought this through. The way it worked, she said, was that "Ruth" would call *her*. That was why she didn't have "Ruth's" telephone number.

Locke now decided to increase the pressure on Nancy. He told her that they had been having trouble locating Jack—while they had experts who were very good at tracking people down, and they'd checked all over Pennsylvania, they still couldn't find him.

"Well, he's in Pennsylvania," Nancy insisted.

Moeller now asked Nancy if she remembered talking to Howard County Detective Block a few years earlier. Nancy admitted that she'd talked to Block due to "some financial problems" she'd had.

Moeller nodded. Then he decided to drop the bomb.

"Nancy," he said, "this charade you've created for yourself is over. I'm Agent Moeller with the FBI. This is Investigator Greg Locke with the Loudoun County Sheriff's Office. We *know* where Jack is. *You* know where Jack is. You know what happened to Jack, and *we* know what happened to Jack. This house of cards you've built has collapsed. We know what happened . . . We've put it all together, everything. You aren't going to jail today, but this is your chance to tell us what happened."

Moeller and Locke both thought Nancy was shocked by this direct approach. She began to fuss over her grandson. While not looking at them, Nancy seemed to deflate. Her psychic armor imploded. Her first thought was apparently that Moeller was lying about her grandson, and that the next thing she knew, she'd be on her way to jail, and some stranger would be arriving to take charge of the child. She couldn't bear the thought of Jennifer knowing that she'd been forced to leave the toddler in the care of someone from the government as a result of her own bad behavior.

"Just don't take my grandson," Nancy told them. "I'll tell you what happened."

"No one's going to take your grandson," Locke told her. "Why would you think that? We're only here to talk about Jack Watkins. It doesn't have anything to do with your grandson." All they wanted, Locke said, was for Nancy to tell them what happened to Jack.

Nancy continued to fuss with the child. Locke had the idea that Nancy was using the toddler as a diversion as she tried to think of what to tell them.

"I'll tell you everything," she finally said, concentrating on the child and crackers and juice bottle. "I want to tell you everything."

Locke fished two pieces of paper from his inside coat pocket. Each had two photographs of the trunk. Nancy glanced at the pictures and began to cry. She turned away.

"I told you I would tell you everything," she said. But nothing came out.

Locke pressed ahead. "How did we get to this point?" he asked, gesturing at the photographs.

Nancy couldn't maintain eye contact with Locke. "I want to tell you what happened." She paused, trying to gather herself.

"I have ruined my family," she finally said. "You don't know what gambling will do to you. It's a terrible addiction that will take control of your life. It's much worse than drugs or alcohol." Nancy thought about this for a moment, probably thinking of Rick and his own ghosts. "Well," she went on, "I've never used drugs or alcohol, but I know it has to be much worse. It will cause you to do things."

Moeller asked how the pictures of the trunk would ruin her family. There were things her family did not know, Nancy said. She again turned her attention to the child.

The telephone rang. Nancy put the child down and went to

answer it. Both investigators were struck by the instant change in Nancy's demeanor. Gone was the emotional Nancy, the woman who had only seconds before had tearfully confessed to ruining her family. Nancy on the telephone was bright, conversational—"upbeat," in Locke's word, later—almost as if none of the preceding event with the trunk pictures had happened. Nancy said nothing to her caller about police investigators sitting in her kitchen.

"Everything here is fine," Nancy told the caller. It was Rick.

"Rick's in Florida on business," Nancy told the investigators after she hung up. Moeller and Locke were both struck by this apparent capacity for mental compartmentalization on Nancy's part. Most wives would have told their husbands almost immediately that the FBI had come to talk, and was asking difficult questions. Not Nancy. It was as if Nancy had jumped from one world into the next and back, right in front of their eyes. Either that, or it was some sort of act on the part of Rick and Nancy—some sort of telephonic duet so the investigators would get the idea that Rick had no idea of what was going on. Perhaps Nancy had already called Rick to let him know what was happening, and this repartee was all an act. Well, they would know as soon as investigators talked to Rick.

Moeller and Locke realized that if they were going to get any further with Nancy, they were going to have to separate her from her grandson, whom she seemed to be using as a shield of sorts. The question was how to do it without upsetting Nancy. They asked if it would be all right with Nancy if they called someone to watch the child while they continued their discussion. Nancy wanted to know who that might be. Moeller and Locke had Jamie Koontz, another Loudoun County investigator, waiting outside the house. Koontz had a 5-year-old daughter. Nancy agreed that Koontz could come in and watch the child while she continued to converse with

Moeller and Locke. Koontz arrived a few minutes later, and Moeller, Locke and Nancy went outside to sit on the condo's deck.

The two investigators thought Nancy was about to confess, but getting her over the hump was proving difficult.

"Ms. Siegel continued to say, 'I'll tell you everything. I want to tell you everything,'" Locke reported later. "When we would ask her to tell us what happened, Ms. Siegel would state, 'I will tell you what happened. I want to tell you what happened.' She would then sit there, without saying anything."

Nancy finally said she wanted someone to call Jennifer, so she could come to the condo to pick up her child. It seemed clear to Moeller and Locke that Nancy wasn't going to say anything more until the child was in his mother's care, so Moeller made arrangements to ask Jennifer to leave work and come to the condo.

Nancy went back inside to check on the child. After satisfying herself that the toddler was okay, she sat at the kitchen table again. Locke joined her.

He asked Nancy if anyone else besides Jack had lived with her at the condo in Ellicott City in 1996. No, Nancy said. Jennifer had grown up and moved out by that time, and Amanda had been in college in Virginia. When Locke pointed out that the college semester in Virginia ended in early May, Nancy said Amanda had taken a trip to Bermuda as soon as school ended.

"Please don't bring my daughter into this," Nancy told Locke. "She doesn't know anything." Neither did Jennifer, Nancy said.

"What did you tell your daughters about where Jack had gone?"

Nancy looked down at the table and didn't answer.

"Did Amanda know Jack was dead?"

"Oh, my God, no!" Nancy said with evident emotion.

"Where did you tell your daughters Jack had gone?"

"I told them he moved away."

"Did they ever ask you any questions about Jack?"

Nancy wouldn't answer.

Locke decided to back off and go back to more fruitful ground.

"How did we get to this point?" he asked again.

Nancy began to cry. "I'll tell you everything," she said. But nothing came out. Finally she asked if Jennifer had been notified yet.

They went back outside to the deck so Nancy could smoke—Rick didn't allow her to smoke in the house.

Locke kept pressing her for details. "I want to tell you everything," Nancy said. "I'm going to tell you everything. Is my daughter on her way? When is she going to get here?"

"Why was Jack found the way he was found?" Locke persisted. Nancy did not respond. Locke tried it another way, suggesting that the person who had left Jack in the trunk where the body could be immediately recovered must have had some compassion for Jack.

"It didn't happen the way you think," Nancy said.

# 16
# "I'M OUT OF HERE"

Locke asked her what she meant, but Nancy wouldn't respond, only asking if Jennifer was on her way. At one point, Nancy told the investigators that she had to take her medicine. She'd had a heart operation a few years earlier and was on medication to reduce her blood pressure. Locke told her that was fine, as long as she let him see what she was taking. He didn't want Nancy taking an overdose—not after what he'd heard Nancy tell Block about the knife five years before. Nancy agreed, and they went upstairs so Nancy could get her medicine. Locke checked the bottles. He watched Nancy take one pill of each kind. She asked if she could use the bathroom.

"Of course," Locke said. "You are free to do anything you wish. We are just here to talk to you." Locke was trying to make the point that the discussion was a "non-custodial interview." In fact, at no point had the investigators ever given Nancy a Miranda warning—the right to silence, the right to an attorney. If Nancy had wanted, she could have asked the investigators to leave immediately, and then they would have had to face the choice of arresting her on the spot, or complying with her demand. But Nancy didn't do this—she seemed to want to appear to be cooperative even as she played for time.

The telephone rang again. Nancy answered it. This time, she was curt. "I can't talk right now," she told the caller. It might have been Jennifer or Amanda, trying to find out what was going on. "I told you, I can't discuss it right now," Nancy said, as the caller apparently persisted. "All right," Nancy said, and hung up.

Now Nancy asked if there were someplace they might go to continue the interview. She seemed to have realized that the investigators weren't going to seize the child and stash him in foster care. Amanda was about to arrive at the house to resume babysitting duty. Nancy told the investigators she wanted to leave before Amanda got there. She didn't want Amanda to see the investigators, or listen to what they were discussing.

Shortly after 3 P.M., Amanda drove up to the condo, just as Nancy, Locke and Moeller were driving away in Moeller's car. Moeller stopped. Nancy told him to keep driving.

"Are you sure you don't want to talk to your daughter?" Moeller asked.

"No," Nancy said. "I do not want my daughter to see me like this."

The investigators drove Nancy to a nearby hotel, where a conference room had been hurriedly set aside at the request of the FBI.

Finally, Nancy began to provide some details of what had happened. She told the investigators that the day after Jack had sold the house on Sungold, they'd both gone to Atlantic City. After they returned, she said, she gone out for a while, then returned to the condo to find Jack drinking. She said Jack was suffering from "dementia"—her word—and had been having gambling problems. That was when she'd taken him to Howard County hospital. This was the first investigators had heard of Jack's six-day stay at Howard County General Hospital in April of 1996.

The investigators asked Nancy what sort of relationship she'd had with Jack. She said that when he'd come to live at her condo, Jack had "different intentions" than she did. Jack had told people that they were going to be married, Nancy said, but it wasn't so. "I never had that kind of relationship with him," Nancy said. "He was like a father to me."

When she'd first met Jack, Nancy went on, she was at a low period of her life. Jack had promised to take care of her. (This, of course, was the opposite of what Jack's close friend Ralph Hodge recalled: Jack had told Ralph that Nancy was going to take care of *him*, as investigators later discovered.) Nancy told Moeller and Locke that her own father had been murdered in 1964, when she was 16. This presumably was supporting evidence as to why she saw Jack as a "father" figure.

All of Jack's talk about marriage made her feel uncomfortable, Nancy continued, because she never had any ideas about marrying him.

"Was it hard to take care of Jack?" Nancy was asked.

It was, Nancy said. At one point, she said, she had called Jack's sister in Richmond to see if she would let Jack live with her. Jack's sister had told her, she said, that she was "too busy" to take care of Jack. (Locke's report on this interview with Nancy noted parenthetically that Jack's sister Doris subsequently told the investigators that Nancy had never called her with such a suggestion.)

She'd tried to have Jack placed in an assisted living facility, Nancy went on, but hadn't been able to find one.

While living with her at the Ellicott City condo, Nancy said, Jack had been diagnosed with "dementia"—her word again—and that he had been acting strangely at times. At one point, she said, he'd waved a shotgun at her. Jack was a different person when he drank, Nancy said.

She'd become concerned about Jack's behavior, Nancy said, and at one point called Jack's personal physician. She said the doctor had prescribed "sedatives" for Jack. Moeller and Locke made a note to check this out, later.

The two investigators now brought out the pictures of the trunk once more, and Nancy again became agitated, pushing her chair back and turning away. She began to cry and covered her eyes. "Can you put that away, or turn it over?" she asked.

"The trunk?" Locke asked. "Yes," Nancy said. Locke put the pictures away.

Locke asked her again: "How did we get to this point?" Nancy wouldn't answer directly. She began another description of Jack's behavior in the spring of 1996. She claimed that one night Jack had jumped out of bed and threatened to go "jump in the river," and according to Nancy, had left the condo, injuring himself slightly. She had convinced him to go back inside, Nancy said, where she treated his injuries.

This led the investigators to ask whether Nancy had ever dressed Jack. She had, Nancy said. Had she ever put him in a pajama top? Yes, Nancy said. On one occasion, she continued, Jack had left the condo, saying, "I'm out of here." Outside, she said, Jack had fallen down, injuring his knee and his head.

"You are describing the same injuries that Jack had when he was found," Locke told her.

"It didn't happen the way you think it did," Nancy said again. But she wouldn't say anything more, even when Locke pressed her to explain.

Locke asked Nancy about the refinancing of the Sungold house, and then the sale in April of 1996. After the sale, she said, there wasn't very much money left. That was when they had gone to Atlantic City. There was only about $5,000, Nancy said.

"Did Jack know that?" Moeller asked. Nancy wouldn't answer. "Jack didn't know that, did he?" Moeller persisted. Again Nancy wouldn't answer.

By now it was nearly 6 P.M. Nancy asked if she was free to leave. The investigators told her she was free to leave whenever she wanted.

"I just need ten or fifteen minutes and I'll come back and tell you everything," Nancy said.

When she left the conference room, no one followed her, according to Locke. The two investigators waited until 7 P.M., but Nancy never came back. Some thought she might have used the time to call Rick or even a lawyer, and then, acting on advice, decided to abandon her interviewers.

# 17
# JAILED

While Nancy had been at the hotel, the investigators served a federal search warrant, giving them the right to search the condo for evidence that might link Nancy to the trunk and the multiple credit accounts in the name of Jack Watkins. Social Security Agent Stephenson asked for the warrant on August 4, asserting that he had probable cause to believe that "Nancy Siegel and Eric Siegel knowingly defrauded the Social Security Administration, New York Life Insurance Company, Visa and Mastercard and other creditors, known and unknown." Rick's name was on the warrant as a suspect because at that point the investigators had no way of knowing if he wasn't a participant in the crimes. After all, Nancy and Rick had known each other since 1991 or so.

Among other things, the search turned up bottles of nail polish. Lab tests would later show the polish was the same as the small spots found on the top of the trunk. (Although polish was polish—all probably acrylic, and therefore not evidentially meaningful—why would Nancy have kept bottles of nail polish around for seven years?) And hair from Nancy's dog, Joshie, matched the hairs found inside the trunk, at least in terms of size, configuration and color.

Meanwhile, other investigators were interviewing Amanda. Shown a copy of the photograph of the trunk, Amanda identified it as hers, or at least, one very much like one she'd owned when she'd been in college. She'd taken the trunk to school in the fall of 1995, and had occasionally used it to steady her feet to paint her toenails, accounting for the polish spots on the lid. She'd brought the trunk back to Ellicott City after the fall semester of 1995. At one point in 1996, Amanda said, she'd asked her mother where Jack was. Nancy had told her that Jack had gone to live with his sister in Virginia. She'd let him take the trunk, Amanda said her mother told her.

Still others were interviewing Jennifer. FBI Agent Tony Crabtree and Loudoun County Investigator Steve Angelo caught up with Jennifer at the cellular telephone sales store where she worked in Delaware. She wasn't in any trouble, the two investigators assured her—they just wanted to ask her a few questions about a possible identity theft. Jennifer confirmed that Nancy was her mother, and that Charles was her father. She initially drew a blank when asked about Jack Watkins. She'd never heard the name, Jennifer said, and didn't think her mother knew him either. Angelo showed her a photograph of Jack. Jennifer didn't recognize him. She thought he looked too old for her mother. Angelo showed her more pictures, including one of the BMW. Jennifer recognized that one, anyway—her mother had been using the car when she, Amanda and Jennifer had lived in Ellicott City.

The picture of the BMW jogged Jennifer's memory. She now remembered hearing Jack's name. She recalled that her mother had told her that Jack had bought the car for her. Angelo showed her a photograph of the trunk. Jennifer said it looked similar to one that had been in the Ellicott City house. At one point, she recalled, she and Amanda had opened it, to find it filled with videotapes with foreign language titles.

Angelo asked if Jennifer knew anything about her mother's financial condition. At first Jennifer said that Nancy had no financial problems, but Angelo could see that the question troubled Jennifer. She began to cry.

"It's the same old crap," she said. "The same old crap." Her mother, she said, was a compulsive gambler. She didn't say anything more, but Angelo and Crabtree knew what she was thinking: her mother had to be involved in yet another grift.

The same afternoon, while Moeller and Locke were interviewing Nancy, Ochsman and Carr arrived at the Carroll County condominium of Cheryl, one of Jack's three step-daughters. The two investigators knocked on Cheryl's door. When Cheryl opened it, Ochsman showed her a Loudoun County sheriff's badge. Cheryl had no idea of why some cop from Virginia would be calling on her.

By that point, "Team Watkins" had done a very thorough job of investigating the backgrounds of people associated with both Jack and Nancy. Ochsman and Carr knew beyond almost any doubt that none of Jack's three step-daughters were involved in the rip-off of his Social Security checks. They'd checked their credit histories and their bank accounts, and found no evidence that anything connected to Jack had ever turned up. None of the step-daughters had any idea that Jack was dead—to them, he had simply vanished, once he had taken up with his "new gal." Their calls to the Sungold house had rarely been returned, and then, one day, the line was just disconnected.

Ochsman had located the sisters the old-fashioned way: with Jack's name in hand after getting the fingerprint identification, she'd gone back through the heart-valve records from Minnesota and found Jack's name among the thousands of recipients. That led her to the hospital where the valve was implanted, and the hospital records in turn led her to Cheryl, and the three step-daughters. That was how she'd wound up on Cheryl's doorstep in early August. This was serious detective work—Jay Merchant had to be proud of his one-time protégé.

Now, in early August of 2003, Ochsman showed Cheryl a driver's license photograph of Jack. Yes, Cheryl said, that was Jack Watkins, who had once been married to her mother, Mary. What was this all about?

That was when Ochsman was finally able to resolve the nagging vision that she and Jay Merchant had shared for so many years, the imagination that had Jack's family members, whoever they were, wondering—what had happened to him? Why had he simply vanished? Ochsman had finally closed the family circle. She could finally put away that gruesome picture of Jack-in-the-box on her desk.

The Jack she knew, Cheryl said, had once been an alcoholic. Her mother Mary had kept him from the bottle. She especially didn't want him driving, so when she helped him get a job at the electronics plant after the Western Auto store shut down, she drove him to and from work. At first, Mary had cooked and cleaned, while Jack took care of the yard at 613 Sungold, growing flowers, vegetables and herbs. Cheryl described Jack as "childlike"—her mother had told him what to do, and Jack did it. After Mary died in 1989, she and her sister Anita tried to make sure Jack didn't get into trouble, like Mary before them. But Jack began drinking again, Cheryl said. Ochsman got the impression that Jack wasn't particularly good at taking care of himself, that he yearned for a woman to cook and keep house for him, and keep him on the sober path, like Mary. He'd taken up with Vera, and had wanted to marry her. But after Vera had broken off their relationship, Cheryl said, Jack was once more at loose ends, desperate for a female companion.

Then Jack called her one day and told her he had a "girl-friend." He'd met her at the VFW, one of Jack's favorite hang-outs. Ochsman asked if Cheryl could recall the girlfriend's name.

"Swartz?" Cheryl guessed. She couldn't recall exactly. Jack one day showed her a picture of the "Swartz lady," as Cheryl now began to refer to her. The "Swartz lady" had blond hair and was half Jack's age. Jack told her she had two daughters and lived in Ellicott City.

"He was totally smitten," Cheryl said. Jack was convinced that the "Swartz lady" loved him.

Cheryl said she and Anita soon learned that the "Swartz lady" sold space in the local mausoleum, and she had sold a small vault in the crypt to Jack. He had shown her a "deed" to the mausoleum space. Cheryl was sure that Jack had been taken for a ride. The only signature on the "deed" was Jack's. Jack told her that he and the "Swartz lady" were going to be entombed together for all eternity. Jack showed her the payment book for the crypt space—$319 down, another $1,900 on time.

After meeting the "Swartz lady," Cheryl told Ochsman, Jack was very happy. But she and her sisters were suspicious. When they called Jack, they soon discovered that his voice had been removed from the message machine, and replaced by a female voice, which they assumed belonged to the "Swartz lady." None of their calls were ever returned, although Jack had always been very dutiful about calling them back in the past. Cheryl thought that their calls to Jack had been erased, so that Jack never got them. When Cheryl went to the house on Sungold Road, no one was ever home.

Jack's best friend, Cheryl told Ochsman, was an elderly man named Ralph Hodge. Ralph's wife Rosalie was a notary public. She'd told Jack before his 1993 heart surgery that he should draft a will. Jack agreed, and Rosalie had helped him write one. This was interesting to Ochsman, so she got Ralph and Rosalie's telephone number from Cheryl, and called them from Cheryl's condo.

Over the telephone, Rosalie—who was in her 80s, but still very sharp—confirmed that she had drafted a will for Jack. Then Jack had disappeared. Rosalie had gone to the Sungold Road house to find out what happened to him. Jack's neighbors didn't know where he had gone, Rosalie said. She later heard rumors that Jack had said that his girlfriend had told him that his step-daughters, Cheryl, Anita and Carol, were trying to beat him out of the modest estate—the only real asset, of course, was the Sungold Road house. Ochsman scheduled a face-to-face interview with Rosalie and Ralph for the following day.

When Ochsman hung up the telephone, Cheryl told her that some years before, she'd received a call from Rosalie. Jack had sold the Sungold Road house, Rosalie had told her— she'd heard this as a rumor at the "Five and Dime Breakfast Club." This had shocked Cheryl—Jack had always told her that he would *never* sell the house. Cheryl had then called Darrel, their younger brother, who went to the house to see what was going on. The new owners told Darrel they'd bought the house from some real estate company, and that they had no information about Jack.

Cheryl gave Ochsman Darrel's telephone number in Texas. Ochsman called Darrel. Yes, he said, when Ochsman got through, he'd gone to the house and talked to the occupants back in 1996. They knew nothing about Jack, or his whereabouts. Darrel, who wasn't a great fan of Jack to begin with, was disgusted. To him, it was typical of Jack to have sold the house and not told anyone. It was particularly galling because his mother had bought the house with her modest inheritance from her father, his grandfather. But Jack seemed to have disappeared with all the money.

By this point, Cheryl was intensely curious. All she knew, she said, was that, first, the "Swartz lady" seemed to be preventing communications with Jack, and the next thing anyone knew, Jack had disappeared. Now Ochsman told Cheryl for the first time that Jack was dead, and not by natural causes—that he'd been murdered. She explained that Jack's body had been found in Virginia years before, but that it had not been identified until recently.

There was a suspect in the murder, Ochsman said. Cheryl had to know that Ochsman meant the "Swartz lady," but

Ochsman gave her no details. More investigation had to be done, she said. Cheryl said she understood.

Cheryl called her sister Anita's cellphone. Anita was riding the train back to Baltimore from her job at a historical preservation project in Washington, D.C.

"What is it?" Anita asked, when she answered. Anita and Cheryl, children by two different fathers with their mother Mary, lived next door to each other, and were very close.

"When you get home, come over," Cheryl told Anita. But she wouldn't say why. Anita closed her phone, thinking something important and probably unusual was going on with her sister. When she got to Cheryl's condo, Ochsman and Carr were waiting for her.

Yes, Anita said, when Ochsman and Carr showed her Jack's picture, that was Jack. And then Ochsman and Carr told the two sisters the story, the one the members of "Team Watkins" had pieced together over the preceding eight months—how Jack Watkins had first been bled white, starved, drugged, then abandoned, dead in a trunk beside the Potomac River.

The next day, August 6, 2003, Ochsman went to see Ralph and Rosalie Hodge in Reisterstown. Jack, they told Ochsman, was a very genial, happy-go-lucky sort who enjoyed playing bingo or bowling. He was not mechanically inclined, Ralph told Ochsman. "He could change a light bulb," Ralph said, "but that was about it. I'm not kidding." He and others from the breakfast club and the senior center had helped Jack maintain the house from time to time—Jack couldn't do it alone.

In the years since Mary had died, he spent a lot of time with the Hodges, who were probably his closest friends. But Jack was "very easily manipulated," Rosalie told Ochsman. "Gullible."

Ochsman produced a driver's license photo of Nancy, and both Hodges immediately identified it as "Nan," as Jack had called her. "Nan" had taken over Jack's life, they said, driving away his friends. Sometimes "Nan" called the Hodges, demanding to know where Jack was. After a few of those calls, Rosalie had told "Nan" never to call them again. The few times they did see Jack after "Nan" had arrived in his life, Ralph got the impression that Jack walked on tiptoe around her, as if he didn't want to make her mad. It seemed to both Hodges that "Nan" completely dominated Jack, much the way Mary had in earlier years, but in a far more prickly way.

Jack's friends at the Senior Center and the breakfast club all warned Jack against "Nan." Most people thought that "Nan" was taking him for a ride. When people suggested that "Nan" was up to no good, Jack would become irritated, indignant, even. People saw less and less of Jack at his old familiar haunts.

Then one day Jack arrived at the Senior Center. Nancy was driving. She stayed in the car. Jack got out, and told everyone at the center that he was moving away, that it was the last time he'd be seeing them. He and "Nan" drove off.

Ochsman found a driver's license photo of Jack, taken in January of 1995.

Yes, Rosalie said, that was Jack. But in the photo, he looked ill, for some reason, Rosalie said. "He looks bad."

That was when Ochsman told the Hodges that Jack was dead—that he had been found dead in Virginia, more than six years before.

The same day, August 6, 2003, Nancy met with Harold Glaser in Glaser's office. By Glaser's own account, this was a stormy session. Glaser later claimed that Nancy was in a state of near hysteria and vomiting—in any case, extremely upset. Assuming that Nancy told him the details of the investigators' questions, Glaser had to know that this wasn't just another one of Nancy's credit card grifts. Glaser told her to keep her mouth closed from then on, although he realized that it was probably too late. Nancy had already virtually admitted to being the person who had left Jack's body in the trunk in Loudoun County in May of 1996, as well as the fact that she'd been the only person in his proximity at the time he died. True, Nancy hadn't said anything about the cause of Jack's death, but Glaser had to know that they weren't asking Nancy all those pointed questions because Jack had died from simply falling over.

The next day, August 7, 2003, the investigators contacted Nancy again, and asked her for another interview. This time Nancy refused, saying Glaser had advised her not to say anything.

That same day or the next, August 8, Rick returned from Florida. It appears that the investigators reached Rick before he talked to Nancy. At first it seemed to the investigators that he thought that Nancy had been up to her old tricks with fraudulent credit card accounts. He sighed, but he didn't appear to be too worried—he knew that restitution could be made. But then the authorities told him that Nancy was a murder suspect. This flabbergasted Rick. It didn't seem possible. Then Rick realized something else: the same authorities were suspicious of him, too.

The details of what Rick told investigators in early August of 2003 were never disclosed, later. But it seems likely that if Nancy was willing to talk—to a point—Rick was a little smarter. He cut short the interview and called Harold Glaser. He wanted to find out what the hell was going on before he said anything more.

On or about August 9, Nancy and Rick met with Glaser in his Baltimore office. What happened next was never fully disclosed, but based on Glaser's later representations to the court, it appears that Rick and Nancy agreed to separate. Rick also appears to have asked Glaser to see if he couldn't figure out what Nancy had been up to with his accounts. There were recriminations back and forth. Nancy and Glaser had words. While no one was watching closely, Nancy took an overdose of her medications. Realizing that Nancy was passing out, that she'd done something to herself, Rick and Glaser took Nancy to a hospital. Later, Nancy would claim that Glaser and Rick had hoped she would die, that they had delayed getting her medical treatment. It wasn't true, but it illustrates something of Nancy's state of mind at the time.

A few days later, Nancy was released from the hospital. Rick made arrangements for her to see a psychiatrist. She returned to the condo to wait to see what would happen next.

On August 14, members of "Team Watkins" met with Assistant United States Attorney Tamera Fine. Fine had been involved in the investigation almost from the beginning. Stephenson from Social Security prepared an affidavit to support Nancy's arrest on fraud and theft charges. The next day, Nancy was arrested at the condo in the early morning, and taken directly to jail. It was Friday, August 15, and that was the last day of her life that Nancy would ever see a glint of freedom.

# 18
# A SCHEME AND
# AN ARTIFICE

On the following Monday, Nancy made her first appearance in court, to respond to Stephenson's criminal complaint charging her with four felony counts: mail fraud, by engaging in a "scheme and artifice to defraud"—using the mails to obtain Jack's Social Security checks; wire fraud, by using the telephone to obtain a replacement check; bank fraud, by her use of Jack's name on credit accounts; and theft, from her conversion of the Social Security checks to her own use.

But by that Monday, the list of charges had grown by two, as amended by Assistant U.S. Attorney Fine: in addition to the first four, Nancy was now accused of identity theft, and aiding and abetting. It seems that the authorities still weren't sure that Rick hadn't known what was going on—that would be one reason for the "aiding and abetting" charge. But the government was handling Rick carefully—so far there had been no evidence linking him to any of the scams, let alone the demise of Jack Watkins.

Nancy had spent the weekend at the Talbot County,

Maryland, Detention Center. By Monday morning she was not in good shape. Glaser, entering an appearance on her behalf, asked the federal magistrate, Paul Grimm, to order a medical evaluation, along with another order to provide copies of all medical records from her incarceration, to the court. Nancy's lawyer wanted to make sure there was a substantial record of his client's mental condition from the very beginning. It could, Glaser knew, be very useful later. Already, Rick's description of her past had suggested to him that Nancy might well have defense of mental disease or defect—after all, Rick had known Nancy for years, which encompassed much of her behavior. Glaser himself had his own experience with Nancy's mercurial moods—after all, he had represented her in the Howard County mailbox-raiding case in 1998.

Glaser told the judge that Nancy was at risk of suicide. He sketched in the events of August 9, when she'd tried to overdose on her medications. Somewhere along the line, Nancy had written a suicide note to her daughters. Glaser didn't immediately produce this note for the judge, but it later came into the record.

"My dearest Jen & Amanda," Nancy had written. And then, in a different pen, as if she'd been interrupted, or wanted to think about it before finishing her thoughts, which seemed a bit scattered, at least in writing: "I love you so much in time you will know . . . I'm sorry for the pain and torment I have put you through. You were my life. Please go on and become the best that you can be."

"It has been reported to the court," Grimm wrote after this appearance and for the record, "that the defendant suffers from depression and has been prescribed an antidepressant . . . further, she attempted suicide and should be promptly evaluated and thereafter monitored as a possible suicide risk." Grimm ordered Nancy held without bail, and told the U.S. Marshal, which had a contract with Talbot County for the care of federal prisoners, to arrange for an evaluation by "an appropriate health care provider."

With that, Nancy was whisked back to jail.

Over the next few weeks, Assistant U.S. Attorney Fine convened a federal grand jury to consider charges against Nancy, and, it appears, maybe Rick. Glaser apparently soon informed Rick that he couldn't represent him, too—there was a possible conflict between Nancy and her husband. Rick was summoned before the grand jury to testify as to his own bank and credit accounts. Glaser gathered up documents about Rick's accounts and turned them over to another lawyer, who would represent Rick when he testified before Fine's grand jury. During this two-week period, according to Glaser's later statements to the court, he and Nancy had numerous conversations, some of them acrimonious. He later said that Nancy wouldn't cooperate with him as her defense lawyer. He said that Nancy believed that he was on Rick's side, that he blamed her for Rick's predicament with the grand jury. Eventually Rick testified, and convinced the grand jurors that he'd had no knowledge of or involvement in Nancy's scams. By that point, the government had come to believe him—in fact, by the end of August, the government had come to see Rick as one of Nancy's biggest victims, besides Jack.

On August 27, 2003, the grand jury returned a seventeen-count indictment against Nancy, charging her with multiple counts of bank fraud, wire fraud, theft and identity theft—the use of the identity of Jack Watkins. The indictment alleged that Nancy had been involved in a long-running "scheme to defraud," the "scheme" beginning around 1995 and continuing through August of 2003. Missing from the indictment was any count implicating Nancy in the murder of Jack Watkins. This was a curious omission, given Nancy's statements to Moeller and Locke. It seemed to show that the federal government wasn't yet convinced that it was Nancy who had actually strangled Jack.

Being indicted by the federal government is an altogether different kettle than, say, being charged in a state indictment. For one thing, the federal government has powers, resources and rights that state prosecutors can only drool over. In fact, the federal government can withhold grand jury testimony against a defendant until the witness testifies in open court. This can be a tremendous advantage—someone accused of a crime has no way of knowing what another person is saying about them until they've already said it—in front of a trial jury.

"You don't mess with the G," defense lawyers often tell their clients. The Congress has stacked the deck against criminal defendants, particularly with requirements to disclose evidence before trial. A defendant would have to be extraordinarily lucky—or demonstrably innocent, *Perry Mason*–style—to beat a federal rap. Only the guileless or the irredeemably guilty take their chances at trial in a federal court—the former because they don't know any better, the latter because they have no choice.

To put her "scheme and artifice to defraud" into operation, the indictment of Nancy contended, Nancy had "sought to cultivate a relationship with Jack Watkins in order to gain his trust and access to his financial resources and financial information which could be used in furtherance of the scheme."

To ensure that the scheme worked, the indictment continued, Nancy had tried to keep Jack away from his family and friends, even going so far as to deleting messages from his telephone message machine. At various times, Nancy had portrayed herself as Jack's "girlfriend," his fiancée, or his daughter. In setting up the "scheme," Nancy used Jack's personal information to establish credit accounts in his name, and then concealed their existence from him by having the statements mailed to her own address in Ellicott City.

At the same time, after Jack's death, Nancy had furthered her scheme by collecting Jack's Social Security checks, and depositing them into bank accounts she controlled, or cashing them. Although Stephenson had identified seventy-two such checks, the government charged Nancy with theft in connection with only nine of them, drawn over a range of years, sufficient to show the breadth of the scheme.

Counts 10, 12, 14 and 15 of the indictment covered bank fraud and mail fraud—when Nancy had opened credit card accounts in Jack's name, and when she'd used the mail to obtain Jack's Social Security and New York Life checks. Counts 16 and 17 covered wire fraud—from Nancy's telephone calls to Social Security in which she had claimed to be Jack's daughter in order to get replacement checks sent. Counts 11 and 13 were for fraudulent use of another person's identity in order to commit the two bank frauds—identity theft.

Altogether, if convicted on the charges, and if she got a maximum sentence for each category of count, rather than consecutive sentences for each of the seventeen counts, Nancy was still looking at a possible total of 73 years in prison—that is, if a judge could find some reason to make the combined terms on each category run consecutively rather than concurrently. Even if the combined counts were sentenced concurrently, the heaviest term, for bank fraud, alone carried a term of 20 years. That meant that Nancy, then 55 years old, was highly likely to spend at least 10 or 15 years in prison—basically, most of the rest of her life, even assuming a parole board was willing to let her out at some distant point in the future. Then, too, there were the possible fines—a maximum total of $1.75 million. Not that Nancy could ever pay them, of course. When the federal government drops the hammer on you, you're squashed—no ifs, ands or buts about it.

But that wasn't the worst for Nancy. Glaser knew full well that if the government believed Nancy had murdered Jack in furtherance of her "scheme," the possible penalty was truly draconian—death.

In conversations with Fine, Glaser learned that the government was still investigating, and that there was likely to be a "superseding indictment," that is, a new charging document to replace the seventeen-count accusation, and that the new indictment, when it came, was likely to include the murder allegation—witness-tampering by death.

Nancy was in one hell of a lot of trouble.

Meanwhile, "Team Watkins" continued to investigate, collecting bank and credit card records, and unearthing other possible witnesses to Nancy's previous scams. Slowly the picture came into focus: after meeting Jack while offering him the cemetery crypt, Nancy had run off with his good name, at least in terms of credit. The logic of probability seemed unassailable: Nancy, a lifelong credit card fraudster, had stolen Jack's credit, and then had strangled him to make sure he never complained.

At one point, investigators talked to one of Nancy's own closest friends, Linda Lafferman. Lafferman had known Nancy since she'd been married to Charles. After Nancy had tried to overdose herself, Lafferman had visited her in the hospital. Nancy had given her the note she'd written to Jennifer and Amanda at that time. And then, according to Lafferman, Nancy had told her how Jack had died—he'd hung himself with a strap, according to Nancy. She'd found Jack dead on his bed in the Ellicott City condo, Nancy told Lafferman, and then, in a panic, had wedged his body into Amanda's trunk and driven it into Virginia, where she'd left it. Jennifer later said her mother had told her a similar story—she'd found Jack dead on the bed next to a rope, and concluded that Jack had killed himself.

Of course, if Jack had killed himself, Nancy couldn't be criminally responsible for witness-tampering, unless her attempt to conceal his identity counted. But the investigators had their doubts about these stories: the autopsy didn't seem to show any evidence of hanging—no ligature marks on the neck, as usually accompanies such a means of death.

True, there were marks on the neck, as well as significant bleeding inside the throat and mouth, almost certainly from some form of suffocation, but they probably weren't caused by hanging. Just how Nancy had managed to strangle Jack, if she did, was left to the imagination, at least in the government's court filings. Fine would later offer a peculiarly chilling theory as to how that alleged strangulation had occurred.

Somehow, in early September, Stephenson learned of Nancy's early 1990s connection with Linda Mayberry. Linda had been arrested the year before for running a prostitution business. It was her second fall in seven years, so Linda decided to get out of the racket. She told Stephenson all about her unhappy adventures with Nancy, including the unpaid-for Toyota, the fraudulent loan obtained in her husband John's name, and Nancy's threat to blackmail her by going to the IRS. It was she, Linda told Stephenson, who had introduced Nancy and Rick back in late 1991 or early 1992.

Meanwhile, Glaser continued to have problems with Nancy, or so he informed the court. Nancy alternated frequent fits of weeping with lashing out at Glaser, accusing him of conspiring with Rick to make sure she died during her overdose of early August. Glaser wasn't sure that Nancy was mentally competent to assist in her own defense. After Nancy was arraigned on the indictment in September, and the case was assigned to a judge, Glaser tried to tell Nancy that it was very likely that the government was soon about to charge her with murder. According to Glaser, Nancy reacted to this with another bout of weeping. He wasn't at all sure that Nancy really understood what was at stake: her own life.

On October 10, Glaser filed a motion asking the court to order a mental examination of Nancy.

In support of his motion, Glaser asserted:

1. That at the initial meeting between defense counsel and the defendant, the defendant became highly agitated, proceeded to vomit uncontrollably, and was unable to communicate effectively with counsel.
2. That at the second meeting in counsel's office, approximately one week later, the defendant had ingested, either in my office or directly prior thereto, a large amount of medication she was taking in her stated attempt to commit suicide. She "just about" passed out when her husband and I arranged for her to be taken to Northwest Hospital Center. Upon her admission to the hospital, her blood pressure was "25/50."

This was very low blood pressure, equivalent to shock, and potentially lethal. Glaser's declaration continued:

3. That the hospital treated her for psychiatric disorders and discharged her some days later.
4. That upon her release, it is my understanding, she continued to see a psychiatrist.
5. That thereafter she was charged by criminal complaint and has been incarcerated since that time.
6. That at the detention hearing on August 18, 2003, before the Honorable Paul W. Grimm, United States Magistrate Judge, the court ordered medical evaluation and appropriate treatment of the defendant . . .
7. That counsel has interviewed the defendant on numerous occasions, both at the "[U.S.] Marshall's lock-up" and visiting her at Talbot County Detention Center. There has been some communication with the defendant in order to prepare a proper defense. She constantly cries and places her head upon the table in the "Marshall's lock-up" and the attorney visiting room at Talbot County. She is not always coherent.

8. That on the date of the arraignment, the defendant indicated she understood the charges against her, the possible maximum sentence and pled not guilty. Nevertheless, there was concern by counsel whether a plea should have been entered at that time. In order to further the proceedings towards trial and to make a determination by the defense for the herein motion, counsel visited the defendant after the arraignment was completed at the Talbot County Detention Center and still feels the defendant should be evaluated for competency.

9. That at the last visit, counsel again informed the defendant that the government has indicated there will be a superseding indictment under which the defendant may be charged with murder in addition to the charges under the original indictment. Counsel avers he owed a duty to the defendant to inform her of the prospective superseding indictment. This exacerbated counsel's difficulty in communicating with the defendant.

10. That counsel has informed the defendant the herein motion would be filed.

In retrospect, it seems possible that Glaser was trying to lay the groundwork for a possible defense based upon a claim of mental disease or defect. Years later, Glaser declined to discuss his approach to the case, citing attorney–client privilege.

Thus, it isn't clear if Glaser intended to eventually argue to a jury that, *at the time of the crime,* May 12 or 13 of 1996, Nancy had been suffering from a mental disease or defect, so she should not be held responsible for her actions at the time of Jack's death. That, under stress, Nancy tended to fall apart, and was capable of anything, whether she knew it or not. And that, under similar stress after being charged, wasn't able to effectively assist in her defense.

But if this was Glaser's strategy, it suggests two other possible conclusions: that in the fall of 2003, when he was representing Nancy, Glaser was concerned that the government had sufficient evidence to convict Nancy of murder if she pled plain-vanilla not guilty, instead of not guilty by reason of mental disease or defect; and second, that Nancy may have told Glaser what actually happened. Nancy's story to Lafferman and her daughter Jennifer had been that she'd found Jack dead on the bed, with a rope or a strap. Well, that was pretty stupid: if Jack had hung himself, why was he on the bed? Why wasn't he dangling from some rafter? Did Nancy really expect the experts in death—medical examiners and detectives experienced in murder—to believe that he had somehow committed suicide by hanging himself, and had then curled up on the mattress, laying the rope or strap down along beside him, before he died? The story had no legs: it was, to "Team Watkins," clearly a lie.

Of course, it's also possible that Nancy had no memory of what occurred on May 12 or 13 of 1996—such blackouts are not unheard of when a person is under a great deal of emotional stress. A blackout, or as a psychiatrist might see it, an effect of post-traumatic stress syndrome, might be evidence of mental disease or defect *at the time of the crime*. Given Nancy's documented history of mental problems—say, by citing his own experience with her, or calling Susan Darvas as a witness—that might be one way of getting Nancy out from under a murder charge.

Then, too, there was the possibility of trying to demonstrate that compulsive gambling alone was evidence of mental disease or defect: the notion that insanity is doing the same thing over and over when it doesn't work. That way, an aggressive lawyer like Glaser might be able to put the casinos in the dock, not unlike the tobacco companies, by portraying his client as also a victim. Clearly the advertising of the casinos wasn't unlike that for Joe Camel—an enticement to the addicted.

In any case, Glaser seemed to be heading for a mental disease or defect defense of Nancy. Still, his motion asking for a competency evaluation lay fallow for several weeks after having been filed. While waiting, Glaser papered the government with his usual snowstorm of other motions: a motion demanding that members of "Team Watkins" retain all their rough notes; a motion to suppress any of Nancy's statements in case they were made involuntarily; a motion to disclose Nancy's prior criminal record; a motion to suppress any physical evidence tying Nancy to the crimes; a motion to suppress any evidence from electronic eavesdropping; and a motion to permit the filing of additional motions after the government turned over all its evidence in discovery.

Fine had apparently offered copies of some of the initial evidence collected by "Team Watkins" to Glaser. But when Fine told Glaser that the government was considering a "superseding indictment," both sides agreed to wait until that happened and to postpone hearings on Glaser's snowstorm.

Thus as October turned into November 2003, Glaser had only the roughest idea of the evidence against his client. He still wanted the mental competency examination, however. Finally on November 17, more than a month later, Judge Andre M. Davis ordered the competency exam. Judge Davis appointed a Baltimore psychiatrist, Dr. John Lion, to determine if Nancy was mentally capable of assisting in her own defense. Glaser had Nancy waive any doctor–patient privilege so that the results of the exam could be shared with the court and the government. Two days later, Lion went to visit Nancy in the Talbot County Detention Center. In this session, and perhaps others, it appears that Nancy may have made new admissions, based on subsequent remarks made in court by Judge Davis.

Lion's assessment of Nancy's mental competency was returned to the court and the parties in late December of 2003. Thereupon it was filed under seal. Glaser later suggested that Lion's evaluation turned up evidence of mental illness on

Nancy's part, but the bottom line was simple: Nancy *was* competent to assist her lawyer. She might be crazy, in a way, but she wasn't insane. The law makes a distinction between the two.

But by then, the government was already working on a way to disqualify Glaser as Nancy's lawyer.

# 19
# A TEST CASE

As Fine had suggested and Glaser feared, the other hob-nailed federal boot fell on Nancy's neck on January 16, 2004. The federal grand jury in Baltimore returned a "superseding indictment," this time charging her with twenty-two criminal counts, including the witness-tampering allegation. The previous indictment was dismissed, not that it made any difference to Nancy.

Nancy, the new indictment claimed, had murdered Jack to prevent him from reporting her to a judge or law enforcement officer, with the intent of protecting her "scheme and artifice to defraud." This was, under federal law, a crime of "witness tampering," or so the government alleged. The first thirty-seven paragraphs of the new indictment, covering ten pages, under the heading "The Participants," recounted most of Nancy's "prior bad acts," beginning with Charles Kucharski, as segments of a long-running "scheme," of which the alleged murder of Jack Watkins was only a part.

Each of the first thirty-seven paragraphs was "re-alleged," or re-charged, as part of the first nineteen counts of the indictment, which meant they could be used as evidence at trial to prove each count. On the last two counts, the government did not re-allege the facts of the supposed long-running scheme, but asserted that Nancy had murdered Jack with the intent of preventing Jack from providing information to law enforcement of "federal offenses, including bank fraud . . . and mail fraud." Just why the government didn't re-allege the supposed "scheme" in the last two counts wasn't clear.

Still, this seemed—maybe—to incorporate the "scheme and artifice to defraud" into the last two counts. Later there would be a great deal of legal squabbling over the way the indictment was written. Of course, there was only one actual "participant" in the scheme—Nancy. All the rest of those named were victims, including Rick Siegel.

With this, the government leapt into uncharted territory, legally speaking. In essence, the federal government was attempting to claim that the murder of Jack—if indeed it *was* a murder—was integral to *all* of Nancy's frauds, going back to 1982 and her first husband, Charles Kucharski. The idea was that if she hadn't murdered Jack, Jack would have been a witness against her, ratting her out for her crimes against him, both before and after, and thence leading to complete exposure of her game plan, her "scheme," which was to commit frauds against all comers, and especially men she had seduced, all the way back to 1982 and her first husband, the father of her daughters.

In many ways it was a stretch—it made Nancy out to be a long-running planner, a scheming, gold-digging bitch, going back more than two decades, when the reality was much more complicated. Nothing was said, for instance, about Nancy's addiction to the casinos' poker machines, or the fact that she had spent twenty years trying to provide for her two daughters. Certainly nothing was said in the new indictment about her claims that both of her first two husbands had abused her, however unfounded. Of course, that wasn't the purpose of an indictment—to give the suspect's side of the story. An indictment was only the government's side. It was up to Nancy's defenders to tell the whole truth, as best as they could spin it, even if it wasn't completely "nothing but."

Much later, faced with opposition to this line of thought, because of difficulties with the evidence, the government realized they had to go a little further than what it had said in the new indictment. It upped the ante on Nancy's supposed motive, and argued that, had Jack reported Nancy to law enforcement, it would have led to Nancy's violation of her 10-years' probation, and therefore a quick trip to the slammer. So, according to the government, Nancy'd had to shut Jack's mouth before he had a chance to tell on her, violate her probation, and send her off to jail for ten years or so—actually, probably much less, given overcrowding in the Maryland pens. That, the government contended, Nancy couldn't allow: she already had Rick Siegel in her sights as her next scam victim, and needed to shut Jack's mouth to snare him. In other words, it wasn't just fraud, it was first fear, then greed.

But this fear-of-probation-violation claim, or greed, wasn't part of the new indictment in early 2004. In those days the government simply argued that Nancy's "scheme and artifice to defraud," as described in her "prior bad acts" in paragraphs 1 through 37, had driven her to murder Jack so she could continue her "scheme"; the next victim of which, in Nancy's "scheme," or "plan," was to be Rick Siegel.

Of course, this theory was based on the idea that Nancy was capable of thinking that far ahead, despite the paucity of evidence that she was able to see much further than the following week. The idea of someone like Nancy organizing a "scheme" in 1982 to cook some senior citizen unknown to her at the time for his Social Security, or his credit, fourteen years later, was bizarre.

Well, it was convoluted, this murder charge by way of "witness-tampering," but it was the only way the federal government had jurisdiction to bring a charge of murder against Nancy, because there is no federal murder statute, except in certain, limited circumstances, such as a killing on federal property. In most cases, murder is a state crime, not a federal offense. So the government had to get creative. The witness-tampering statute was essentially an appendix to federal legislation designed to hamstring organized crime. Bringing it against Nancy was a bit like using a howitzer to swat a fly. But it worked, as far as the federal authorities in Maryland were concerned. And it did have certain usefulness—if it worked, in court, the government would have expanded its authority. It would be able to connect old things to new things—bad stuff of the past, unchargeable because of the statute of limitations, or adjudication by local jurisdictions, to bad stuff now: the supposed murder of Jack Watkins.

It was all inextricably linked, in the new indictment, to the "prior bad acts" on Nancy's part, as well as to things she'd done after selling Jack his above-ground crypt at the cemetery. There was something circular about the government's reasoning, though. It was subtle, but it was there: there had to be a "scheme" by Nancy in order to establish any intent on Nancy's part to get rid of a witness. No scheme, no witness—it was as simple as that. The new indictment proposed to make new law as to the use of "prior bad acts" as evidence against a criminal defendant, and in time, it would become a landmark case, of sorts.

Ordinarily, the rules of evidence generally don't permit the use of earlier crimes—"prior bad acts"—to convict a defendant of the crime with which he or she is presently charged. The idea here is that jurors who are told of earlier, unrelated crimes might unfairly conclude that the defendant's earlier propensity to commit crime, as evidenced by the earlier acts, more likely than not proves that she's committed the charged crime.

After all, just because someone did something bad once doesn't mean they did something bad again. Common sense might say yes, but common sense isn't proof beyond a rea-

Jack Watkins, a few years before meeting Nancy Jean. Born in 1920, Jack seemed much younger than his years. *Cheryl Jenkins*

Carol, Anita and Cheryl, the three daughters of Mary Triplett, step-daughters of Jack Watkins. They had the deepest suspicion of "the Swartz lady," as they recalled Nancy Jean Sweitzer Kucharski Geisendaffer, as she was then known, but when Jack vanished from their lives, they had no idea that foul play was involved.

*Carlton Smith*

The house on Sungold Road in Reisterstown, Md., purchased by Mary Triplett and inherited by Jack Watkins after her death. Nancy Jean convinced Jack to borrow tens of thousands of dollars against the house's equity. Until he met Nancy, Jack owned the house free and clear of any debt. *Carlton Smith*

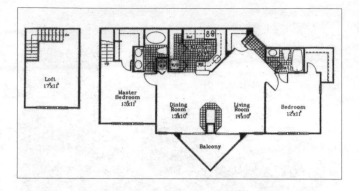

A schematic drawing of Nancy's condo in Ellicott City, Md. Police believed that Nancy kept Jack Watkins in the loft above the bedroom, preventing him from leaving her and reporting her defalcations, which had left him penniless by early 1996.

*Exhibit at the trial of Nancy Jean Siegel*

Ralph Hodge, Jack Watkins' closest friend in Reisterstown. Ralph warned Jack that Nancy Jean would take him for every cent he had. He had no idea, however, that Nancy would also be convicted of taking his very life.

*Carlton Smith*

After allegedly suffocating Jack Watkins, Nancy Jean stuffed his body in this trunk, and left it by the side of a highway in Harpers Ferry National Park. It took almost 7 years to identify his body. Jack's body was naked from the waist down, and his head was covered with a duffel bag. The trunk was sealed with heavy tape.

*Loudoun County Sheriff photo*

Nancy during the search of her condo in 1998. Both before and after meeting Jack Watkins, Nancy Jean obtained money by falsifying other people's identities, then cashing checks in their names. Police in Howard County, Md., eventually caught her, and searched her condo for evidence. They came close to discovering Nancy's biggest secret, but didn't know it.

*Howard County Sheriff photo*

Nancy on her way to cash one of Jack Watkins' Social Security checks in early 2003. By February of that year, the state/federal team of investigators wanted to learn if there were others involved in the death of Jack Watkins, and as a result put her under covert surveillance.

*Photo still from FBI surveillance video*

Loudoun County Investigator Bobbie Ochsman, at the Potomac River turnout where Jack Watkins' body was discovered in the trunk in May, 1996. In 2003, Ochsman was finally able to identify the remains, which led her and a team of federal and state investigators to Nancy Jean Siegel.

*Carlton Smith*

Nancy Siegel, at the time of her arrest in 2003, more than 7 years after Jack Watkins vanished.

*Maryland DMV photo*

My dearest Jen & Amanda,
I love you
so much in
time you will
know
I'm sorry for
the pain and.
torment I have
put you through,
You were my
life
Please go on and become
the best you can be

After her arrest, Nancy attempted to commit suicide in her lawyer's office. While recovering at a nearby hospital a day or so later, she wrote this note to her two adult daughters.

*Exhibit at the trial of Nancy Jean Siegel*

Loudoun County Investigators Jamie Koontz, Greg Locke and Bobbie Ochsman were commended by the federal Social Security Administration for their work in unraveling Nancy Jean's fatal fraud. By the time she was arrested, 7 years after Jack Watkins' body was found in the trunk, Nancy had ripped off hundreds of thousands of dollars by posing as Jack Watkins' daughter, niece, fiancée or friend.

*Loudoun County Sheriff photo*

Jack Watkins' step-daughters, Anita and Cheryl, receive the flag used to honor his military service in World War II during a moving memorial service at the national cemetery at Arlington, VA in August, 2009.

*Photo by Kraig Troxell, Loudoun County Sheriff's Department*

sonable doubt. The first can't prove the later unless it's connected, in, say, an ongoing "scheme."

But even then, there usually has to be something tying the first act to the later crimes—the same victim, say, or the same objective of the "scheme," such as a pension fund, property or the same bank. With its new indictment, the government was breaking new ground—it was trying to say that a lifetime of grifting was all one "scheme," and that evidence of a "scheme" led inevitably to the conclusion that the "schemer," Nancy, was guilty of murder, or in this case, witness-tampering, in order to protect the "scheme."

But as usual with the rules of evidence, there were exceptions. Previous crimes can be admitted against a defendant if the authorities show the earlier crimes demonstrate motive, intent, pattern, or, as noted, "a common scheme or plan." Here the boundary line between a "scheme" and *modus operandi*, *m.o.*, was blurry. In its new indictment, the federal government wanted to show that *m.o.* and "scheme" were the same thing. This would be a significant expansion of the exception to the evidence rule on "prior bad acts," Evidence Rule 404.

Thus, in order to show that Nancy's motive in killing Jack was to protect her "common scheme or plan," the federal government wanted to show that *all* of Nancy's "prior bad acts," going back to 1982 with her first husband, Charles Kucharski, were related, and connected, part of her "scheme"—her supposed ongoing plan to commit frauds—all the way up until August of 2003, when she was arrested. That's why the government "re-alleged" all the prior bad acts for each of the first nineteen counts of the new indictment. Just why the government didn't re-allege for the last two counts wasn't entirely clear, but the linkage between the supposed "scheme" and the final two counts was implied by the use of the words "federal offenses, including."

Nancy's defense lawyers, though, would argue tooth and nail the notion that there had ever been any sort of "scheme" behind Jack's death, and still are. It's the way law is made in this country, one crime at a time.

For the defense, while there might have been a "propensity" to commit fraud on Nancy's part, that didn't necessarily mean that it was all part of one "plan," or that Nancy's grifts were "in common," and certainly not one "scheme." After all, Nancy's whole history seemed to indicate that Nancy, like most grifters, operated by the seat of her pants—by impulse and instinct, not long-term planning. Just because she had a documented history of grifting didn't necessarily mean she'd killed Jack to hide it.

Even assuming she killed Jack, it might have been for other reasons—for instance, that she didn't really like him, or that she just didn't want him around anymore. It was also possible that they'd had some sort of fight, a mere domestic dispute. The killing of Jack—if it *was* a killing—wasn't necessarily part of some sort of twenty-year "scheme." It might well have happened on the spur of the moment. Who knew for sure? Where was the evidence, other than surmise based on Nancy's history?

Using the earlier acts to prove Nancy's intent in disposing of a potential witness against her was like saying, once bad, always bad. It proved nothing beyond a reasonable doubt, certainly nothing that had to do with any "scheme." So the old, bad stuff shouldn't be used to smear her with a jury—it was "character evidence," forbidden under the rules. That was the defense position, and they were sticking to it. In short, Nancy was nothing like Mafiosi, who, of course, have been known to "scheme" over years and years, and pass their "schemes" down from father to son. Then, if a witness wound up as a corpse in the New Jersey pine barrens, it might be part of a "scheme."

Applying this to a grifter like Nancy was like saying that using someone else's credit card in 1982 or 1983 meant that such an act was connected "in common" to a garroting in the Bronx fifteen years later. As far as the defense was concerned, there had to be a connection besides the perpetrator and the "propensity" to commit a crime, that made it part of a "scheme."

The difficulty for both the government and the defense in the Siegel case was that the parameters of the "prior bad acts" rules of evidence had never been clearly delineated by higher courts, and they were something of a moving target. Motive might well be different from intent; intent could usually be separated from "common scheme or plan." The passage of time changed these things.

What one might want at one point in time could well differ from what they might want years later. An intent in one year could be wiped out by another intent in another year. A person might scheme or plan something in 1991, then adopt another scheme or plan in 1992. Even "pattern" and "preparation" could be different, depending on when and where, or who.

The key word was "common," which seemed to require, in the law at least up until then, a linkage between acts, something that tied one act to another, later one—such as the same victim, or objective. The government liked to argue that motive, or pattern or intent, or even *m.o.* was such a linkage, irrespective of who was victimized, or when, or where, but defense lawyers usually vigorously contested this—to them, *all* "prior bad acts" were separate until a proven connection, something in common beyond motive or pattern, was established. Without this connection, something in common between the acts, the earlier should not be used to convict an accused of the later. That was particularly true when different, unconnected victims were involved.

Would, for instance, a shoplifter have any sort of "common scheme or plan," if he or she had filched a Slurpee from a 7-Eleven in 1991 and a pearl necklace from Nieman Marcus in 1998? Anyone reading the federal evidence rule would probably say no. A shoplifter and a grifter were a world apart from some Mafia caporegime conspiring in a Bensonhurst social club to control a vulnerable garment workers' union. The first were separate, unconnected acts, while the latter involved something that might extend over months or years and involve many separate acts, yet still involving one common victim, the union.

In short, the evidence rule on "prior bad acts" was a morass of conflicting interpretations, a sort of hydra with many heads. Every time one was sliced off, another two or three popped up. One could find almost anything in the rule, if one tried hard enough. It was like the Bible, for believers as well as agnostics.

The government's contention was almost Rube Goldbergian in reasoning, Nancy's lawyers maintained—it relied on a series of assumptions, like a pinball rolling down a chute to trigger a lever which unleashed a weight which flipped a switch which triggered another pinball, etc. It was balderdash, assumption piled atop assumption. If the government's reasoning prevailed, an accused's teenage candy snatch could be used to show his bank heist thirty years later was part of a "scheme," and assumed that a witness to the candy snatch would have exposed the perpetrator to prosecution for the bank heist. It was ludicrous, the defense said. Well, that was why the defense lawyers got the big money, when they could actually collect it.

Of course, the U.S. Attorneys Office in Maryland *did* have an alternative: they could have charged Nancy with the federal fraud counts—wire fraud, mail fraud, theft, identity theft and the like—convicted her on those in federal court (after all, the bank frauds were worth as much as 20 years themselves), and then turned Nancy over to Maryland authorities for the alleged murder of Jack as a separate offense.

True, that would have meant two separate trials, one in federal court for the frauds, the other in state court for the alleged murder of Jack. But the opportunity to expand the law on admissibility of "prior bad acts," to expand the definition of "scheme," and who it might apply to, apparently proved irresistible to the U.S. Attorneys Office.

The United States Constitution, as amended, has often been described as a "living document." When people say that, they mean it evolves; and over the past decade or so, the use of "prior bad acts" against criminal defendants, under the Fifth Amendment's guarantee of "due process," has been expanding. What would have been legally unthinkable even twenty years ago on "prior bad acts" has increasingly become part of the arsenal of prosecutors against criminal defendants. As society has become ever more complex, as crime has become ever more a national obsession, governments, whether local, state or federal, have sought to expand their powers to convict.

In short, the *United States of America* against *Nancy Siegel* was about to become a test case.

# 20
# NOT GUILTY

In asserting that Nancy's "scheme" extended all the way back to 1982, the government in its new indictment included allegations that Nancy had cheated both of her first two husbands, Linda Mayberry, her own daughters, and a wide swath of credit card companies and banks both before and after meeting Jack Watkins. Then, the government contended, Nancy proceeded to cheat her third husband, Rick Siegel. While the government didn't charge most of these acts as crimes, it included all of them in the factual background supporting the indictment as evidence of Nancy's twenty-year "scheme." The government wanted to demonstrate that Jack's murder was necessary to protect the "scheme," once her attempt to have Jack committed as suffering from "dementia" failed, and she was forced to take him back to her condo.

Then, the government contended, Nancy had furthered her "scheme" by "drugging him and depriving him of food." When that didn't work—when Jack didn't die—Nancy had strangled him to death.

*As part of the scheme and artifice to defraud, when Watkins threatened to leave the home, defendant manually strangled him until he was dead in order to prevent her fraud from being communicated to law enforcement officials.*

This was the witness-tampering part of the "scheme," Count 22.

With Jack disposed of, the way was clear for Nancy to continue her "scheme" by converting Jack's Social Security payments to her own use. And Nancy continued her "scheme," the superseding indictment said, by going on to victimize Rick Siegel:

*As part of her scheme and artifice to defraud, defendant established a romantic relationship with her current husband, Eric Siegel, gaining access to his personal financial information. By making material and fraudulent misrepresentations and concealing material facts, the defendant used Eric Siegel's personal financial information to gain access to his financial accounts and to establish new accounts in his name, all without Eric Siegel's knowledge or consent. In so doing, the defendant caused a substantial financial loss to Eric Siegel.*

So there it was, all the elements of a pattern, or *m.o.*: again and again over twenty years, Nancy had gotten close to someone, obtained their personal financial information, then used it to open fraudulent accounts. Kucharski, Geisendaffer, Mayberry, Watkins, Siegel, all of them victimized in similar fashion. To the government, this *m.o.* was proof of Nancy's "scheme," which was to get money that didn't belong to her. All of which justified the government in seeking Nancy's conviction on the witness-tampering-by-murder charges, by preventing Jack from possibly exposing her.

The new indictment then listed the specific counts of criminal wrongdoing for which the government was seeking to try Nancy. Like the original indictment, the bill began with the cashing or deposit of a representative sample of Jack's Social Security checks—seven counts, this time, instead of the nine in the first indictment, but still sufficient to establish the scope of the offenses. All of these counts dated from after Jack had died—it wasn't until after Jack had been found in the trunk that Nancy had begun to rip off his Social Security.

Counts 8 through 12 were all bank fraud counts. The government alleged that Nancy opened credit card accounts in Jack's name by falsely asserting that the applications for credit were made by Jack himself. These counts referred to applications that had been made in 1994 and 1995, while Jack was still alive, but presumably unaware of her actions. The fact that the bills for the new accounts were sent to Nancy's address instead of Jack's seemed to show that Jack didn't know about them.

Counts 13 through 20 again encompassed allegations of bank fraud *after* Jack's death, when Nancy had opened more credit accounts in Jack's name; identity theft, for using Jack's name unlawfully to open the accounts; mail fraud, when Nancy "caused to be delivered" Jack's February 3, 2003, Social Security check and the February New York Life check to herself; and wire fraud, from her two telephone calls to Social Security to get replacement checks, in February 2003, and again in June 2003.

Count 21 was for obstruction: when Nancy had put Jack's corpse in the trunk and left it in Loudoun County, she had corruptly impeded an official investigation, according to the government. This one was a little iffy—what investigation? Until almost seven years later, there hadn't been any investigation, at least of Nancy, so it might be hard to prove that Nancy had "impeded" anything "official," especially something that hadn't begun at the time Nancy had done this. Of course, if the government had wanted to be clever, it might have contended that the very concealment of Jack's identity was itself "tampering with a witness"—the prevention of identification of the corpse could have been construed as an effort by Nancy to corruptly "impede" with "intent" Jack's cadaverous "testimony"—tampering, in a way, by preventing dead witness Jack's post-mortem evidence. Clearly, if Jack's body had been immediately identified, an investigation leading to Nancy would have been begun by Jay Merchant.

Count 22 was the big one:

> *On or about May 13, 1996 . . . the defendant herein killed Jasper Frederick Watkins, Jr., a/k/a Jack Watkins, willfully, deliberately, maliciously, and with premeditation, and with the intent to prevent the communication to a law enforcement officer or judge of the United States of information relating to the commission or possible commission of federal offenses, including bank fraud . . . and mail fraud . . .*

In essence, Nancy had killed Jack with premeditation, the government contended, to seal his lips. That meant she'd planned to do it, although how the government knew about the premeditation relied on the government's theory that Nancy was trying to protect her "scheme," the existence of which itself had yet to be proved.

And there was this kicker: the government provided a "notice of special findings" asserting that, due to the fact that the victim, Jack Watkins, was "particularly vulnerable due to his old age and infirmity," the government intended to seek Department of Justice approval to ask for the death penalty: in the government's view, Nancy had committed senior abuse to the max.

Nancy was re-arraigned on the "superseding indictment" two weeks later, on January 30, 2004, in front of Judge Grimm.

At this re-arraignment, Judge Grimm read the charges, while Nancy stood silently at Glaser's side. She and Glaser still weren't getting along, at least according to Glaser. After he read the last count, the witness-tampering-by-murder allegation, the judge informed Nancy of the possible penalty if convicted.

"If you are found guilty of this charge," the aptly named Grimm told Nancy, "the maximum penalty you could receive is death, and in that regard, this makes that count a death penalty–eligible charge. This triggers certain important additional rights that you have."

One of the most important of those rights, he continued, was that a person facing a federal death penalty was entitled to a second lawyer, a specialist in the death penalty. The law on the death penalty was so complicated, Grimm explained to Nancy, that it usually required someone who was an expert in the field, a "Keenan counsel." The court would appoint such an expert for Nancy, if she requested it.

Nancy didn't say anything. Glaser spoke for her. He'd explained to Nancy about the superseding indictment and the notice of special circumstances, and Nancy had agreed to ask the court to appoint a death penalty specialist, he said. But on balance, Glaser added, he still wasn't sure that Nancy really understood what was happening.

His client, he said, wanted the court to make the appointment of the Keenan counsel. Moreover, she would need the government to pay for the specialist. For all practical purposes, Glaser said, Nancy was broke. She and Rick "in a sense" had separated, which meant she could not draw on his funds.

While he'd originally been hired by Rick to represent Nancy, Glaser told the court, it soon developed that Nancy, in her evaluation by Dr. Lion, had made a number of statements disparaging of Rick, and suggesting that he'd been involved in some sort of illegality.

"Forgetting any other thing that was said, the doctor indicated she was competent to stand trial," Glaser told Grimm, "although there were some comments in there that really concurred with my reasons for requesting her to be examined in this respect to competency." Glaser wanted Grimm to read the evaluation, which had been sealed. Grimm said he didn't know what was in it. Glaser was prepared for that. He'd brought a copy for Grimm to read. He gave him the copy. Grimm began to read, but was interrupted by Glaser, pointing to several paragraphs near the end of Lion's report. Grimm halted Glaser—he wanted to read it himself before hearing any more from the feisty lawyer. Apparently this had to do with some sort of conflict between Nancy and Rick, and maybe Glaser himself.

"Your Honor," Glaser said, when Grimm had put the evaluation down, "she now has no wherewithal to get any funds whatsoever." Glaser launched into an abbreviated discussion of Nancy's suicide attempt, and other findings of Dr. Lion, but Fine cut him off. She suggested that the lawyers discuss the matter privately, at the bench, because of the sealed nature of the document. This had to do with Nancy's mental condition after her arrest. The last thing Fine wanted was some sort of public airing of Nancy's supposed mental problems. It might publicly taint Rick, or possibly prejudice a jury in Nancy's favor. Or perhaps Fine was simply fastidious about breaching a sealed document.

What followed was a short, disjointed colloquy between the judge and the lawyers, in which Glaser wanted to make sure that the court knew that Rick wasn't going to pay for Nancy's defense. Fine didn't want to get into the details of any of this. She told Grimm that the government had no objection to a ruling that Rick's assets be excluded from Nancy's eligibility for a publicly paid-for defense, for alleged crimes before Nancy's marriage to Rick, including the cost of the Keenan counsel. These legal fees might total in the hundreds of thousands of dollars by the time the case was over, but it was worth it to Fine—she had other plans for Rick Siegel, and wanted to make sure to separate him from Nancy's defense. Glaser was offering her an escape hatch.

Grimm agreed—there was no reason to include any of Rick's income and assets in figuring Nancy's eligibility for a public defense, and since Nancy was for all practical purposes now a pauper, he said he would approve public compensation for a Keenan counsel.

All that was left, Grimm said, was for him to re-advise Nancy of her rights on self-incrimination, a formality. Everyone was agreed that Nancy would stay in jail. Right?

"Well, I just have one more comment," Glaser said. "She has been crying. I mean—she would not read the superseding [indictment]. So I had to go over it with her. She has never read it. But I did go over it, the new counts with her, and the old ones she already knew."

Nancy had told Glaser that she couldn't bring herself to read the last two counts, the ones about Jack's alleged murder, and the stuff about the trunk. She just couldn't read them herself, she was crying so much, Glaser said.

Glaser wanted this on the record in case the issue of Nancy reading the complete indictment ever came up later. But he'd explained the counts to her, Glaser said, and the possible consequences of conviction. That was sufficient, Grimm told Glaser.

Now he asked Nancy how she pled to the indictment.

"Not guilty," Nancy said.

# 21
# PREDICATE ACTS

Grimm soon appointed Nancy's second lawyer, the Keenan counsel. This was Thomas J. Saunders, one of Maryland's pre-eminent experts on defending against the death penalty. While Saunders had begun his career as a public defender in Maryland, he eventually came to specialize in the ultimate sanction, which almost always eventually involved appeals; his trial expertise was in the arcana of the penalty phase, with its emphasis on aggravation and mitigation.

As with the first indictment, the case was tracked to Judge Andre M. Davis.

At 54, Andre M. Davis was a native of Baltimore, and an eight-year veteran of the federal bench. After graduating from the University of Pennsylvania with a degree in history in 1971, Davis had worked for several years as a housing administrator in Baltimore, then enrolled at The University of Maryland School of Law, graduating cum laude in 1978. He then served as a law clerk to U.S. District Judge Frank Kaufman for a year, and another year as a clerk to Francis D. Murnaghan, Jr., judge of the Court of Appeals of the Fourth Circuit. Subsequently he worked as a civil rights attorney for the U.S. Department of Justice, then as an assistant United

States attorney in Baltimore, leaving in 1983 to go into private legal practice. In 1987 he was appointed associate judge of the Baltimore City District Court, then the Circuit Court for Baltimore City. In 1995 he was nominated to the federal bench by President Bill Clinton, and confirmed by the Senate in August of that year.

In Maryland legal circles, Davis was known most for his geniality and even temper. Defense attorneys considered him a "good judge," one who was fair to both sides. In some ways, given his background, this characterized him as a "liberal." He also had a doggedness in making sure he understood the facts and the issues, stamina not always being a trait shared by federal judges in light of their lifetime tenure. Before the Siegel trial was over—it would take years, as things turned out—Davis was rumored to be one of President Obama's first nominees to the U.S. Court of Appeals of the Fourth Circuit, replacing his one-time mentor, Judge Murnaghan, who had died in office. After the trial was over, he was in fact nominated and confirmed by the Senate Judiciary Committee. But these developments were still to come, and certainly had nothing to do with the case against Nancy Siegel.

Then, on February 11, 2004, the government filed a motion to disqualify Harold Glaser as Nancy's lawyer. The move probably didn't come as a complete surprise to Glaser, given his previous relationship with Rick. For one thing, the government had already included Rick in the indictment as one of Nancy's victims. The government contended that Glaser had a conflict between two clients—Rick and Nancy.

All of this unfolded against a backdrop of another conflict, this one over strategy between Glaser and Saunders. Glaser wanted another competency evaluation of Nancy. Saunders was against it. There was no point, he told Glaser, to subject their client to still more probing of her mental state by a psychiatrist appointed by the court, especially when the results had to be given to the opposition. Saunders worried about any more admissions Nancy might make while Dr. Lion tiptoed through her brain. Glaser still seemed to think the evidence was sufficient to convict Nancy, and the best way out was a mental disease or defect defense.

But Saunders had been reading the indictment carefully. He thought he saw some fatal flaws. He thought it might be possible to convince a jury to acquit Nancy on the witness-tampering charge, the big one. That charge required the government to prove that Nancy had killed Jack with the "intent" to prevent his reporting Nancy for her federal offenses, according to the indictment. As far as Saunders could see, there were only five alleged "federal offenses" that Jack could have been a witness to: Counts 8 through 12, all alleged bank card frauds from 1994 and 1995. Those were the only alleged crimes in the indictment that had occurred before Jack died, to which he could possibly have been a witness. Everything else happened after the death—the Social Security thefts, the wire and mail frauds. Jack couldn't be a witness to things that hadn't happened yet, or so Saunders believed.

If Saunders could demonstrate that the government wasn't able to prove Nancy guilty of the five 1994–1995 bank fraud counts, these charges would go out the window, and with them, the intent, and after them, the witness-tampering. How could Jack be a witness if there were no crimes yet?

How did the government know for sure, Saunders asked himself, that *Jack* hadn't applied for the 1994–1995 bank cards? Where was the proof beyond a reasonable doubt that Nancy had forged the credit card applications in Jack's name? Hadn't Jack signed the papers in 1995 encumbering the Sungold Road house with a mortgage used to pay off some of those same credit cards? There was no definitive evidence, not a shred, that Jack hadn't signed the mortgage papers willingly. Who could then say he hadn't willingly signed the credit card applications, too?

The record, in fact, seemed to show that Jack *had* known of the credit cards. Why else would he have agreed to the mortgage and its pay-offs to the same credit card companies? True, the bills had gone to Nancy, but where was the evidence that Jack hadn't appointed Nancy as his representative in collecting them and paying them? Saunders had an idea that the government wouldn't be able to make those five charged pre-death bank fraud charges stick, and if it couldn't, the witness-tampering claim would have to be thrown out. If *Jack* had applied for the credit cards, Nancy would be off the hook. And who knew for sure?

Exactly why the government hadn't charged Nancy with *all* the pre-death supposed credit card frauds—all fourteen—as separate counts wasn't clear. It was possible that the government had treated them in the same fashion as they had the later Social Security thefts, as representative examples. The records from discovery seemed to show that Nancy had opened these accounts in Jack's name, using his Social Security number and date of birth, besides the seven charged in the formal indictment.

But there were some other facts in Nancy's favor. If she'd *really* intended to murder him in order to keep his mouth shut, to keep her alleged twenty-year "scheme" secret, why had she taken Jack to the hospital the month before he died? Jack could have blabbed everything then, if he knew—if he was a potential witness. That surely showed that Nancy never had an "intent" to protect her so-called "scheme"—in essence, Nancy's seeming willingness to let Jack possibly tell on her at the hospital showed there was no "scheme," no plan, nothing to be protected by the alleged murder, at least in Nancy's mind—in short, no intent to tamper with a witness. (Of course, that assumed that the hospital people had been willing to listen to Jack—the evidence seemed to show that even when he'd wanted to talk about money, no one wanted to hear him. To them, it was just more proof of his Korsakoff's syndrome. This was not a point for Nancy's side, though.)

Still, why would Nancy take the risk of taking Jack to the hospital, if she was such a schemer? Surely if there had been a twenty-year "scheme," she would have killed Jack *before* ever taking him to the hospital, where the "scheme" might be exposed. So surely Nancy had no plan, no motive, to murder Jack, at least at that point, no "intent" to protect her so-called "scheme," and certainly nothing going back to 1982. For Nancy, as Saunders saw her, everything was impromptu, the usual sort of grifter's scramble.

Of course, the government didn't see it that way. It believed that Nancy, not Jack, had filled out those credit card applications in 1994 and 1995. If it couldn't explain why Jack had agreed to mortgage his house in order to pay them off, it didn't matter much. To the government, Jack was besotted with Nancy, and Nancy used his infatuation to manipulate him. Her whole history of fraud showed that likelihood. That's why they wanted the entirety of the "scheme" brought before the jury, to prove that Nancy had in fact committed the bank card frauds during the seventeen months before Jack's death, just as she had conned Charles Kucharski, Ted Geisendaffer, the Mayberrys, and others. The more the government could pile on Nancy, the more a jury would be likely to believe Nancy had filled out the applications—that she'd committed the crucial bank card frauds. To the government, once a grifter, always a grifter.

In seeking to toss Glaser, the government's motion to disqualify him noted a number of circumstances not favorable to Glaser's continued representation.

For one thing, said Fine in her motion, Glaser had represented the "Siegel family" in "other matters, principally investigating the extent of Ms. Siegel's fraudulent conduct against Eric Siegel, and assisting Eric Siegel in resolving those debts." Fine was referring to Glaser's actions in early August of 2003, before Nancy was arrested, in which Glaser had helped Rick unravel Nancy's victimization of him. Fine's use of the words "Siegel family" was intended to include Rick as someone within the penumbra of the attorney–client relationship, although there was no evidence that Glaser had ever formally represented Nancy's third husband, even if Rick had signed the checks for Nancy's legal fees to Glaser.

Still, Fine contended, that put Glaser in a position of conflict, because the government intended to call Rick as a witness against his wife.

There was more.

Glaser, Fine contended, had personal information about Nancy, related to crimes of which she had been accused in previous years. Clearly Fine was thinking about the mailbox-raiding of the later 1990s, the crimes that Block had investigated, and for which Glaser had represented Nancy in 2000. Fine also asserted that Glaser had information, in the form of documents, which was relevant to the current case against Nancy.

Here the implication was clear: not only was the government going to fold Nancy's husbands into the "scheme" as victims, to show the long-running "scheme" as contemplated in the superseding indictment, the government also intended to include, in its presentation to the trial jury, the material from Howard County detective Block's 1998 investigation of Nancy as well. The "scheme" was now expanding.

With this, Glaser's prior representation of Nancy might become evidence in the demonstration of the "scheme." Fine asserted that she knew that Glaser had provided documents to Rick's lawyer to help prepare Rick for his appearance before the grand jury the previous August. And the kicker: just about the same time the government had subpoenaed these documents from Glaser, he'd passed them on to Rick's attorney for the grand jury; Fine was suggesting that Glaser, in his prime interest in protecting Rick, had tried to hide the ball.

Third, Fine asserted, Glaser knew from his own personal knowledge that some of the things Nancy had told Dr. Lion during her competency evaluation were "false."

"This information maligns Eric Siegel, and Mr. Glaser has already spoken at defendant's re-arraignment hearing regarding some of these matters in Dr. Lion's report, which is sealed," Fine said in her motion.

The fact was, Fine continued, Glaser was in no position to represent Nancy. Rick had provided money to Glaser to cover his fees for Nancy in the present case as well as previously; that created a financial conflict for Glaser if and when Rick should ever testify against Nancy, and Glaser had to put him under cross-examination. How could Glaser ask hard questions of a man who was signing the checks for his fees?

"Finally," Fine added, "Dr. Lion's report, as well as comments made by Mr. Glaser as recently as [the re-arraignment hearing], clearly reflect that Ms. Siegel cries continuously in Mr. Glaser's presence and sometimes walks out on meetings with him, making it virtually impossible for Mr. Glaser to discuss important case-related matters with her. In light of this fact, the early stages of this case, and the recent appointment of Thomas Saunders as co-counsel for this capital-qualified case, it does not appear that replacement of Mr. Glaser will prejudice the defendant's ability to assist in the preparation of her defense, and may enhance it."

In short, Nancy would be better off without Glaser, as Fine saw it. Of course, as the prosecutor, Fine wasn't all that concerned about Nancy's legal welfare—she was thinking that Nancy might well have significant appeal issues if Glaser stayed on.

Glaser's own statements and actions since Nancy's arrest showed that he had a conflict, Fine asserted. When Rick learned that Nancy had been cheating him by opening credit accounts without his knowledge, he'd turned to Glaser for advice. "He provided Mr. Glaser with copies of documents to assist him in ascertaining the extent of the fraud and determining how best to deal with the fraud Nancy Siegel had perpetrated against him . . . Mr. Siegel is expected to be an important witness in the government's case against the defendant."

After learning that Rick had told Glaser that the frauds

Nancy was accused of perpetrating against Jack Watkins were similar to those she'd used against him, the government had asked Glaser to turn over the records Rick had given Glaser to demonstrate his innocence. "These documents exculpated Mr. Siegel, but implicated defendant Nancy Siegel," Fine said. At that point, the government sought permission to subpoena the records from Glaser. Instead, Glaser had turned them over to the lawyer who represented Rick before the federal grand jury. Eventually the government got them, however, which enabled them to clear Rick of any involvement in Nancy's scams.

Even more significant, Fine said, Glaser's dealings with Nancy from the time of her arrest created a personal conflict—Glaser knew that Nancy had said things about Rick that weren't true, and that she had repeated those untrue things to Dr. Lion during his evaluation of her mental competency. In fact, Nancy had told Lion that Glaser and Rick had hoped she'd die when she took her overdose in Glaser's office in early August.

"Mr. Glaser's personal knowledge exculpates Eric Siegel of the criminal conduct of which he is accused by the defendant." That meant Glaser might be called as a witness himself, if Nancy chose to blame Rick at trial. Glaser might have to swear that Nancy was a liar. There was no way he could then act as her lawyer.

Glaser fought back, saying the government was wrong—there were no conflicts; or, there were no conflicts that couldn't be resolved by waivers of Rick and Nancy. He'd never represented Rick, Glaser said, and in any case, Rick waived any rights he might have if Glaser had to cross-examine him. As for Nancy's statements to Dr. Lion during the evaluation about being uncooperative with Glaser because she thought he was "unsympathetic," all that was in the past, Glaser said. "The latest meetings with the defendant have been fruitful and productive," he told the court.

Of course, this may have been an effort by Glaser to claw back some of his claims as to Nancy's mental competency. Having spent months asserting that Nancy might not be competent to assist him because of her crying and other recalcitrant behavior, Glaser may have decided that he'd gone a bit too far—it was a fine line between madness, and just being mad. Now everything was sweetness.

A week later, Davis convened a hearing on the government's motion to throw Glaser off the case. The court record doesn't reflect what happened at this hearing, but something seems to have transpired, because the hearing was continued for a week. A document was filed with the court three days later under seal, and the judge convened a telephone conference between the lawyers four days after that. On March 16, 2004, Davis granted the government's motion to disqualify Glaser as Nancy's lawyer. Fine later asserted, in other court filings, that Glaser had voluntarily removed himself because of another conflict, unspecified. Saunders later said he doubted that—as far as he could tell, Harold Glaser had removed himself because of the conflicts that Fine had raised.

A month later, Nancy got a new lawyer, Andrew D. Levy, a prominent Baltimore lawyer and professor at the University's law school. If Saunders was an expert in capital punishment defense, Levy was an expert in constitutional law. The papers were approved assigning the costs of Nancy's defense to the public—sure to be very expensive for the treasury, given the government's interest in giving her a lethal injection.

# 22
# "SURPLUSAGE"

Now the Siegel case moved into its discovery phase—when, under the rules, the government had to provide all its evidence against a defendant. This was laborious. There were literally thousands of pages of documents assembled and boxed up by "Team Watkins," and the defense team was entitled to see every one of them. These included page after page of loan agreements, credit card applications, bank statements, postal records, Social Security records, mortgage documents, the BMW lease papers, investigative reports, court records—it was a geyser of paper that kept on gushing. The defense team of Saunders and Levy had to read all of them, and then parse them—who knew what, and when did they know it?

Meanwhile, Nancy continued to reside at the Talbot County Detention Center, and by all accounts, was something less than a model prisoner. Not only did she have some serious medical issues, stemming from her heart surgery several years before, her mercurial mood swings did not enamor her with her jailers. Some thought the one-time Queen of the Hop was much too imperious. The doctors had prescribed various drugs for Nancy; sometimes she got them, sometimes she didn't, it was alleged. It all depended on how cooperative Nancy was with her keepers. Of course, there's also an underground economy for certain sorts of drugs in jail, and the jailers aren't always above stiffing an uncooperative inmate and finding a more cooperative buyer. That's how it is when you're in jail.

Saunders and Levy tried to sort through the flood of paper on Nancy. Both knew that the stakes were enormous—so far, the government was still intent on asking for the death penalty for Nancy. If the government succeeded, Nancy would be the first woman executed by the federal government since Ethel Rosenberg in 1953. As far as Saunders and Levy could determine, Nancy was at that point the only female federal prisoner who might be subject to the ultimate sanction, if convicted. That was a sobering thought.

The death penalty notice required the government to adhere to certain rules and procedures. First, the appointed United States Attorney for the District of Baltimore, Thomas M. DiBiagio, had to approve; then the matter had to go to the federal Department of Justice in Washington, D.C. for further review there by a special panel. All along, Saunders and Levy would have a chance to argue that the death penalty should not be applied. All this took time to organize; but until that issue was decided, it was difficult for both sides to plan.

The government twice asked Judge Davis for a waiver of time so that the court's speedy trial rules would not apply. Saunders and Levy were agreeable—if anything, they had even more work to do than the government. Davis granted both requests.

On September 1, Fine sent a letter to Davis briefing him on progress to date, and asking for an additional time waiver.

"As I informed you last month," Fine wrote, "the parties were scheduled to meet regarding the appropriateness of the death penalty in this case, and that meeting did occur on August 16, 2004. At that time some options were discussed, and defense counsel were afforded additional time to discuss a matter with their client which might have rendered it unnecessary to respond to motions."

Reading between the lines of Fine's letter, it appears that the government offered to refrain from seeking the death penalty if Nancy pleaded guilty to all the charges, and accepted a federal prison sentence, probably life without the possibility of parole. Saunders and Levy were obligated to communicate this offer to Nancy. It appears that Nancy rejected it. She denied killing Jack.

The two defense lawyers communicated Nancy's rejection to Fine on August 23, 2004, a little less than a year after she was first charged by the grand jury. At that point, Fine forwarded the formal request for the DOJ death penalty review to Washington. Fine told Davis that she believed the review would be completed by December 1, 2004. In fact, she was wrong—it later appeared that the request for review got lost somewhere in the government's bureaucracy between September and December.

In the meantime, both sides were gearing up to argue pretrial motions. The defense had "adopted" all of Harold Glaser's snowstorm from the previous fall, and added some of their own. In one, they wanted the government to furnish a "bill of particulars," that is, a more definitive description of the illegal acts in Counts 21 and 22, the dumping of the trunk as an "obstruction"; as well as the allegation that Nancy had tried to forestall an investigation by causing the death of the witness. That, of course, was the big one, the tampering charge. The defense wanted the government to spell out exactly when and where these acts had taken place, in a "bill of particulars," a formal statement of the details.

On Count 21, the defense demanded to know exactly what sort of "official investigation" Nancy had supposedly impeded. The fact was, there was no "official investigation" underway when the trunk had been left in the turnout in Loudoun County, the defense contended. In fact there was even doubt that any crimes had actually been committed, if Jack indeed had himself signed the credit card applications. So how could Nancy have "impeded" any "investigation," if none had yet begun?

And as for Count 22, the witness-tampering-by-murder charge, the defense demanded to know which of the "predicate acts" Jack might have been a witness to, for the purpose of silencing him. The law on tampering with a witness required some sort of underlying federal offense—there couldn't be any tampering with a witness if there wasn't a federal offense that had yet taken place.

Since the "prior bad acts" from 1982 weren't charged as crimes in the indictment—in most cases they couldn't have been, since the statute of limitations had already run out, although they had been described in the indictment as part of the "scheme"—that seemed to leave only the 1994–1995 credit card applications as "predicates," the underlying "federal offenses" that made the witness-tampering charge possible.

If so, the defense believed it might have caught the government on the horns of a conundrum: if Jack didn't know about the credit cards, how could he be a witness? If he *did* know, how could there be fraud? It was tricky, technical, maybe, but that's what lawyers are good at.

Saunders and Levy tossed a few other obstructions in front of the government juggernaut that was shaping up against their client. In another motion, they asked the judge to "strike the surplusage" from the second indictment under Evidence Rule 403, which prohibited evidence that was prejudicial to a defendant's right to a fair trial. That meant they wanted all the stuff about Charles, Ted, Rick and the Mayberrys, the "prior bad acts," taken out of the indictment, the re-alleged "prior bad acts" in paragraphs 1 through 36. It would hardly do Nancy any good with twelve tried-and-true of her peers to hear how she'd habitually stiffed her husbands and friends; it would, they thought, be highly prejudicial. And finally, they asked for an outright dismissal of the obstruction-by-dumping count on statute of limitations grounds: the depositing of the trunk was too remote in time to the charging—more than seven years, when the statute said obstruction had to be charged in five.

Fine responded to the defense motions in October. She swept Glaser's old motions off the table as mostly irrelevant. There'd been no electronic surveillance of Nancy, except for the pin register on the telephone, and that had been approved by a judge when the government was trying to determine if anyone else might be involved in the frauds, so it was legit. As for most of the rest, the government had ample grounds for probable cause to search the condo, and whatever statements Nancy had made to Moeller and Locke had been freely given, The defense already had all of Nancy's prior criminal history in the boxes of discovery.

As for the "bill of particulars," Fine said, it wasn't necessary. There was no rule that said the government had to do the defense's investigation for them. If Saunders and Levy wanted to know the specifics of a particular crime, all they had to do was look through the boxes of discovery. Nor should it be required to specify any "official investigation" that Nancy had obstructed by her use of the trunk—that one was obvious: the investigation that Jay Merchant had begun on May 14, 1996, was certainly "official." The government didn't have to prove these things because the counts covered Nancy's intent, not the government's. In Counts 21 and 22, it was what was in Nancy's mind that mattered, not what the government knew or didn't know at the time of the alleged murder. The intent of obstruction and tampering was in the mind of the perpetrator, no one else.

As for the statute of limitations on obstruction, that shouldn't apply because it was Nancy who had taken steps to conceal Jack's identity by leaving him semi-naked in the trunk without any means of identification. It was Nancy who had frozen the statute of limitations by her own acts, in 1996. That alone revealed her "intent."

Well, all of this was typical lawyerly pre-trial maneuvering, where the game plan for the defense is to whittle down the charges and evidence as far as possible, while the prosecution tries to get in as much as it can, including the 1982 Kucharski kitchen sink, if possible.

All of this was still awaiting hearing before Davis when, on December 1, 2004, Fine sent another letter to the judge. Fine was chagrinned to have to admit to the judge that the request for consideration of the death penalty had gotten lost somewhere between Baltimore and Washington. "I have been trying to determine its status for several weeks now," Fine said of the request, "and was told yesterday that the department [of Justice] has no record of receiving the referral." Fine said she'd made a new referral, and the DOJ said it would need until March of 2005 to consider it.

The defense was not happy with this—Saunders told Fine he would not agree to a further delay on this crucial question.

On January 26, the defense struck back with a motion to bar the government from asking for the death penalty. Failing to meet the previously agreed-upon deadline of December 15, 2004, for the decision, was tantamount to the government waiving its right to ask a jury to put Nancy to death, the defense said. It was now too late to ask for death, according to Levy.

No way, Fine said, in a response filed by the government the following month. There were extenuating circumstances for the foul-up, and the government shouldn't be penalized. While it was true that the "package" of the office's recommendation for death had been "misplaced," the government had been hampered by the sudden resignation of U.S. Attorney Thomas DiBiago in early December of 2004. Fine seemed to be hinting that the "package" may have gotten lost in DiBiagio's in-basket as he was looking for another job. DiBiagio was replaced by his principal deputy, Allen Loucks, on an interim basis. Loucks tried to pick up the pieces, but it took a little time. Now the Department of Justice was ready to hear the defense lawyers' pitch for why death was not appropriate in Nancy's case. A meeting with the DOJ was scheduled for April 18, 2005.

That was one week before Davis was scheduled to rule on all the motions, nearly twenty months after Nancy had been arrested, and almost nine years after Jack's body had been found in the trunk.

# 23
# BACKFIELDS IN MOTION

The warring parties gathered in Davis' courtroom on the fifth floor of the U.S. District Courthouse on Lombard Street in downtown Baltimore's Inner Harbor on April 22, 2005. Right off the bat, Fine asked Davis to allow the lawyers to approach the bench for a confidential discussion. Davis waved them up.

"Briefly, Your Honor, in the past we have by consent sealed matters with regard to Ms. Siegel's health," Fine began. "I just wanted to note for the court that I do believe there are members of the press here. To the extent that we're going to address mental health issues, we may want to do that at the bench instead of back at counsel table . . ." Fine suggested that if Nancy wanted to listen in, she should be given an earphone. That way no one else would know what was being discussed, particularly the news media.

Davis said he wasn't sure what Fine meant.

"Why those issues are going to come up?" Fine asked, perplexed. She wasn't sure what Davis was asking.

"No," Davis said. "I mean, why they are not publicly available. She's a defendant in a criminal case and this is a public proceeding. Why is her mental status . . . Why does she retain some privacy interest . . . Why does she retain a heightened privacy interest that we need to do that matter in camera?" If Nancy had mental health issues, Davis suggested, why was the public not permitted to know about them?

She was only trying to follow the decisions that had been made by the magistrate Grimm earlier in the case, Fine said, when he'd ordered such matters sealed. Actually, it had been Davis himself who had ordered Lion's mental competency report sealed, and that at the request of the government.

Saunders interrupted. He told Davis that he agreed with Fine that some aspects of Nancy's mental health should be discussed in private.

"My client has [been] interviewed today," he said, "[and] said certain things that are of grave concern to me, that I wanted the court to be aware of, and in front of her family and others, she felt uncomfortable." Saunders was suggesting that Nancy had been threatening to kill herself again, but didn't want Rick and her daughters to know this.

"I'm generally uncomfortable with attempting to handle a criminal case in camera," Davis said. "Is there a question of competency here?"

"A question of safety," Saunders said.

"Safety?"

"That she may suicide."

"Doesn't that call into question competency?" Davis asked. He could tell from the lawyers' expressions at the bench that it wasn't necessarily so. "Maybe not," he said.

Saunders tried to explain.

"At this moment," he said, channeling Carnac the Magnificent, "I see the distinct possibility [of suicide] in the future, because over the last six weeks her situation has deteriorated very badly from when . . . I have worked with her for a long while now and see her often, and she has deteriorated very badly. I am concerned for the future, but not the present, in terms of competency." Saunders meant that Nancy wasn't incompetent to assist her defense, it was just that she might kill herself. Of course, a client who killed herself wouldn't then be competent to assist in her defense, because she would be dead. Sometimes the law is crazier than the client, but there was a certain bizarre logic to Saunders' assertion.

Davis figuratively scratched his head. He knew that Nancy had been evaluated by Lion, but that had been more than a year earlier, when Nancy was still represented by Harold Glaser. Saunders, of course, had been against any more mental evaluations of Nancy almost as soon as he'd been named as the Keenan counsel. Davis decided to put off any more discussion of the mental health problem for the time being, and turn to "more mundane matters," like the pending motions. But first he wanted an update: what was the status of the government's request to DOJ on the death penalty?

"We are waiting [for] the department's decision," Fine told him.

"Why is that taking so long?" Davis demanded. "Am I correct that it's taking an extraordinarily long time? I understand there's a new attorney general [this was shortly after former Attorney General Alberto Gonzales resigned], but this case was indicted in August of 2003, and the superseding indictment came down sometime after that."

In January, Fine told him.

"In January of . . . ?" Davis asked.

"Of 2004," Fine admitted.

"So it's been going on now for sixteen months. Isn't that far in excess of anything that's reasonable?"

Saunders and Levy by now had to feel that Davis was leaning in their direction on the death penalty question, maybe even falling over.

Fine was discomfited, but fought back gamely, saying that changes in personnel at both the U.S. Attorney's Office and in the DOJ had complicated the matter. But otherwise, everything was ready to go. All that had to happen to precipitate action from the Department of Justice was the setting of a trial date, by Judge Davis. Once that happened, the DOJ would swing into action.

Davis didn't seem to be buying this, but let Levy take a hack at the pitch. Levy was happy to do it.

Calling the foul-ups "an incredible delay," he complained that the government had given conflicting explanations for what had happened. "Apparently," he said, "the current explanation is the department is just too busy to decide whether it's worth trying to execute our client." Levy's sarcasm was usually drolly delivered, and this was no exception. Fine's statement that the DOJ was ready to act as soon as Davis set a formal trial date was "outrageous," he said.

Fine took umbrage. "In response, *that* statement is outrageous," she shot back. There had never been conflicting explanations from the government over the delay. "And it's not outrageous for the Department of Justice, in a world of limited resources, to focus its attention" on cases that already had a trial date set. Of course, it wasn't as if the Department of Justice was approving death penalty requests left and right—the federal government wasn't the state of Texas, even if the former attorney general had once been a judge there.

"It shouldn't take a United States district judge setting a trial date to get the Justice Department to do its work," Davis said. "It shouldn't matter one bit, frankly, who the attorney general is, or who the attorney general was . . . if there are too many death penalty cases brought, then more people ought to be signed up to do the work." The idea that a case had to have a firm trial date for the DOJ to decide such matters shouldn't matter one whit, he continued. "This is an important decision."

By now, Saunders and Levy were probably giving each other mental high fives. But Fine tried to persist, asking to respond to the judge's remarks.

Davis shook his head. "That doesn't really call for a response, Ms. Fine. The court was just thinking out loud, not to rule, but for what it's worth, that's this court's view of the matter. It's not bureaucratic efficiency that's in play here."

Fine tried one more time. Former U.S. Attorney DiBiagio had actually met with Nancy, she said. Numerous meetings had been held on the decision, some with the defense. It wasn't as if nothing had been done. "Great resources have been committed to this case already, with regard to this determination, but a final decision has not been made, and that decision rests with the attorney general, as I understand . . ."

"Thank you for that, Ms. Fine," Davis said. He could be droll, too.

Davis now turned to the "more mundane matters," the outstanding motions. Saunders went first, on the "bill of particulars."

"In the bill of particulars, we're not asking for the government's evidence or theories," Saunders told Davis, "we simply want them to name the federal crimes that are the predicates, so that we may ask our client about that." All the government had to do, he said, was specify the alleged crimes, the "predicates," those that had occurred before Jack was dead—the ones alleging that Nancy had Jack murdered Jack to cover up, which he might possibly have been a witness to.

The way the indictment was worded, with all its "surplusage," allegations about Charles and Ted and Rick and the Mayberrys, and then the stuff that had taken place after Jack's death, like the Social Security checks and the wire and mail frauds, had left the defense in doubt. "We just don't want to be surprised at trial," he said. That was the only reason the defense had filed the motion for the "bill of particulars."

"We're not fishing," Saunders said. "We have the unique situation of a federal crime that does not stand on its own. If they simply come in here and prove that a murder occurred and prove that our client did the murder, that's not enough. There would have to be an acquittal. It has to be with the intent to keep them from a reporting a particular kind of crime." It had to be a federal offense, according the statute on witness-tampering. Saunders thought that cashing or depositing Jack's Social Security checks after he was dead, or calling Social Security years later, wasn't covered by the statute—Jack couldn't report something that hadn't happened yet.

Davis asked Fine what she thought the law required.

"I think it means what we have here," she said. "We have a situation in which an individual was killed . . . in order to prevent communication to law enforcement officials that federal crime, that is, the bank fraud, the wire fraud, the fraud scheme that Ms. Siegel was involved in, with regard to Mr. Siegel, and with regard to Mr. Watkins specifically."

"The problem is the word 'including,'" Davis said, referring to Count 22, in which Nancy had been accused of murdering Jack to prevent his reporting federal crimes, "including" bank fraud and mail fraud. (Fine had misspoken. It wasn't wire fraud, but mail fraud, that had been specified in Count 22. Davis passed over her error.) "That's how you drafted the indictment," he said. "The indictment says, 'including' bank fraud and mail fraud. That's the problem here. You've clearly left yourself some wiggle room."

By using the word "including" in the indictment, Davis suggested, the government was attempting to give itself latitude to include any federal offense, even the Social Security checks, as well as all the other post-death allegations. Those post-death allegations were buttressed by the thirty-six nasty paragraphs, all the prior bad acts. The way the indictment had been written, the "scheme" encompassed acts that Jack could not have been a witness to.

It was all part of the broader context of Nancy's scheme, Fine reiterated.

"I guess I don't quite understand what you mean by 'within the context of that broader scheme,'" Davis said.

"The bank fraud and the wire [mail] fraud were simply acts taken in furtherance of the broader scheme, Your Honor."

"But—there is no federal crime called 'scheming,'" Davis pointed out. "That's not a federal crime."

Here Davis had put his finger on the nub of the problem. How could the government throw the kitchen sink at Nancy, dredge up all of her past offenses, as a means of proving the present charges, then even using those post-death, as "predicate acts" as Nancy's "intent to tamper with a witness," that is, the murder of Jack?

Yes, maybe Nancy had done nasty things in the past, and then again, after Jack was dead, but it didn't prove that she'd committed them with Jack. It certainly didn't prove, beyond a reasonable doubt, that Nancy had strangled him.

To try to get them into evidence as part of a "scheme"—to use them as proof that Nancy had committed murder—wasn't that an end run around the law requiring Nancy to have committed "federal offenses" that Jack could have been a witness to? By alleging the before and the after, wasn't it like summoning the spirit of Jack as a witness to things he couldn't have known about at the time? And if so, even if he was Marley's Ghost, who could swear him in?

In the face of Davis' skepticism, Fine retreated. The predicate counts, the federal crimes the government was using to make Jack into a witness for the purpose of the tampering count, were Counts 8, 9, 10, 11 and 12—all the bank card applications of 1994–1995, she now said.

Saunders broke in. The government had been telling him that all the stuff from 1982 forward, the "scheme," the first thirty-seven paragraphs of the indictment, was going to be used as a predicate for the witness-tampering count. Now it seemed to be saying something different.

"I want to make sure I hear what I think I'm hearing," Saunders told Davis. "If what the government is saying is that the counts that are charged, Eight through Twelve, are in fact the underlying federal offenses on which Counts Twenty-one and Twenty-two are predicated, then we have our answer and we have no need to be surprised, that there's going to be another universe of things that are going to be predicates."

"That's what I'm hearing," Davis agreed.

"Yes, Your Honor," Fine acknowledged. But, she persisted, Counts 8 through 12 were still part of the "scheme" that had begun in 1982, as described in the first thirty-seven paragraphs of the indictment under the heading of "The Participants."

"Ms. Fine," Davis said again, "there is no federal offense called *scheming*. I understand you keep referring to 'the scheme,' but I don't understand the relevance of that reference." It was true that federal law criminalized "schemes" that used mail and wire fraud, but mail and wire fraud were not included in the predicate counts, 8 through 12. In those counts there was no allegation of either mail or wire fraud.

"The freestanding notion that a 'scheme' is sufficient here simply leaves me somewhat puzzled," Davis told her.

But the concession that the rest of "the scheme," if there was one, couldn't be used as predicates for the witness-tampering-by-murder count was what Saunders and Levy wanted. Now that the "predicates" underlying the tampering charge had been limited, they could go to work trying to get evidence of the "prior bad acts" of the early 1990s thrown out, suppressed, so a jury would never hear about them. That would give them a better chance to convince a jury that no bank fraud had been committed in Counts 8 through 12, which would knock the foundation out from under the murder count. They already were pretty sure that the post-death counts, 1 through 7 and 13 through 20, couldn't be used as predicates for the critical witness-tampering count, and Fine had just admitted as much to Davis.

\* \* \*

Well, this was a lot of legal mumbo-jumbo—stuff like "predicates" and "surplusage" and "prior bad acts"—lots of lawyer talk designed to shape the limits of the trial to come. But this is where the law is made, and cases are won and lost. It doesn't have all that much to do with guilt or innocence—it's how you can frame the debate. That's what we pay lawyers for, both public and private, prosecutors as well as defenders. We may call them sharks, but the best ones know just how much to bite off in any one chomp. That's why they get the big money.

Levy made the defense argument for dismissing Count 21, the obstruction charge, on the statute of limitations grounds. He said the law had a limit of five years after an underlying act, for the government to charge obstruction of an investigation. The only exceptions were when someone might be involved in a conspiracy with others to continue the conspiracy after the underlying act.

When Nancy had put Jack's body in the trunk and left it in Loudoun County, she had been conspiring with no one— she'd done it all by herself, at least according to the government's own allegation, Levy said. And in fact, even if one believed that Nancy had actually had a "scheme" since 1982—that was still in dispute—no one was saying that anyone else was involved, Levy pointed out. So—*what* conspiracy?

Fine disagreed. She said the statute of limitations had stopped running the instant Nancy took steps to conceal Jack's body.

"This is a situation in which a dead body was bundled up and essentially folded into a duffle bag. That duffel bag was placed in another duffle bag, and that duffle bag was placed in a trunk, and the trunk was taped shut. The trunk was then transported a substantial distance across state lines, and dumped by the trash on an access point to the Appalachian

Trail in Virginia." (Fine meant the wayside on U.S. 340 in Harpers Ferry National Park.)

Davis was already shaking his head.

"And it wouldn't have made a bit of difference for present purposes if it had just been buried in the back yard, with all respect," he said, perhaps thinking of Dorothea Puente. "Isn't that so? I mean, you're concealing the body. The law doesn't contemplate the methodology, does it? Or the distance?"

The methodology did make a difference, Fine said, because it was a means of attempting to obstruct by way of concealment, by way of distance from the scene of the crime. An investigation couldn't begin until after the body was identified, which showed there was obstruction. When Nancy had admitted disposing of the trunk and the body so far away from Ellicott City, that was an obstruction.

Just because the identity of the body was concealed, Davis countered, didn't mean the crimes connected to it—presumably the bank frauds—were also concealed. "The crime isn't concealed," he said. "The body is concealed. Is there not a difference?"

Fine said there was no difference—Nancy had taken steps to isolate Jack from his family and friends in order to conceal the bank frauds. When Nancy had left the body with no way to identify it, she'd been bent on concealing the crimes she'd committed using Jack's name and credit.

Davis said that as far as he could see, if Fine was right, there wouldn't be any point to Congress having approved the law on the five-year statute of limitations. "Persons who commit criminal offenses generally don't want to get caught," Davis observed, "and generally take steps to avoid detection of the crime . . ." There had to be something more than mere concealment to avoid triggering the limit, he said. Like a conspiracy.

Fine disagreed. If the government couldn't charge Nancy

with obstruction, the court was rewarding her for her misconduct in trying to conceal Jack's identity in the way she had.

"To not allow the government to include this count as an indictment is essentially giving criminals the go-ahead, to go ahead and try to hide your crime, and if you hide it long enough, then the government's going to miss the statute of limitations, and you're not going to be tried at all."

Levy intervened, saying that the government's position seemed to be that unless and until Nancy had come to the police and admitted putting the trunk by the side of the road, the five-year limit didn't start. But Fine pointed out that Nancy had the opportunity in 1998 to do exactly that, when she was interviewed by Detective Block, and said that Jack was in Virginia. "Which was technically true," she added.

"I think I've heard enough," Davis said. "I don't fault the government for seeking to create some law. Partly that's what the government does, the Department of Justice tries to do. But here it seems to me perfectly clear that this is a case [that's outside the exceptions]. It's not at all clear why the government thinks it's so important, with all respect, to include this count."

The answer to that, of course, was that the government wanted the obstruction count to buttress its notion of the long-running scheme, another brick in the wall of its case.

Davis ruled that the obstruction count would be dismissed.

This was the second indication in the hearing that Davis wasn't all that enamored with the government's theory about Nancy's so-called "scheme." First he noted that there was no such federal crime as "scheming," and now he'd knocked out one of the main bricks of proof there was such a "scheme."

Fine wasn't happy.

"Your Honor," she said, "I would just note the reservation of our right to either seek a reconsideration of that, or to seek interlocutory appeal." This was Fine's way of saying that the government didn't intend to take this lying down—it would go to a higher court, if necessary, before trial.

# 24
# RULE 404

Now the defense turned to its strike-out pitch—the effort to get all the "prior bad acts" struck from the indictment as "surplusage," irrelevant to the charges Nancy was actually facing about Jack Watkins. It had succeeded in pinning the government down to the 1994–1995 bank frauds as the predicates for the witness-tampering, and had the obstruction count dismissed. They were on a roll of sorts.

If they could get all the stuff about Charles and Ted and the Mayberrys and Rick removed from the indictment as "surplusage," they had a chance of convincing a jury that Nancy hadn't committed any bank frauds while Jack was still alive. If there were no crimes and therefore no witness, there could be no tampering.

If they could get that far, then all Nancy would face was the Social Security thefts, the later wire and mail frauds, and the identity thefts, all of which had occurred after Jack's death. The maximum for these crimes was 20 years. Since Nancy had already spent more than 2 years in custody, there was a chance—albeit a slim one—that with a lesser sentence than the maximum, Nancy might get out of prison in time to enjoy her own Social Security. It was a world away from a hot shot on a gurney, which the government still seemed intent upon.

"Specifically, Your Honor," Levy began, "we are moving to strike allegations of crimes and wrongs that are alleged in the ['scheme' portion of the] indictment on the grounds that they are an improper attempt by the government to inject in the indictment and to get before the jury evidence which is necessarily barred . . ."

Levy meant all the assertions about Charles, Ted, the Mayberrys, and Rick Siegel. It was the defense position that any mention of those "prior bad acts" was not permitted by the federal rules of evidence. This was the "surplusage," as the defense referred to it. Levy was quite familiar with the rule, 404, which touched on evidence of "character." It was the same in every court, local, state, and federal in the United States:

(a) Evidence of a person's character or a trait of character is not admissible for the purpose of proving action in conformity therewith on a particular occasion . . .

(b) Evidence of other crimes, wrongs, or acts is not admissible to prove the character of a person in order to show action in conformity therewith.

But there was an exception to the rule:

It may, however, be admissible for other purposes, such as proof of motive, opportunity, intent, preparation, plan, knowledge, identity, or absence of mistake or accident . . .

In alleging that Nancy had engaged in a "scheme" going back to 1982, in which the death of Jack Watkins was only a part, the government was saying that Nancy's "other crimes, wrongs or acts" *were* admissible—that they proved her "motive, opportunity, intent, preparation, plan, knowledge, identity, or absence of mistake or accident." Of course, the language of the rule covered a universe of hydra-headed possibilities, some or all of which had been wrapped together in the government's word "scheme." The evidence rules giveth and they taketh away.

In short, in re-alleging Nancy's previous grifts in the first thirty-seven paragraphs of the first nineteen counts of the indictment, the "scheme," the government was saying that Nancy's previous frauds made it very likely that she had committed a similar if not identical fraud with regard to Jack Watkins and her use of his credit, both before and after his death. This was circumstantial evidence, but very powerful circumstantial evidence, because it was only common sense. Was there a juror in the world who wouldn't believe that Nancy had stolen Jack's good credit history for her own use, once the government was able to argue she'd done it so many times before?

The question was: did these "prior bad acts" of Nancy constitute admissible evidence of "plan or preparation"—in other words, some sort of "scheme," something that had formed in Nancy's mind years before she ever knew Jack Watkins? The line was very blurry between *modus operandi* and a long-running "scheme." It wasn't as if Nancy had decided, back in 1982, to find an old geezer fourteen years later, and take him to the cleaners—that wasn't how life really worked. This was where the law met the human mind, and where evidentiary rule-making usually fell apart.

The problem for the defense was that Nancy's track record—whether one called it "intent," or "motive," or "knowledge" or "preparation," demonstrated that she knew exactly how to take advantage of Jack. She'd been there, done that. So the defense wanted to find some way to keep this poison away from a jury. That was what the "motion to strike surplusage" was all about—the defense wanted to get all the bad stuff about Nancy away from a jury. Just because she knew how to do it didn't necessarily mean she *had* done it.

If the defense had a right to ask the judge to toss out all of Nancy's "prior bad acts," the prosecution had an equal right to ask that they be kept in, under some reasoning from the exception of 404(b): "It may."

But the burden was on the prosecution to find the exception, whether it was "motive," "plan," "intent," whatever. "Scheme" was a nice shorthand word for what the government was trying to say, but it wasn't one of the words used in the rule. The prosecution had to prepare its own motion to justify letting all the bad stuff in, under one of the recognized exceptions.

Davis wanted to know how soon the prosecution would file its motion to let Nancy's past stand as part of the indictment. He thought it made more sense to consider both the defense motion on "surplusage" and the prosecution's justification for it at the same time, since both were dealing with the same topic. Fine agreed that made sense, and the defense acquiesced. Davis said he'd reserve any ruling on the matter until both sides were ready. That, it turned out, would be a very, very long time later.

Now Davis returned to the issue that had been raised at the start of the hearing—Nancy's mental condition. This was a problem, Saunders told Davis, that had been significantly exacerbated by her treatment by her jailers.

Saunders sketched in the background: up until March of 2005, Nancy had been incarcerated at the Talbot County Detention Center. Then she was moved to a new jail, this one in northern Virginia. Not only was this much farther away, the jailers there were withholding her medication.

He wasn't blaming the U.S. Marshals for the situation, Saunders said. It was hardly their fault they had to contract with other law enforcement agencies for housing federal prisoners, since they had no adequate facilities for federal female prisoners in Baltimore. The Congress had so far failed to appropriate money for an adequate facility for female federal prisoners in Maryland, and the Marshals had to negotiate for space with local lock-ups.

"But I have to deal with the situation of my client," he said. "She is fifty-seven years old. She has had bypass surgery, she is on heart medications. She had a documented history coming into the court system years beforehand of depression and treatment of depression by mental health professionals with Zoloft and sometimes sleep medication . . ." Zoloft is a trade name for anti-depressant medicine often used to treat major depression.

"What happens, what is reported to me is . . . I'm not saying it's the facts, but what was reported to me, is that at the Talbot County Detention Center, she began hoarding . . . a portion of her medications, and an inmate reported to the Talbot County Detention Center that she intended to make a suicide attempt . . . They searched her cell, found the medications, and as a result of that, she was put out of the facility."

This was the reason Nancy had been transferred to the jail in Virginia.

Davis was surprised—ordinarily inmates on medication are monitored when given the medicines, to make sure they take them. "How is a detainee able to hoard medications?" he demanded.

Saunders said he didn't know, but guessed that the jail people at Talbot hadn't been watching Nancy closely. In any event, Saunders said, he'd been trying to find out what was up with Nancy from the northern Virginia jail officials, but no one there would talk to him. In fact, they wouldn't even return his calls.

"For an entire month she has been there without seeing a doctor," Saunders went on. "Without medications, initially none of her heart medications . . . now she is receiving what she believes is her heart medication, but she's not being told what she has been given. She has been given some crushed pills. She has been told clearly she's not getting her Zoloft and not getting her sleep medication. She saw a doctor very briefly within the last week for the first time, on two occasions. There was no mental status examination done, no questioning of her about her history. It was simply, 'What is your issue?' It was a matter of thirty seconds or less. 'We will look into this,' or whatever. She's called back a couple of days later and told she's not going to be treated at all, no Zoloft, no medications, no mental health examination, no issues."

As far as he could tell, Saunders continued, Nancy was deteriorating very fast, "very rapidly over the past month. She is extremely anxious, extremely depressed. She has reason to be depressed now. She is facing a death sentence, possibly. She is incarcerated. She is away from her family. She has every reason in the world to be depressed, but this is more severe than anything I have seen before."

Just before the hearing, Saunders said, Nancy had confided that while she had no "plan" to kill herself, she did feel as though she wanted to die.

"She feels like she's going crazy. She's just tired. She feels closed in and depressed. She's getting nothing from [the facility in Northern Virginia] that I can make any sense of."

Saunders asked if Nancy could be transferred to another jail.

Davis asked Fine what she thought. Fine said the prosecutors wanted to make sure Nancy got appropriate medical care, but that it might be difficult to find a place if Nancy had once violated the rules by hoarding her medication. Davis cut her off.

"Well, she's not going to stay down there," he said, referring to the northern Virginia facility.

"I—" Fine began, but Davis was emphatic.

"She is absolutely not going to stay down there," he said again. The last thing he needed was for Nancy to die before the trial was even held, especially due to a lack of adequate medical care while in jail.

Fine said her office would look around for a more suitable facility, but Davis didn't seem to be listening.

"I'm going to direct the court reporter, as soon as she can get to it, to prepare a transcript of Mr. Saunders' representations to the court, which I intend to take directly, first thing Monday morning, to the United States Marshal ... This court is not going to permit this situation to continue." He asked where Nancy was going to be taken after the hearing. Told she was due to be returned to the facility in northern Virginia, Davis said that wasn't going to happen.

One of the Marshals offered the judge a brief written summary of Nancy's medical treatment at the northern Virginia facility—it had arrived by fax from the jail when it emerged that Saunders was going to make an issue of the matter. Davis looked at it.

"This isn't worth the paper it's printed on," he said. He suggested that he might issue an order for the jailers to come to court the following Monday with the complete file. There's nothing more to be dreaded in the justice system than a federal judge with his dander up.

A deputy Marshal informed Davis that there were no jails in Maryland that accepted female federal prisoners, except on a voluntary basis. Once Nancy had hoarded her meds, none of them would take her—it was a possible liability question. "When she was kicked out of Talbot," the deputy said, "that virtually closed the door on every other jail."

Now Davis asked Saunders a profoundly disturbing question:

"Do you want a transfer of venue?" Davis meant shipping the case to another federal jurisdiction, one that did have facilities to provide care for female inmates with psychological issues.

"We might ask for that," Saunders said, cautiously.

"In all honesty, I would seriously consider that," Davis said. "I would seriously consider a transfer of venue to get this case heard in a district that can at least provide humane treatment to a female detainee. I think any defendant is entitled to that."

Saunders said he wanted to consult with Levy before making any decision on changing districts. There were positives and negatives: Nancy might get adequate medical treatment, but logistically, it would make things much more difficult for the lawyers.

Davis turned to the schedule. There had been no date yet selected for the trial. Nor had the DOJ acted on the death penalty request. It seemed an Alphonse/Gaston routine was shaping up—the DOJ wouldn't act until there was a trial date; Davis didn't want to set the trial date until he knew what the DOJ recommended on the death penalty. Maybe this was just politics? Who knew? He ordered the government to get the DOJ to act on the death penalty recommendation within the following month. Then he set a tentative trial date for March of 2006.

But even that was too optimistic.

# 25
# AT THE HOP

It is said that justice grinds exceedingly slow, but exceedingly fine. As far as Nancy could see, it was a lot more slow than fine. Shortly after the hearing, she was transferred to a federal detention facility in Philadelphia. There she would spend the better part of the next two years, waiting for her trial to begin. At least in Philadelphia she received adequate medical care, including mental health treatment. Her cousin Larry Kaskel and his wife, Mary Jeanne, often visited her there, as did other members of her family. It was Larry's impression that Nancy felt far more comfortable in Philadelphia than she had anywhere else on her odyssey so far. Slowly, he thought, Nancy was becoming adjusted to her fate. She still insisted that she hadn't killed Jack, though. And indeed, it seemed hard to believe that "Little Nancy," all 105 pounds of her, could have committed such a violent act.

Despite Judge Davis' order, the Department of Justice took its time on its death penalty determination. Finally, just as the case was supposed to go to trial in March of 2006, the DOJ rendered its verdict: no death penalty for Nancy.

Later, Saunders remarked that the whole process was shrouded in secrecy. No papers were filed with the court;

there was nothing to go on, nothing to evaluate as far as the fairness of the process. It was one of those things, like the Spanish Inquisition, or national security like the case of Jose Padilla, that the government liked to keep classified. Just why anyone believed that death was an appropriate penalty for a 58-year-old woman, no matter how egregious her acts, wasn't clear. Doubtless, there were scores of people locked up in the federal system more deserving of the ultimate sanction than Nancy Siegel. But in the end, the DOJ made the right decision, or so, at least Saunders believed.

Then a new problem emerged: Davis had another trial, another death penalty case involving three defendants, and the Siegel case had to be delayed for yet another year.

Thus it was March of 2007 before Nancy returned to Davis' courtroom. Now almost 59 years old, Nancy was a little more hefty than the sylph-like figure she had presented in earlier proceedings. The one-time Baltimore Queen of the Hop on the *Buddy Deane Show* was ready to make a deal with her pursuers.

# 26
# THE RUBBER MEETS
# THE ROAD

Having had Nancy as their client for almost three years, and having reviewed every jot, squiggle and tittle of the evidence against her by late February of 2007, Saunders and Levy were ready to separate the sheep from the goats—that is, what was indefensible [in a legal sense] from the charges that, they felt, could not be proven beyond a reasonable doubt—the ones they could fight and have a chance to win.

These were the witness-tampering-by-way-of-murder charge in Count 22, and the predicate charges, the pre-death bank credit card frauds of 1994–1995, alleged in Counts 8 through 12, without which there could be no witness-tampering conviction, as Fine had already admitted, if one threw out the supposed "scheme." The defense still believed that if there was an actual trial, Nancy had a chance to beat the rap, that is, convince a jury that proof of actual fraud on the bank card counts was lacking—that it was Jack, not her, who had filled out those applications for credit cards in 1994–1995, or changed the billing address to Nancy's condo in Ellicott City. That was the main reason Saunders and Levy wanted to find a way to ditch those ugly first thirty-seven paragraphs, re-alleged for each of the first nineteen counts in the indictment. Who would believe Nancy if she was packaged with years upon years of cheating, including victimizing her own husbands? Her daughters? To the defense, whatever Nancy had once done with Charles or Ted or the Mayberrys or Amanda and Jennifer was irrelevant to the charge—something done then didn't mean it was done later.

As Saunders had said, from the very beginning, even if the government was able to prove the murder of Jack Watkins at Nancy's hands, there was no federal cause of action against Nancy unless the government could also prove that she had killed Jack intending to prevent him from being a witness against her in the alleged bank card frauds, the predicate "federal offenses." A jury, based on the law, would have to acquit.

Finding Nancy guilty, he thought, might prove very difficult to do. Just using the word "scheme" to smear her didn't cut it. Of course, Nancy still insisted she hadn't murdered anyone. Finding a way to get the "prior bad acts" out of the alleged "scheme" would give her claim of innocence a boost of credibility. That was, in fact, the first line of defense, for the defense.

That still left the first seven counts: the post-death Social Security thefts, and the other post-death counts, 13 through 20: wire fraud, mail fraud, and the identity thefts. The obstruction charge, concealing Jack's identity, Count 21, had already been tossed out by Judge Davis. There wasn't any way to get Nancy off the hook on any of those that were left, 1 through 7, and 13 through 20. The evidence for these was overwhelming. Nancy had cashed or deposited the Social Security checks, she'd made the telephone calls to Social Security, she'd used the mails in furtherance of obtaining money, and she had falsely claimed to be Jack after his death—identity theft. She had admitted as much to Lion, and the prosecution had Lion's report.

So on February 20, 2007, the defense lawyers offered a "proffer"—that is, a proposed guilty plea: Nancy would admit guilt on all the post-death counts: the Social Security thefts, and the others. In return for which, the government would dismiss the bank card frauds, the required federal "predicates," Counts 8 through 12, and the witness-tampering murder, Count 22. Saunders and Levy asked that their "proffer" be sealed by the court. If they had to go to trial on the whole enchilada, they certainly didn't want potential jurors reading about Nancy's proposed admissions ahead of time.

Nothing doing, said Fine, in her response. The limited proffer didn't begin to address Nancy's depredations, especially if it didn't acknowledge the totality of the "scheme." The government might have removed the death penalty from the equation, but it certainly wasn't willing to let Nancy plead to anything less than Jack's murder as part of her twenty-year-long "scheme."

"The counts charged in the indictment reflect a much larger scheme involving defendant's fraud against Jack Watkins both before and after his death, as well as other victims of the same fraud scheme, both before and after Jack Watkins' death," Fine asserted. She guessed that Nancy had victimized between ten and fifty people or institutions over the years, with one sort of fraud or another, but all rooted in her "scheme," which involved conning other people.

Moreover, Fine wasn't willing to allow Nancy's lawyers to keep their proffer secret. While she'd once been anxious to keep the lid on Nancy's mental condition, that didn't apply to the plea offer. The case law on proffers, she said, allowed the government to use the admissions to some crimes if the proffer wasn't agreed to by both the court and the prosecutor, and then was later withdrawn.

In her response to the proposed plea offer, Fine again reiterated the history of the "scheme"—all of Nancy's bad behavior with Charles, Ted, the Mayberrys, Rick, Jack and now, the 1998 mailbox raids and even the wallet thefts of the early 1990s. This was like rubbing salt into the open wound—publicly reiterating Nancy's "other crimes and wrongs" was a rather emphatic way of saying *No, forget about it*, and on the public record, too. Fine didn't ask that her response, which spelled out the terms of the defense offer, be sealed. So then the whole world knew what Nancy was willing to admit, according to her own lawyers. Wham-o!

The lawyers held three-way telephone conversations with the judge on three different occasions, trying to work out an agreement of the plea offer. The defense backed off its proposal for the government to drop the five "predicate" bank card frauds and the witness-tampering count. It knew that the government wasn't about to collapse on those, not with a murder at stake. But it still wanted to wipe out the "scheme" evidence under Rule 404. For the defense, it was a fall-back of sorts: the partial plea of guilty on the post-death theft counts, and the wire fraud, mail fraud and identity theft counts was a way of getting a truncated trial on the five "predicate" bank card frauds and the witness-tampering charge, sans, maybe, the "scheme." Again, this was the role of the defense: to pare the charges down to the minimum as best it could.

Fine indicated that the government was willing to accept the partial plea, and the truncated trial, but only if the evidence about the "scheme" was allowed to be used at trial, and certainly at sentencing. That, of course, would defeat the whole purpose of the partial plea, as far as the defense was concerned. In that case, what was the use of a partial plea at all?

This is how high-stakes criminal cases are negotiated—each side has to estimate the cost of litigation against the downside damage: prison time for Nancy, and major embarrassment for the government's political leadership and its hired attorneys, along with potentially millions in costs for the government, if it can't prove its case. It is, in fact, a game of judicial chicken—the first one to blink gets to take out the trash.

The two sides arrived in Davis' court on March 14, 2007, to thrash out their differences.

The problem at issue, Davis told the lawyers, was still the supposed "scheme." Could the "scheme" be used to as evidence against Nancy at trial? This was the "surplusage" issue of 2005 in just another form.

"The government has alleged a scheme going back to 1982 and continuing through August 2003, a twenty-one-year scheme," Davis summarized. It was just that "scheming," as Fine had admitted two years before, wasn't a federal crime. The government didn't need to allege a "scheme" with respect to the Social Security checks, he said.

Fine agreed that the government didn't have to allege a "scheme" with regard to the Social Security checks—that was simple theft, and in themselves a "federal offense," albeit not one that Jack could have been a witness to, since he was dead by the time the thefts had occurred.

"However," she said, "in the government's view of this case and as it has been indicted, the scheme incorporates those charges, as part of the way in which the scheme was effectuated and as substantive charges, as well, within the indictment."

This was a bit like saying that while it was true zero was nothing, nothing wasn't always zero. "Scheming" might not have been a federal offense, but that's what had happened. In order to show that Nancy was likely to have committed thefts as well as the predicate bank card frauds, that she was likely to have killed Jack to shut him up about those, the whole story was necessary. That was what the "scheme" was all about, and why the grand jury had indicted her.

"Okay," Davis said. He seemed a little dubious.

He called on Saunders to see if he could offer an alternative.

The government had gone a bridge too far with Nancy, Saunders said, when it tried to say that she had murdered Jack as part of some sort of two-decade-long "scheme." There had never been a "scheme," some sort of well-thought-out plan on Nancy's part that had lasted for twenty years. Using that as a means to convict her of murder by tampering with a witness was inherently unfair—the charge of fatal witness tampering should be tried on its own, Saunders said, without all the prejudicial trimmings going back to Charles Kucharski.

"We have proffered that our client will admit that, without any right, authority, et cetera, and with the intent to defraud, she signed his name and sent that in, in the hope if getting a VISA to use . . . she is prepared to admit that her scheme was to defraud either the institution or the government by signing the name of Jack Watkins without any right . . ." Saunders said, referring to those bank credit cards Nancy had obtained after Jack's death, Counts 13 and 15, as well as the Social Security checks. That didn't apply to the pre-death credit cards, though. Those were still in dispute. Whatever—the idea that Nancy had some sort of twenty-year scheme that led to Jack's death was preposterous, he said.

"The government believes, somehow, that if they claim a scheme that is twenty years long, that is, from the very beginning, she has enticed men, married them, or been with them, and used that to steal . . . they're really talking about a character issue, not a scheme that is necessary to be in place, piece by piece . . . you know, the government has had this theory about a 'scheme,' as broad as they have painted it, but from the very beginning, we have contested whether or not that is really relevant to the set of actions that occurred."

Saunders admitted that Nancy might have had a motive, an intent, "all of those things," under 404(b), but he wasn't yet ready to concede even that. But even an intent to get money by theft wasn't the same thing as a "scheme," Saunders said. In his view, the federal government was trying to cobble together a whole series of disconnected actions as part of an effort in order to demonstrate a "scheme," and then use the "scheme" to undergird its notion that Nancy had killed Jack to protect the unproven "scheme." It was using something that didn't necessarily exist in order to establish some sort of act that also didn't necessarily exist—it was bootstrapping, relying on one assumption to prove another assumption.

Without all the "prior bad acts," the inference of the "scheme" simply fell apart, Saunders believed. That's why the government wanted to throw the Kucharskis' kitchen sink at Nancy. Saunders was referring to the "wiggle room" that the indictment contained, the "including" word, which the government had used to backdoor its way into witness-tampering by way of all the evidence on the pre- and post-death "wrongs," even if they weren't part of the "predicates." It was trying to use Nancy's character to convict her of murder by way of witness-tampering, and that wasn't allowed by the rules.

"*Scheme* here is not necessarily whatever the government constructs, in terms of a twenty-year-long . . . belief that she has been involved in fraud through a good portion of her adult life," Saunders told Davis.

The only crimes Nancy was accused of that could legally trigger the witness-tampering statute, he insisted, were the bank card frauds of 1994–1995, and the defense was willing to take those to trial, to show that the government couldn't prove them beyond a reasonable doubt. Saunders still thought he could make a case that Jack Watkins had applied for those credit accounts, not Nancy.

"Okay," Davis nodded. "So I think we're now at the point where the rubber meets the road, because here's the court's ruling, and frankly, to me it is very obvious."

If Nancy pled guilty to *any* of the post-death counts from 13 to 20, Davis said, because those counts encompassed the "scheme" re-alleged from the first thirty-seven paragraphs of the indictment, the government was free to use the prior bad act material against Nancy at the truncated trial and at sentencing. In effect, she would be admitting the "scheme."

"If Ms. Siegel pleads guilty to a count that incorporates paragraphs one through thirty-six [sic] as the description of the scheme, she has pled guilty to a scheme which the grand jury says lasted for twenty-one years," Davis said.

This was putting the rubber on the road, all right. A guilty plea by Nancy to any of the post-death counts, say to Count 13, one of the post-death bank fraud counts, meant that the government could use all the bad old stuff at trial in support of any of the disputed predicate counts, 8 through 12, since the witness-tampering count encompassed the word "including"— meaning a "scheme" that went back to 1982. That was the way the superseding indictment had been worded—in for a dime, out for nearly two million dollars, in fines anyway, not to mention life in a federal prison.

Saunders wanted to talk this over with Levy. If this was going to be the case, it made no sense at all for Nancy to offer a partial plea.

Levy wanted to make sure of what he was hearing from Davis.

"As I understand the court's ruling, through the artifice [Levy was using that word appreciative of the irony, but applying it to the government, not Nancy] of an extensive 'scheme,' the government and the grand jury can effectively trump Rule 404(a), that, if they allege a scheme of inadmissible propensity evidence in the course of attempting to prove the scheme, they can put in lots of evidence that would be irrelevant under 404(a) . . . I don't understand how that can possibly be the case." Levy couldn't understand how all Nancy's prior bad acts could ever be used against her to prove the charges about Jack without violating the character evidence rule.

That was about the size of it, Davis told Levy. There wasn't anything yet to show that Nancy didn't have a "scheme" in mind when she'd allegedly killed Jack Watkins.

"The indictment is coherent," Davis said. "It is logical. Certainly, there's a certain, I don't know, Tom Wolfe quality about it, frankly. Who could believe such a thing?" Davis meant that the whole story of Nancy's life since leaving Charles had such a melodramatic aspect to it that it was hard to accept as really true. It had to be fact masquerading as fiction, a Tom Wolfe specialty.

"This Count One [encompassing all the bad old stuff] reads sort of like a bad novel, with all respect," he said, perhaps unconsciously serving as Wolfe's literary critic. "Yet there's no irrationality or implausibility in it. It recites a narrative that is rational, that is coherent, that is easily within the realm of human capacity.

"So, if the grand jury heard from these many witnesses and the agents, and discussed it and thought, 'Yeah, we think she had it in her mind to do all this, starting two decades ago, and all this evidence we have seen over what happened over the last twenty years, is simply the way she is, the way she lives, the way she pursued her life,' then the grand jury says it's a twenty-one-year scheme." In short, it really was possible that Nancy had been "scheming" for two decades.

Levy still wasn't buying it.

"Your Honor, unless the jury is going to be instructed [by Davis] that they cannot find the defendant guilty of the counts which incorporate this 'scheme'—unless they find that twenty-one years ago, when she allegedly defrauded her first husband, that this was part of a 'scheme,' [one] that she intended to culminate with the death and defrauding of Jack Watkins—they have to acquit her."

Without such an instruction, Levy insisted, the evidence about Charles and everything else about the supposed "scheme" would be purely propensity evidence, and not allowed under the rule. The only way it could come in at all was if the judge then afterward instructed the jury to ignore it—an absurdity, because why then admit it at all?

Davis said he wasn't sure about that—he'd make up his

mind on any jury instructions when the time came. Of course, he said, the defense was free to try to get any of the prior bad act evidence suppressed on a case-by-case basis, if it thought the evidence was weak. Of course, Davis knew that if the defense disputed the prior bad acts, the trial would last weeks if not months. Examination and cross-examination might well be excruciating, lasting day after day. Argghh!

Saunders, Levy and Nancy held an intensely whispered conversation. They apparently were thinking about withdrawing the partial plea offer.

"Your Honor," Saunders said after the conversation ended, "we will need to set a trial date." This seemed to be one way of saying—*No deals, they were willing to go to the mattresses*.

"Okay," Davis said.

After considerably more discussion on whether the partial plea meant Nancy would have admitted the whole "scheme"—Fine said it did, and Davis said it didn't necessarily mean that Nancy was admitting to the *entirety* of the "scheme," but maybe just a portion—the proceeding became entangled in a thicket as to the legal significance of *any* admissions Nancy might make as part of the plea offer. Precedents and interpretations of precedents flew thick and fast in lawyerese. Davis pointed out that if Nancy pled guilty to some of the counts, he would be the one to sentence her on those counts, and it would be up to him to evaluate the relevance of the supposed "scheme" for that purpose, that is, figuring out just how long Nancy would have to be in prison.

Fine continued to insist that the "scheme" could be used in the trial on the remaining counts, as well as Davis' sentencing; Levy and Saunders said it couldn't be used for either, once Nancy made her admissions as part of the partial plea, and it especially couldn't be used to prove any "scheme," and certainly not any "scheme" that had to do with Nancy's supposed intent to cook Rick. It thus appeared that the government and the defense simply could not agree about the supposed "scheme," its duration, or its relevance and admissibility. It was a case of the irresistible force against the intransigent objectors.

Whatever the facts of the supposed scheme, Davis now pointed out, the defense was certain to appeal. He told this to Fine.

"If the jury returns a guilty verdict [based on hearing about the "scheme"]— I mean, they [Saunders and Levy] couldn't have been more clear about this. Mr. Levy and Mr. Saunders, quite apart from what Ms. Siegel will or will not admit, don't believe, as the professionals that they are, that this is a valid indictment.

"They are going to test it. Whether it's after a plea or after a conviction by a jury verdict, they're going to contest whether federal law actually permits what Mr. Levy says is an end run around 404(b), in an indictment that alleges a twenty-one-year scheme. That's not a specious issue. I don't think it's specious. I don't know how the appellate court would rule on it, but . . ."

This perception of Davis created some consternation among the lawyers, and after another ten minutes or so of additional wrangling between the parties, Davis grew exasperated. All the squabbling over the validity and relative importance of the "scheme" was beginning to seem like debating dancing, tutued angels on the heads of pins. It was becoming more and more abstract, as each side tried to slice the issue thinner and thinner.

"Look," Davis said, "we're going to trial. We are *going* to trial. I hope when all is said and done, somebody can explain to me what this dispute is about. I am absolutely in the dark. I am totally in the dark."

# 27
# IRRELEVANT AND
# PREJUDICIAL

By late May of 2007, the case was once more nearing a potential jury trial. Both sides continued fencing about the "scheme" question, with the government insisting it was part and parcel of Nancy's motive in killing Jack, and the defense adamant that it was an impermissible, new-fangled evasion of the rule barring "character evidence." The defense filed a motion *in limine*, that is, a request that the "scheme" evidence not be allowed at trial. This joined the still-pending motion to strike "surplusage"—good defense lawyers try to cover every bet. Davis convened a hearing on May 22 to go over some of the ground rules for the trial, and to sort the damn "scheme" thing out. Nancy had maintained her not guilty plea to all the counts in the indictment, even though Saunders had already told Davis that the defense didn't plan to vigorously contest any of the post-death counts, 1 through 7 on the Social Security checks, and 13 through 20 on the frauds and identity thefts, all counts that encompassed things after Jack was dead.

Where the defense would dig in was around the five 1994–

1995 bank card fraud counts, the "predicates" to the all-important witness-tampering charge, the only charged crimes that Jack could have been a witness to. Saunders still thought the defense could establish reasonable doubt on those.

Davis invited Levy to respond to the government's latest effort to get the "scheme" into evidence. By this point, the government had added still more "prior bad acts." Now the wallet thefts of the early 1990s were part of the "scheme." To Fine, it was just more evidence of Nancy's "plan"—to get credit and money by pretending to be someone she wasn't, just as she'd done with all the credit card frauds, from Charles to Rick. Levy insisted that even if the evidence was remotely relevant, it was too prejudicial to let a jury hear.

Fine reiterated her position—the evidence was not just remotely relevant, it was directly relevant. All of Nancy's prior actions came directly to the likelihood that Nancy had done the same thing to Jack Watkins, before his death. And then, in order to permit her scheme to continue, to safely pursue her romance with Rick, and fearing that if Jack complained about her rip-offs, she'd be busted on her decade-long probation in Howard County, she'd decided to kill him. The appellate courts had ruled that even when evidence might be prejudicial, if it was directly germane to the current charges, it was admissible, she said.

Davis said he'd thought a lot about the "scheme" issue.

"Here's the court's ruling," he said. "This to me is clearly a case of government overreaching, and I don't say that pejoratively, or to suggest any improper motive . . . What I mean by that is, this strikes me as the kind of case prosecutors sometimes come upon where's there's so much evidence, the prosecutor doesn't know what to do with it."

The court had a responsibility, Davis said, to balance the defendant's rights against those of the government. To that end, Davis said, he intended to prohibit the government from mentioning the "scheme" in its opening statement to the jury, and to prohibit it from introducing any evidence about the "scheme" during the presentation of its case.

"The defendant's motions to strike surplusage and to exclude 404(b) evidence are granted." That meant all the bad old stuff about Charles and Ted and the Mayberrys, and the wallet thefts and the mailbox raids, was out. Absent certain developments, the jury would never hear about it. Davis wanted the lawyers to understand his thinking.

"As the law has long recognized," Davis explained, "the fact that a person is a criminal, or has engaged in criminal acts or wrongful acts of a like or similar character, to the layperson, of course, it's relevant." It was only human nature, he said, to believe that if someone did something wrong in the past, they were likely to have done some similar wrong in the future.

"But that's exactly the point in our system, of Rule 404(b)," Davis said. "We don't try people on criminal propensity. That's *exactly* the point. So what we have in this case in a very real way is a clash of doctrines, a clash of interests, a clash of principle. On the one hand, the government quite appropriately is arguing, 'Judge, to the extent that she's stolen others' identities twenty years ago, that's relevant.' In a very meaningful way, that's true. It *is* relevant. But it's relevant in exactly the way that 404(b) says . . . is not admissible."

Davis said he was particularly concerned about the "wrongs" that involved Nancy's family. He worried that some family members—Nancy's husbands, her daughters—might come into court and testify against her emotionally as part of an attempt to "expiate" their own responsibility for failing to stop her in her "scheme" over so many years. He noted that Rick had paid off about $300,000 that Nancy had scammed in his name, "rather than turn in Ms. Siegel," before her arrest in August of 2003.

"And I had to think to myself," Davis said, "in all candor, do these witnesses, Mr. Siegel, Mr. Kucharski, maybe the daughters—I don't know, do they feel some guilt here? Because in effect, what they did—I say this most respectfully—they enabled the defendant, taking as true the grand jury's allegations.

"If perhaps they had been less loving, less forgiving, less understanding, whatever it is that drives a family member to cover three hundred thousand dollars in theft losses, committed by another family member, maybe we wouldn't be here today in federal court on a murder case.

"This case is not the place, with all respect for those persons, to expiate their differences. This is not the forum for that. The grand jury wasn't the forum for that. I'm not even sure—I don't want to go too far down this path—but are they even victims? I mean that, in the sense that . . . just like the fifteen-year-old who steals a twenty-dollar bill from her parents' purse to go to the movies, is that really stealing? If the mom says, 'Don't ever do that again, I'm not going to punish you for it this time,' is that stealing? Is that a criminal offense?

"Well, of course the government will say, 'Of course it is, Judge.' I'm not a theologian. I'm a judge. But what is the role of forgiveness? I go down this path just to point out why it clearly would be very likely an enormous waste of time to permit ex-husbands to come in here over the course of days and days, of what I understand, is likely to be hours and hours of testimony."

Once the government got into Nancy's checkered domestic relations, the trial would certainly get bogged down in ancillary issues—things like whether Rick loved Nancy, whether Ted had really abused her, why Charles hadn't known about the gambling, why Jennifer and Amanda had allowed their mother to act as she allegedly had, with regard to the "scheme."

"Clearly we open up the whole panoply of issues relating to the defendant's state of mind, her mental health, his knowledge of it," Davis said. "It's not a family law case. It's a murder case."

All the material about Charles, Ted, the Mayberrys, and anything else that happened before Nancy met Jack Watkins—including the wallet thefts—would be inflammatory and prejudicial to Nancy's right to a *fair* trial, Davis said, one based only on the actual allegations involving Jack Watkins. Therefore, it was out—"preliminarily," he said, unless the government could show that they were entitled to present it, in rebuttal, say if Nancy took the stand and denied ever using anyone else's identification for purposes of fraud.

Presumably, that applied to the mailbox raids of 1997, too: since those had happened after Jack was dead, how could they be evidence of Nancy's intent with regard to Jack—to remove him as a potential witness to acts that hadn't yet happened?

The only way any of that material could become relevant, Davis said, was if Nancy took the stand and denied ever conning anyone.

Of course, the government and Fine knew the chances of that were minimal—no defense lawyer who wasn't chewing peyote on an hourly basis would ever, *ever* allow Nancy to take the witness stand. Fine and the government lawyers would devour her if she tried to testify, shred her credibility into tiny pieces. They would expose lie after lie, two decades of grifting, the cheating of husbands and daughters and friends, revealing her as a predator. It wouldn't take a jury given that information much more than a millisecond after all that to decide that Nancy had throttled Jack to shut him up.

But if Nancy never took the witness stand, it meant, for all practical purposes, that the long, sordid, "Tom Wolfe" tale of Nancy's scams of the 1980s and 1990s would never be heard by her jury. The defense had won the last round—now they had a chance to convince twelve of Nancy's peers that she never conned Jack Watkins, that it was Jack himself who had applied for the critical, five "predicate" credit cards of 1994–1995, that he could never have been a witness to any scam of Nancy's, that she could therefore never have had an "intent" to silence him, and that therefore, there could be no witness-tampering.

And of course: Nancy still insisted that she hadn't killed Jack, only that she'd disposed of his body after he killed himself, using her daughter Amanda's trunk.

The government was not happy with Davis' decision. They appealed his ruling to the Court of Appeals for the Fourth Circuit in Richmond.

The appellate court received the case with all its attendant briefs and transcripts, boxes and boxes, reflecting the long odyssey that the matter of *United States* versus *Nancy Siegel* had been wending its way through the district court since August of 2003, as the government attempted to expand the reach of the law. Nancy went back to the federal detention facility in Philadelphia. The lawyers on both sides took up new cases, new problems, while a three-judge panel in Richmond pored over all the documents, trying to decide whether Judge Davis had done the right thing in throwing out the "scheme."

Fourteen months later, in August of 2008, two of the three judges on the appeal panel said he had not. They said the "scheme" was valid evidence, and could be admitted to prove that Nancy Siegel had murdered Jack Watkins to shut his mouth, forever, even if he wasn't the sharpest crayon in the box.

# 28
# TO COMPLETE THE STORY

The appellate court in Richmond had a rather schizophrenic reputation. On one hand, it was widely reputed to be the most conservative appellate court anywhere in the United States. It had, for instance, accepted the federal government's claims that the executive powers of President Bush allowed the government to keep any person the government designated as an "enemy combatant" outside the penumbra of rights guaranteed by the Constitution, even U.S. citizens, such as Jose Padilla, the putative "dirty bomber" from Chicago, who was kept in a Naval brig for years, while the government tried to figure out what their actual legal cause of action against him might be. This was, lawyers both left and right acknowledged, a major claim to expansion of the government's power. The left said the government couldn't do it, while the right said it had been done before—in the Civil War. It was all politics—it depended on how one envisioned the rights and powers under the Constitution. The Fourth Circuit might have been conservative at the time of the government's appeal, but it certainly was no rubber stamp.

Because, at the same time, the court also had a reputation for standing up for individual rights, say, on the First and

Second Amendments, especially when it was alleged that the federal government had violated those rights. In short, it tended to favor the government on its right to exercise its authority, while also giving scrupulous adherence to citizens' rights under the Constitution—say, to pray or speak out or bear arms. It was all in the balance of those rights, the court's judges had said over many years—in short, it was a form of politics.

The Fourth Circuit was also significantly understaffed—vacancies to its bench had been caught up in the politics of the courts as practiced by the Congress. Liberal nominees were stymied by the Senate's conservatives in the 1990s, and conservative nominees were similarly blocked by liberals in the following decade. This would be the bench that Davis would join, years later, after the Siegel case was finished. It was a place where he had worked, as a law clerk, years before. It is fair to say that the three judges asked to rule on Judge Davis' ruling on the critical "scheme" evidence against Nancy knew full well the political import of their decision, both nationally as well as collegially. They had to guess that at some point, a district court judge like Davis was likely to join them, and would be looking over their shoulders. It was politics, in a way—there are always politics in every court, all the way up to the top.

The appellate court's majority opinion by Judges William Byrd Traxler and Robert Bruce King, both appointed by Bill Clinton in 1998, essentially held that the government's effort to expand the interpretation of facts allowed under 404(b) was reasonable and necessary under the facts of Nancy's depredations. The dissent came from Judge Jackson L. Kiser, a Virginia district court judge, "sitting by designation," that is, pinch-hitting in a way, since the appellate court was short-handed. Kiser partly agreed with his two higher court colleagues, but asserted that Davis, as the judge assigned to try the case, had every right to set limits on the cornucopia of evidence. That was for a district court judge to decide, District Court Judge Kiser said, and if Davis thought much of the "scheme" was superfluous, unnecessary to decide the central issues, it should be within his power to determine. It's possible that Kiser was looking over his shoulder—once an appellate court asserted the authority to tell a trial court how to run a trial, what was the point in having a district court at all?

But the two majority appellate judges maintained that the government had made its case for inclusion of the "scheme." Traxler wrote the opinion. He cited a 1994 case from the Fourth Circuit that said under 404(b), other acts or wrongs *were* admissible before a jury, if it was "necessary to complete the story of the crime on trial." Another case suggested that other wrongs could be admissible if they were "necessary preliminaries to the crime charged."

That was the situation with Nancy Siegel, Traxler wrote. He bought the government's argument that Nancy had already measured Rick for a scam, and in order to pull it off, had to keep Jack quiet. "She needed to find a way to end her relationship with Watkins that would not jeopardize her freedom or her access to Eric's financial resources," Traxler wrote. If she'd simply abandoned Jack, Jack would have had no choice but to turn to his step-daughters or the Hodges for help. Then, it would have all come out—how Nancy had conned him out of everything he owned. So Jack had to die.

Similar reasoning applied to the wallet thefts of the early 1990s. Nancy was on a decade's probation from those—she couldn't afford to have Jack report her for new crimes, because then she'd be sent to jail, ruining her "scheme" to plunder Eric. Jack might not have known about her probation, but once he was on the street, derelict, wiped out financially, someone was sure to have exposed Nancy's grift with Jack.

Of course, this summary of the facts by the appellate court skipped over Howard County General Hospital's opportunity to do exactly that, back in April of 1996, when Nancy had brought Jack to the hospital after the trek to Atlantic City. Had the hospital acted then to separate Nancy from Jack, to check out their conflicting stories, rather than simply categorize Jack as a Korsakoff's syndrome–demented alcoholic, the chances were very good that none of what happened would have happened.

The awful fact was, the doctors had only *assumed* Jack's ailment, and the assumption was based mostly on Nancy's story—doctors at work. While there are a number of biological tests for Korsakoff's syndrome that can be interpreted from brain scans, none were performed for Jack. To Howard County General Hospital, at the time, he was just another drunk.

Finally, Traxler concluded, all of the rest of the evidence about the "scheme" was admissible against Nancy because it showed her *modus operandi,* her *m.o.* All of the earlier and later crimes in the scheme were similar in the way they were pulled off, Traxler noted—Nancy got inside information about her victims, like Social Security numbers and banking information, then used it to get money. The *m.o.* proved that all the crimes were part of a "scheme," Traxler concluded, and the established "scheme" connected Nancy's cheating of her first husband, Charles, with the cheating of her last, Eric. Poor Jack was just collateral damage as the twenty-year "scheme" unfolded.

So Nancy would go to trial, with her whole history of scams in the dock with her. Davis might have been in the dark, but the appellate court was not.

Fine and her colleagues in the Maryland U.S. Attorney's Office were very happy.

The August 2008 decision of the Circuit Court allowing the bad old stuff to be heard by a jury left Saunders and Levy with one last escape hatch, before having to defend Nancy in front of a jury. A trial date with Judge Davis presiding had been set for mid-January of 2009. If they could get the U.S. Supreme Court to overrule the Richmond appeals court, they might still get all the "prior bad acts" thrown out—to validate Judge Davis' initial ruling. In November, the defense filed with a request for a writ of *certiorari*—a plea for the high court to take the case to resolve the "scheme" issue. In mid-December, the request was turned down. The Supreme Court justices weren't ruling on the merits, only on its timeliness, in effect saying that there would be plenty of time later for Nancy to appeal to higher courts once a trial was over, and if she was convicted. Well, of course, the Supreme Court has halved the number of cases it has accepted under *certiorari* since 2001. It's politics.

With all the bad old stuff back in, the government had estimated that a trial might take as long as six weeks. Davis realized that the defense was going to fight every old claim, every "prior bad act," down to whether Nancy had ever told Charles Kucharski that she did or did not love him. In his view, the appellate court had erred—they'd just allowed the whole case to fall into a largely irrelevant, emotional swamp. What did Nancy's behavior with Charles or Ted or her daughters have anything to do with what had happened to Jack? Where was the nexus, the connection, the commonality, other than the indisputable fact that Nancy was a thief?

Going down that road was certain to add days and days, probably weeks and weeks, of irrelevant and inflammatory, prejudicial testimony. And why? The government had overwhelming evidence even without all the bad old stuff, as far as he could see. But the higher court had spoken: he added two more weeks to the schedule—eight weeks, almost two months of litigation, all to prove the point of a "scheme's" admissibility, which would probably swamp the real issue— had Nancy really killed Jack? Now, he was not happy.

Apart from the admissibility questions of the prior bad acts, there was the matter of time—eight weeks? Good grief, Davis had presided over much more complicated trials than *U.S.* vs. *Siegel* in far less time. So there had to be another agenda—the government wanted to pry open the rules on 404, "character evidence," and intended to use Nancy Siegel, a slam dunk, to do it.

It appears that Davis leaned on the lawyers. Couldn't they find some way to pare down the time—maybe with stipulations? Cut to the chase? A stipulation is a written agreement between litigants as to certain facts. If Nancy's side admitted certain facts for the purpose of a trial, there wouldn't be a need to put on what was likely to be interminable—and perhaps emotional and even inflammatory—testimony. After all, she had already offered to plead guilty to much of the indictment—was it really necessary to spend hours and days proving the obvious? The January trial date was continued while Davis pressed the parties to work out agreements on some of the prior bad acts.

In the end, the wallet thefts went—in return, Nancy's side agreed to let the jury see the state court records of her earlier convictions. The 1997 mailbox raids were allowed in, but only through the testimony of Detective Block. Evidence from Jennifer and Amanda would be permitted, along with that from Charles, Ted and Eric, but only that which encompassed her frauds. The Mayberrys were left on the cutting room floor. It was one way to clear the emotional, prejudicial chaff from the case, but still follow the appellate court's decision.

By early March of 2009, both sides were ready to go.

# PART III
## THE TRIAL OF
## NANCY JEAN

# 29
# NO QUESTIONS

So now—finally—more than five years after Nancy was arrested in August 2003, and almost thirteen years after Clark
Jackson found Jack's body in the trunk, sixteen years after
the wallet thefts, twenty-four years after Nancy deserted
Charles Kucharski's hearth and home, leaving him holding
the bag on almost $100,000 in debts, justice is about to be
served. The merry-go-round has stopped, the calliope isn't
playing anymore. She wasn't there, but now she is. The citizens of Maryland are in the jury box, Judge Davis is admon-
ishing them to ignore anything printed or broadcast about the
case, and Nancy, still short, still blonde, still blue-cyed, still
cute, is sitting at the counsel table, waiting for the judicial
video poker reels to spin. It's "the time of the season," as the
Zombies once sang, years before—"Who's your daddy?"
Her real daddy might have been beaten to death in an alley in
Fell's Point in 1964, when she was sweet sixteen, but this is
the last gamble of her life, the biggest plunge of all, and
Nancy has no edge. The horrible, awful truth is, she never
did. Grifters usually don't run long, and Nancy's run, if anything, has been far longer than most.

Fine has had half a decade to think about this—she knows

what she wants to say, and she's arranged her witnesses with care. In her mind, the government's case against Nancy Siegel is open and shut—a woman who seduced and lied and cheated men for most of her adult life, from a kiss to a murder. It was light years, at least in moral distance, from Ricky Nelson and the *Buddy Deane Show*. Who's your daddy?

In the face of the evidence, Saunders and Levy are at the Little Big Horn with cap pistols—a little bang to no effect. There is almost nothing they can do to stem the onslaught. They are already planning to run away to fight another day—probably not in the Court of Appeals of the Fourth Circuit, which has already reached its verdict on the crucial issue, Rule 404, but in the United States Supreme Court, which hasn't yet said a definitive no.

For Saunders and Levy, the case of Nancy Siegel has grown beyond Jack Watkins—it is now about the government's use of unrelated "prior bad acts" to prove charges of crimes that occurred many years later. Once the government is allowed to do this, they think, Evidence Rule 404 will fall, be effectively eviscerated, and virtually everyone in the country who isn't a saint will be at risk of prosecution for present allegations on the basis of evidence of what they might have done in an earlier part of their life. It was simply wrong, Saunders and Levy thought—a thorough perversion of the rules of fair justice, and a violation of the Constitution's guarantee to due process under the Fifth Amendment. This is what they're all about.

But for now they have lost. Judge Davis had agreed with them, but he'd been overruled by the higher court. Now the world will hear the lurid, if bowdlerized-by-stipulation story of Nancy's history of grifting, and quickly conclude that because Nancy is a crook, she has killed Jack Watkins.

They will fight at trial, as best as they can, to refute Nancy's guilt on the actual charges, but they know—and probably Nancy now knows—it's going to be a losing battle. The defining clash will come long after the trial, at the Supreme Court, if they can get that far. It may take years. By the time it rises to the Big Black Robes in Washington, D.C., Nancy may well be dead—it can take that long. It's the principle of the thing that drives them on. That's why they get the big money. Well, it's not really about the money—they just don't like the idea of the government going too far, and taking so many whacks at the Constitution. If they didn't think that way, they would be prosecutors.

Larry Kaskel and his wife, Mary Jeanne, a former nun and another child of Fell's Point, sit on the hard wooden benches of the courtroom, watching, listening, hoping. But even they know that it's like ascending Mount Everest on a unicycle—it can't be done. Nancy is guilty, and it's just a matter of time before a jury figures it out. They don't want to admit it, even to themselves, but sometimes the cards don't lie.

Fine's opening statement is standard procedure for a prosecutor. Assisted by Assistant United States Attorney Richard Kay, her goal is to lay out the facts that her side will present—the facts that, when put together, add up to the inevitable conclusion that Nancy murdered Jack Watkins to zip his lip.

She begins with Jack, tries to humanize him by recounting his love of gardening, singing and bingo, his life with Mary, the breakfast club of senior citizens, and then moves on to the discovery of his body in the trunk. Then she lays out the crimes the government expects to prove against Nancy—theft, mail fraud, wire fraud, identity theft, and witness-tampering. All of these crimes involved Jack Watkins, she tells the jury, but all of them were only incidents in a lifetime of fraud and deceit, in which Nancy cheated and stole, including her own husbands and children, all the way up until the day she was arrested.

"The evidence will reflect the pattern of the defendant, Nancy Siegel," Fine says. "Time and time again she gained personal information, information about themselves, information about their accounts, and then stole from them." That's what she did with Jack, and in order to silence him so she could continue her lifelong "scheme" with Rick, she knew she had to kill Jack and conceal his identity. Otherwise, she would be exposed, sent to jail, and her plan to victimize Rick would be wrecked. That was how Nancy had led her life—one grift after another. It was what she was, *who* she was.

Now it's Levy's turn for the defense. He wants to disarm the jury quickly, or at least back it up a bit after Fine's litany of Nancy's malefaction, by shifting the focus away from Nancy's history, and onto the predicates, the 1994–1995 bank card frauds, without which there is no proof of the big one, the witness-tampering-by-murder claim. This is where he and Saunders have staked their defense of Nancy. Conceding the impossible to defend, the defense hopes to direct the jury's attention to the more narrow issues—the so-called predicates, the 1994–1995 credit cards. Their theme is: yes, Nancy's been a crook for half her adult life, but that doesn't mean she killed anyone. They will try to establish that it was possible that it was Jack, not Nancy, who had applied for the critical 1994–1995 credit cards. It's all they can do. Without evidence of who actually applied for the cards, it's reasonable doubt, they think.

"There will be a number of things in this case that frankly . . . we don't disagree with," Levy tells the jury. But, he adds, "there are certain things in this case that we very *much* disagree with." The jury would be hearing lots of things about Nancy, he continues. Many of them were not very nice—"quite frankly, not pretty"—and no one would say she hadn't done them. But just because she had been bad in the past didn't mean she was guilty of murdering Jack Watkins.

Levy asks the jury to distinguish between cynicism and skepticism, and tells them they aren't the same. Being skeptical was fine, being cynical was not. "You will hear many things about Nancy Siegel, many that are not pretty . . . you're being told about these things, not to show she's a bad person, but to show an alleged pattern. We disagree that there *is* a pattern. You have to resist the natural human emotion, that, based on these other acts, she must be guilty of the things she's charged with in *this* case."

It isn't necessarily so, Levy says. One does not have to follow the other, even if it seems logical. "If this was a made-for-TV movie," Levy says, "it would be logical. But as Judge Davis told you yesterday [during jury selection], this is not TV, it's real life. The story is not always obvious. I ask you to keep these things in mind."

This is a bit like trying to put up protective padding around Nancy. Fine in her opening statement has already placed the explosives from the past—two former husbands, all of Nancy's criminal history, the supposed "scheme." All the defense can do, in its own opening statement, is try to shield her from the inevitable blast, try to minimize the fall-out to come.

Levy urges the jury to separate the alleged crimes into three separate categories: those they would soon hear about from the distant past, not charged in federal court; those said to have taken place *before* Jack's death—the five critical bank card allegations—and those that took place *after* Jack had been found in the trunk.

There isn't much dispute about what happened before Nancy met Jack, or *after* Jack died, he says. The evidence would show that Nancy had disposed of his body, and then had committed theft and fraud afterward, using his identity.

"But none of them make Nancy Siegel a murderer," Levy says. Well, it was true on paper. But murder cases aren't won on paper, but in the eyes and minds and hearts of jurors. Levy has fired off the first shot from his cap pistol, but it isn't likely to do much good. Once the jury hears about Nancy's history as a grifter, as background to her admissions of stealing Jack's Social Security checks and his credit—along with the admissions that she disposed of his corpse and tried to conceal his identity—the jurors will have to be rubes at the carnival not to reach the obvious conclusion: that she had murdered him. Who else had the motive and the means and the opportunity? It's *Murder, She Wrote*. And the people in the jury box are not nearly as simple—or as sophisticated—as Levy and Saunders believe, or hope. They know a spiel when they hear one. It isn't cynicism, it's skepticism.

Fine has set up her case in classic fashion—the first thing she wants to do is drop the body through the roof. That means calling Clark Jackson, the Loudoun County patrol officer who first opened the trunk back in May of 1996. Jackson skips over the part about his scavenging contest, or how Jack's corpse soon became known as "Jack-in-the-box." He is somber, serious, a professional through-and-through. With his testimony, Fine has established the discovery of the body.

"No questions," Levy says. Fine runs through all the forensic evidence: more Loudoun County sheriff's deputies, including the criminalist Brian Harpster: duffle bags, pillowcases, dog hairs, toenail polish and DNA. Wheel tracks in the dirt, where the trunk was dragged from a car to the wayside. The unfolding of Jack's corpse at the hospital in Leesburg.

"No questions," Levy says once more. No one's disputing that Jack's dead body was found in the trunk in the early morning hours of May 14, 1996, at the wayside along the Potomac River. There's nothing to be gained by the defense for prolonging this, it's already ugly enough.

The next two witnesses, from the Virginia Office of the Chief Medical Examiner, Dr. Field, and an expert from the state forensic lab, establish the cause of death—strangulation of some sort, but likely not by ligature. So much for Nancy's suicide-by-hanging story.

In questioning Dr. Field, Fine brings out a crucial detail without much elaboration—the bruise found on Jack's neck back in May of 1996 was a sort of "L" shape, as far as Field could see. Fine and Kay will come back to this with devastating effect later in their closing arguments. In effect, they're trying to sandbag the defense—they don't ask Field her interpretation of the mark at this point. They want the defense to go too far and skip over its possible significance. Then they will try to catch the defense on their backside, unaware—where they haven't paid enough attention.

It isn't exactly fair, but it's legal.

Levy seems to have overlooked the significance of this "L-shaped mark," based on his questions to Field. He could smoke out Fine's landmine with sharper cross-examination of the medical examiner, but apparently has missed it. Either that, or the defense has some alternative in mind. He still tries to mitigate the effect of Dr. Field's limited testimony. Can she be absolutely sure that Jack didn't hang himself? That the marks on the neck were *not* from a strap or a rope? Field says she can't be completely sure, but it's highly unlikely.

Levy can't push much further than this—he lets Fields go, without any questions about the bleeding on the opposite side of the brain, the evidence that Jack was clouted about the time of his death, or anything useful about the "L-shaped mark" on the neck. The facts are, nothing about the pathologist's official report helps the defense. The best Levy can do at this point is make Fields admit that she can't rule out suicidal hanging. But even this comes with a non-verbal, shrugging dismissal from Fields: the jury can see from her face and her body language that it's highly unlikely. The L-shaped bruise on Jack's neck lies there in the weeds as the bomb that will ultimately blow the defense case to smithereens.

An expert from the Virginia toxicology laboratory testifies: it appears that Jack was loaded to the gills with over-the-counter sedatives when he was strangled. Here Fine goes a bit too far. She takes the residual amount of the Benadryl-like substance in Jack's liver as evidence that Jack was given a massive overdose of the stuff just before being killed. The tox expert tries to explain: no—it was more likely that the drug had piled up in the liver over a period of time, and that, in fact, some significant portion of it may have wound up in the liver after death, a result of a sort of drainage that accompanies the post-death blood flow, lividity. Fine is possibly misunderstanding the power of this evidence, or maybe she's going too far in her enthusiasm for her case—she has conceived that the tox results showed that her culprit, Nancy, overdosed her victim just before strangling him. In fact, the tox evidence shows that the dosing with over-the-counter sedatives might have taken place over many, many days. In turn, this seems to show that Nancy, if she gave Jack the medicines, had done so repeatedly in an effort to keep him docile. Mixed with alcohol, the meds would have made him easy to control, even for a 105-pound woman. The defense tries to exploit this error, but it doesn't help them at all with the jury. Saunders and Levy certainly don't want to explain its true meaning—how can it help their client? All they can get out of it is the possible inference on the part of the jury that Jack had given himself the medicine, not Nancy. But it's ephemeral, only a wisp of reasonable doubt.

Ochsman is called as a witness. She tells the story about the FBI and the fingerprint databases—how there was at first no match, then in late 2002, a hit: Private First Class Jack F. Watkins, born March 21, 1920, a veteran of World War II, a twenty-something who had served in the Army Air Corps in India, a lifetime ago, when most people tried hard to be who they said they were.

"No questions," Levy intones.

Soon Fine is into other damning evidence: Nancy's February 2003 telephone call to Social Security, to report Jack's "missing check," Count 19, and once again, in June 2003, Count 20. The witness, from the Social Security Administration, has the records of notes taken from the telephone calls—what was said in the attempt to get a replacement check. The caller's telephone callback number is Nancy's. There can be no doubt that Nancy has called Social Security at least twice to collect Jack Watkins' Social Security benefit, almost seven years after his body was found in the trunk. Wire fraud, worth at least ten years a pop, if convicted.

"No questions," says the defense, because they have none worth asking.

Mark Carr, the postal inspector testifies. He was in the Ellicott City post office on February 4, when Nancy arrived to pick up Jack's Social Security check—the day she was under the FBI's videotaped surveillance. He claims to have seen Nancy come inside the post office, then go to the box to retrieve the mail, including Jack's Social Security check, along with the meager monthly annuity from New York Life. Then, he says, he watched Nancy do the same over the next few months, and had even induced her to fill out a form claiming she was authorized to pick up mail for Jack—mail fraud.

"No questions," the defense says.

Over the next few days, Fine calls more witnesses: Jennifer and Amanda, then Charles, Ted, and finally Rick Siegel. The first four are to establish Nancy's "pattern," if not her "scheme." Rick is intended to be the capper—Nancy's grifts cost him about three hundred grand from 1996 to 2003. Fine wants to ram that point home—the idea is, with Rick in Nancy's crosshairs, ready to be picked off, Jack had to be disposed of, to facilitate Nancy's "scheme."

Jennifer is first. Born in 1972, she is taller than her mother, but has all of her blond-haired, lean beauty. As she takes the witness stand, Nancy puts her hands over her eyes—she seems to be crying. Jennifer is also upset. Testifying in a court of law against one's mother has to be the worst—who could imagine doing it? Fine asks her: did she ever meet Jack Watkins? Jennifer says she did, a few times—she remembers him as an elderly, smaller, thin man who was acquainted with her mother. She remembers that her mother said that Jack Watkins had acquired the car, the BMW, for her.

Fine asks if she was ever told by her mother what had happened to Jack. Jennifer says Nancy told her, at first, that he had gone to live with his sister in Virginia. Fine shows her several checks from New York Life, which have her name on them. Were those endorsements her signatures?

"No," she says. She begins to weep.

"What did she tell you happened to Jack Watkins?" Fine asks.

"She told me that she came home and he was dead," Jennifer says. "That there was a cord or something around his neck." This is something Nancy told Jennifer after she was arrested, when Jennifer confronted her in the hospital after her attempt to kill herself.

"Did she say what she had done with the body?"

"She put it into a trunk." By now Jennifer is sobbing. "She drove it through Maryland . . . to somewhere in Virginia."

Fine is relentless.

"Were you a victim of identity theft?"

"Uh-huh." Jennifer is still crying. So is Nancy.

"Did you ever have trouble getting credit?"

"Yes."

"Do you know she stole your identity?"

Jennifer doesn't know what to say. She wants to explain about Nancy, her mother, about her compulsive gambling, but doesn't know where to start. "My mom," she starts, but Fine cuts her off.

"Did you ever confront her?"

"Yes."

"What did she say?"

"That she was sorry."

No questions, the defense says.

Is there anything worse than this, for a defendant? Having one's own child testify that her parent was a liar and a cheat,

and probably a murderer? No wonder Jennifer is in tears—
she loves her mother. And who can blame her? Jennifer
knows her mother has problems, but having to get on a witness stand and give testimony to help send her to prison for
the rest of her life—who could do such a thing? But the government has insisted.

The same situation applies to Amanda. She takes the
stand after Jennifer. Kay questions her. And if her older sister
is weepy, Amanda is made of sterner stuff. She seems angry,
whether at Kay and the government, or her mother, isn't
clear.

Amanda identifies a photograph of the condo in Ellicott
City, and says she met Jack there as a friend of her mother.
Kay shows her copies of New York Life checks that have her
signature on the backs as endorsements.

"Was that your signature?"

"No."

Kay shows her a picture of the BMW. Did her mother
ever drive a car like that? Yes, Amanda says. Amanda says
she believes Jack helped her mother acquire the car.

"Was there a credit card opened in your name that you
didn't apply for?"

Yes, Amanda says. It was opened when she was living
with her mother and Rick in 1999. She had no idea.

Kay shows Amanda a photograph of the trunk. Amanda
identifies it as once having belonged to her—she'd taken it
to college in 1995.

"Did there come a time when you asked your mother
what happened to Jack Watkins?"

Yes, Amanda says—in 2003, when Nancy was in the
hospital after her attempted suicide.

"What did she tell you?"

"That she came home one day . . . he had committed suicide. There was a cord around his neck. She said she freaked
out. She didn't know what to do. She didn't think anyone
was going to believe what happened. She put it [the body] in

the trunk. She didn't want anyone to find out what happened."

"No questions," the defense says.

The following Monday, March 9, 2009, the government calls Greg Locke to the witness stand. He testifies about the confrontations with Nancy back on August 5, 2003, in the post office, the Siegel house, and the hotel, in which she kept saying she wanted to tell what happened, but never did. A tape and a transcript of these interrogations come into evidence, with all of Nancy's admissions about gambling, and the trunk, along with Nancy's repeated statements: "I'll tell you what you what happened," but nothing much beyond that.

Detective Block is called, and tells of his taped interview with Nancy in 1998, in which she said she had a "tendency to scheme." Block recounts seeing the BMW, and asking Nancy about Jack Watkins.

"She said she hadn't seen him for two years, that he was in Virginia," Block says.

"No questions," the defense says.

Now Fine calls Cheryl, one of Jack's three step-daughters, who sketches in Jack's life before Nancy—the house on Sungold Road, the breakfast club, the bingo, the singing.

"He could be very naïve," Cheryl says. Jack told her that Nancy taught Sunday School in a church someplace. "He planned to marry her," Cheryl says. She didn't file a missing persons report on Jack, because she heard, from some of the other seniors, that Jack had moved in with Nancy, the "Swartz lady," as Cheryl recalls her.

"No questions," the defense intones.

Fine calls Anita, Cheryl's sister. She recalls Jack as a very sociable person, very responsible with his meager resources—not someone likely to sign up for a $44,000 car, with only a $1,200-a month income.

"Prior to 1994, did he have any financial problems?"

"None that I know of."

"Did he have a drinking problem?"

"No."

"A gambling problem?"

"No."

Fine shows Anita a photograph of Nancy. She isn't sure, but it looks like the person whom Jack said was his "girl-friend" back in 1994 and 1995, the "Swartz lady," as her sister Cheryl had called her.

"He was real happy, excited," Anita says. "We started hearing less and less from him."

"Did you call him?"

"Yes."

"Did he return your calls?"

"No."

"Did you file a missing persons report?"

No, Anita says. "We were told he sold the house after that, and just that he'd gone off with her."

From the defense: "No questions."


Fine marches through other evidence: pawn shop records from Baltimore, including a karaoke machine that Jack used while singing at the senior center—Nancy hocked them in April 1996, a month before Jack was found dead in the trunk. The pawn records identify the borrower as Nancy Sweitzer.

Kay calls Ralph Hodge, who tells of Jack's leave-taking, in Nancy's company, in the spring of 1996, shortly before he was found dead.

"He said he was in love," Ralph says. "They were going to be married."

Ralph tells how he tried to dissuade Jack. "Jack," Ralph remembers telling him, "you've got to be out of your mind. She's half your age." And Jack protesting: "She's going to take care of me." Ralph: "She's going to take you for every-thing you've got." But Jack wouldn't listen, Ralph says.

Finally from the defense, on cross-examination: Saunders asks—did he seem happy? Ralph admits that yes, Jack seemed happy. "But from what she was saying," Ralph adds, "I wouldn't advise anyone to go with her."

Kay calls one of Jack's near neighbors, John Radka. Radka and his family lived next door to Jack and Mary. He recalls Jack as friendly, sociable, dedicated to his garden. After Mary died in 1989, Jack often talked to him when he came home from his job. Once, Jack gave him a box of tomatoes he'd grown.

"He was just a nice old guy, as far as I'm concerned," Radka says. He remembers seeing Nancy at the house, picking up mail. "He told me he was going to get married," Radka says. "He was going to live at her condo." Jack told him he was going to sell the house, and that he'd already given Nancy money for a down payment on the condo.

"One day, he was just gone," Radka recalls. "He never said goodbye, or anything like that."

By this point, Nancy's lawyers have decided that they have to try to blunt the effects of some of this testimony. The Jack the initial witnesses have described could be a simpleton, an easily manipulated dolt. They want to show he was more complex, capable of making his own decisions. How else can they raise the prospect that it was Jack who applied for the crucial 1994–1995 credit cards?

"Did you ever notice a deterioration in his mental faculties?"

"No," Radka admits.

"Did he ever complain in any way about her conduct?"

"No."

Then a crucial question, from the defense: how many times did Radka see Nancy pick up Jack's mail? Radka admits that it was only a few times.

"Did you ever see anyone interfere with his interaction

with others?" This comes to the testimony of Cheryl and Anita and Ralph, to the effect that Nancy tried to isolate Jack from his friends and family.

"No," Radka says.

The government calls Charles Kucharski to testify.

# 30
# FOR BETTER OR WORSE

Charles doesn't want to be here—this was his former wife, the mother of his daughters, someone he once loved, and maybe, in a way, still does. Yes, Nancy took him for a ride, but he doesn't want to see her hurt. Anyone can see it in his demeanor. If he isn't willing to lie for his former wife, he also isn't also willing to help the government trash her. He keeps his answers short, to the point, never going beyond the minimum necessary to respond to the prosecution's questions. He's treading a fine line between his love for his children, the life he once had with Nancy, and the government's demands on him as a witness. It's a horrible place to be in.

He and Nancy had married in 1967, he says. They were divorced in 1985. While they were married, Nancy kept all the records of the accounts. He never checked on her—he trusted her. Then he became aware that Nancy had obtained credit accounts in his name, without his knowledge, and that the bills for these were not being paid. Nor were the income taxes. Eventually he'd had to file for bankruptcy on debts of nearly $100,000 that Nancy had incurred, including back taxes and interest from 1982 to 1984 or so.

"Did you ever ask her where the money went?"

"I did," Charles says. "She only told me I wouldn't understand."

"Did you ever call the police?"

"No."

Levy has only one question for Charles.

"Do you recall anything she ever did in those seventeen years that was violent?"

"No," Charles says.

Now Ted comes to the witness stand. He and Nancy were married in 1985, he tells the jury, and divorced in 1993. "We were having financial problems," Ted says.

"She had a gambling problem?" Kay asks.

"Yes."

Ted says he first learned that something was going on when his sister-in-law told him that Nancy wanted to borrow money from her. Then he found out that Nancy hadn't been paying the mortgage, converting the payments to herself. After that, he'd found several plastic bags crammed with unpaid bills stashed behind the washing machine. One of them was a dunning notice from the IRS for taxes on Nancy's winnings at casinos in Atlantic City. When he discovered that Nancy had gambled away his daughter's school tuition, Ted says, he became so angry at Nancy that he'd shut himself inside a closet.

"I didn't want to strike her," he says.

Until then, did Ted have any idea of Nancy's deceptions?

"I was totally unaware," Ted says.

"Did you call the police?"

"No."

By now, Nancy has told her lawyers that Ted was abusive and a mean drunk. The relevance to the charges at trial is a little iffy, but they figure that if the prosecution can attack Nancy by reputation, the defense ought to at least be able to do the same to her accusers.

Levy suddenly becomes aggressive with Ted, asking him

whether he and Nancy had ever had physical altercations. The defense probably hopes that this might make Nancy more sympathetic to the jury. To their side, it's worth a shot—at Ted.

"Once you beat her so badly she had to go to the hospital?" Levy asks.

"No," Ted says. Ted explains that Nancy had once broken her wrist trying to hit *him*.

"You used to beat her up pretty good, didn't you?"

"It never happened," Ted says.

Levy can't take this any further. He has no real evidence, and it's already on the line as far as relevancy. He desists.

Afterward, Ted's third wife remarked that Ted was chagrinned and embarrassed at the way the news media covering the Siegel case had characterized him—"I'll always be known as the guy who hid in a closet in fear of his wife," he ruefully told her. Of course, to Ted it wasn't that way at all. He'd hidden in the closet so he wouldn't have to see Nancy—otherwise he might have killed her. It was probably the smart thing to do at the time.


Now Eric Siegel comes to the witness stand. He first met Nancy in November of 1991, Eric says, without elaborating on where or how. They married in December of 1998, after seven years of an on-again, off-again relationship. They began living together in the fall of 1997, Eric says, after his marriage to Faye ended.

Fine marches Eric through a series of documents, including one that shows that Nancy became a signatory to one of Eric's bank accounts. Was that his signature, authorizing Nancy?

"No," Eric says.

What about various credit cards issued in his name? Had he applied for them?

"No."

"Did you ever receive mail at a post office box in Ellicott City?"

"No."

He only discovered what Nancy was up to when some of the credit companies called Faye, who then called him, Eric testifies. He confronted Nancy, and she then admitted having opened accounts in his name, without his knowledge—six of them, in fact. All the statements were mailed to the Ellicott City post office box, the one he'd never known about.

"At that point, it came to a head," Eric says. Nancy went into the hospital for treatment, and Eric arranged for her to see someone at a credit counseling service. Fine doesn't go into the suicide attempt, or Nancy's treatment by the psychiatrists. That appears to be a morass that neither prosecution nor defense wants to step into.

Instead, she asks Eric about deposits of some of Jack Watkins' Social Security checks to a joint checking account he had with Nancy. He never knew about the deposits, Eric says. In fact, it appears he never even knew about the joint account.

"Did the time come when you were contacted by the IRS for a failure to report income?"

"Yes."

Fine produces another exhibit—this one, an IRS form proposing to change the Siegels' 2001 tax return to account for Nancy's gambling winnings that year. Again, the form only reflects the upside, not the losses, because Nancy has put those out of her mind.

Fine asks if Eric ever thought of reporting Nancy to the police.

No, Eric says.

Fine asks how much money Nancy cost Eric with her grifts.

"A couple of hundred thousand," Eric says. "Maybe, possibly three hundred thousand. I never added it up."

Levy cross-examines Nancy's third husband. Eric acknowledges that he knew Nancy was a compulsive gambler when he met her—he himself was a recovering alcoholic.

"So, there's a similarity in demons?"

"Yes, that's true."

When he confronted her about the credit card scams in his name, or the IRS notice, had Nancy gotten violent?

No, Eric said.

"Did you ever see her get violent about anything?"

"Never."

"She was fun to be with?"

"Absolutely," Eric says, and his smile lights up his face. He looks down at Nancy at the counsel table. At that moment, Nancy knows that Eric loves her, no matter what.

Nancy bursts into tears at this. This is when she knows for sure, if she hasn't guessed it already, what she has really lost—not money, not even her freedom, but a lifetime of love with a man who cares for her still, for better or worse. It wasn't anything she could buy, or even steal, but something beyond any price.

# 31
# DOCTOR, DOCTOR

The next day, the government calls on the doctors. First up is Craig Haber, who cared for both Mary and Jack. Kay asks the questions. He saw Jack Watkins in November of 1995, Haber says, referring to his files. He weighed Jack—128 pounds. Then, in March of 1996, he received a telephone call from Jack's "girlfriend," reporting that Jack had been acting erratically. Haber thought then that Jack might be having some sort of cerebral incident, possibly a stroke. He wanted Jack to come in for an examination as soon as possible. Three days later, Jack was given a brain scan. His brain looked completely normal. Then, a month later, the "girlfriend" called to tell him that Jack had been admitted to Howard County General Hospital with dizziness. That was the last he ever heard of Jack Watkins, Haber tells the jury. He doesn't explain why he never called the hospital to find out what was then going on with Jack.

Haber's medical records on Jack are admitted as an exhibit—they seem to show that Jack's weight has generally been around 130 pounds for over two decades. In November of 1995, he weighed 128 pounds. Fine wants this before the jury—she wants the panel to recall that when he was found

in the trunk in May of 1996, he weighed only 111 pounds.
The implication she wants to leave is that Nancy has tried to
starve Jack to death, once he came to live with her at the
Ellicott City condo. What else could explain Jack's drastic
loss—almost 18 pounds, a little over 14 percent of his normal
weight?

When it's his turn, Saunders has Haber review all of
Jack's weight measurements, going back to 1977, and Haber
admits that in 1993, after the heart valve replacement, Jack's
weight had fallen to 118 pounds. Saunders wants to show the
jury that the apparent weight loss suffered by Jack isn't necessarily Nancy's doing.

"No other questions," Saunders says.

Fine counterattacks. "If his weight had dropped from one
hundred and thirty pounds to one hundred and eleven,
would that be a concern to you?"

"Yes," Haber says.


Fine now veers away, for the time being, from Jack's medical history. She wants to get to the meat of the predicates,
the bank cards, and it appears that the rest of the doctors,
from Howard County General Hospital, aren't available just
yet as witnesses to follow Haber.

She calls Margaret Stansbury, an expert on fraud from
one of the banks, and has her testify to the authenticity of
a variety of documents connected with the credit accounts
opened in Jack Watkins' name between 1994 and 1999. The
address on the accounts is always the same—Nancy's condo
in Ellicott City.

"Is the identity of the person applying for credit essential
for granting or denying it?" Fine asks.

"It's essential," the official says.

Saunders now zeroes in on one of the predicate accounts—a
bank credit card that Jack opened in 1983, years before meeting Nancy. The records show that the billing address for the
account was changed to Nancy's condo in late 1994. Eventu-

ally, the account was "charged off"—determined to be uncollectible—resulting in a loss of $14,000 to the bank. This was the "federal offense" alleged in Count 12 of the indictment—while Jack had opened the account in 1983, Nancy, according to the government, illegally seized it in late 1994 by fraudulently changing the billing address to keep Jack in the dark about what she was up to.

"Do you know who changed the mailing address?" Saunders asks.

"I do not," the fraud expert admits.

"Do you know if he authorized it?"

"I do not."

With this, Saunders is trying to lay the foundation for the defense—the notion that there's no proof that Jack himself hadn't opened all the credit accounts, besotted as he was by his "new gal." If the defense can establish that there's reasonable doubt as to who was responsible for the crucial credit cards, Nancy might yet be acquitted of the witness-tampering charge.

Fine now covers a lot of financial ground—credit reports, the two mortgage deals, the 1995 payoffs of the credit card balances that Nancy had rung up. Saunders tries to establish that the only evidence that Nancy, not Jack, made these financial arrangements was that Nancy's address was used. He establishes that Jack signed the mortgage papers, including the payoffs, and that to the finance people, he seemed perfectly coherent when he did so. He even endorsed the checks for the payoffs.

Now the other doctors arrive. First up is Nandakumar Vellanki. He was the physician on duty at Howard County General Hospital on April 11, 1996, when Nancy brought Jack in. Fine provides him with a copy of Jack's hospital record.

As far as he could tell at the time, Vellanki says, after looking over the hospital records, Jack appeared pretty normal. He seemed oriented as to where he was in time and place, and he was speaking coherently. The admitting form completed by the triage nurse, however, had Jack slurring his words with dizziness and a loss of balance. Jack had fallen down, the admitting form said. The contradiction between Vellanki's observation of Jack and the notes on the form suggest that it might have been Nancy who described Jack's symptoms to the admitting nurse, rather than Jack himself.

He asked Jack to say why he'd come to the hospital, Vellanki says. Jack said he'd gone to Atlantic City with Nancy, to celebrate their imminent marriage, and there he'd had too much to drink. Vellanki asked him how many drinks he'd had, and Jack estimated that he'd had about ten. From this, Vellanki tells the jury, he surmised that Jack might soon be suffering from delirium tremens, the "DTs," the result of the celebration binge.

Vellanki now says that according to the records, he had Jack admitted to the hospital as an alcoholic, and ordered him treated with intravenous fluids to rehydrate, vitamins, along with an appointment with a neurologist to see if there was any brain damage—"routine hospital management" for people with alcohol problems.

A few days later, satisfied that Jack was capable of taking care of himself, Vellanki prepared to release him from the hospital.

Fine directs Vellanki to a paper in Jack's file—one that Vellanki wrote back in 1996—and asks him to read it aloud. Vellanki reads it.

"'Discuss with the caretaker, Nancy, he could not, he cannot go home. He is too confused at times. Sometimes he is sharp. She wants him to go to a group home. He says that he, she's going to be his fiancée. In fact, it is not true. He's getting alcoholism, secondary to alcoholism and his confabulations. Hold discharge and obtain a psych consult.'"

Vellanki's notes are not exactly the best record of who said what to whom, or details of what was going on at the time—but then, he'd had no idea when he wrote them that they might later become a critical exhibit in a murder trial. And also, English was not Vellanki's native language. Sometimes subjects, tenses and verbs might get confused. Vellanki was qualified to look at the body, not necessarily the soul—or at least a soul that had grown up in a place like Richmond, Virginia, in the 1920s and 1930s. It was a cultural thing—it was hard for Vellanki to separate fiction from truth, because he'd never been there, at least in Richmond. He hadn't spent much of his life hearing the calliope, and dealing with grifters.

"You mentioned confabulation," Fine asks. "What was the basis of your determination that Mr. Watkins was confabulating?"

"Well, if the gentleman, he is telling all kind of stories, saying that he's getting married or he has all kind of future plans, and some are not true."

"And how do you know that they're not true?"

"If he is talking, which is— I had the experience, I cannot explain. Whatever he is talking, it does not make sense at the time."

"Okay. Let me ask you a question. You indicated in the first part of this note that you had a discussion with the caretaker, Nancy?"

"Yeah."

"And did you receive information from her with regard to whether or not she and Mr. Watkins were going to be married?"

"He says that he wants to get married, she is going to be his fiancée. In fact, when I heard this, this I remember, I said no. The other part, Nancy said, 'I'm not going to marry him.' So this is the discrepancy we had. That is one reason, also, is the confabulating. He is infatuating or confabulating, I don't know at the time. That is a reason for me to get a psych consult, too."

"And do you happen to know who did that psych consult?"

"Dr. Alix Rey."

Saunders cross-examines Vellanki.

"Doctor, you had a fair amount of, you had contact with Jack Watkins during the time period from the emergency room on through to his discharge?"

"Yes."

"Okay. Did he ever complain to you that Ms.—I believe she was then Ms. Sweitzer, I'll call her Nancy because that's the reference in the note—that Nancy, the caretaker, was stealing from him, controlling him, or any complaint of that nature?"

"No."

"The complaint, I believe, the conflict was, he said they were getting married and she said they weren't?"

"Yes. She said, he says it was his fiancée . . . That's the reason for the jubilation of the drinking on the day. But on the next couple of days when I was talking to them, and just clear to me that she says, 'I'm not going to marry him.'"

"Well, Doctor, my question is that, other than that, and I'll call it a complaint for what it's worth, other than that, there were no other statements that Nancy was doing something wrong to him?"

"No."

"Did he ever ask you to contact the police or authorities of any kind to make any statements or talk to them about problems?"

"No."

"Did he have the opportunity to do that if he wanted to?"

"Yes."

"I have no other questions."

Alix Rey testifies next. He's a psychiatrist, now retired. Fine gives Rey the hospital file. She directs him to his initial consultation notes. He reads them, then summarizes for the jury.

"It was a consultation done on a seventy-six-year-old male with histories of DT's, post-alcoholic binge, severe confabulation, and dementia, Korsakoff's syndrome, psychosis type. Recommendation to put him on Haldol."

"On what were you basing your determination that he was suffering from confabulation and dementia?" Fine asks.

"He was stating that he was going to marry Nancy Sweitzer. And when I did talk to her, she denied that it was the truth. And he was acting on it and celebrating his future marriage."

"You recommend point five milligrams of Haldol. What is Haldol?"

"Haldol is an antipsychotic. Point five milligrams of Haldol at bedtime and placement in a senior citizen house. Patient tends to wander and has been dangerous to himself without supervision. And transfer to psychiatry if proper setting not available."

"Okay. So your recommendation at this point was a placement in some sort of senior center?"

"Yes."

"And what were you basing your assessment that the patient tends to wander off and has been dangerous to himself?"

"I was basing it on information that I got from Nancy Sweitzer, that he invited people from the street into the house and he would take off at times and go drink."

"And other than your discussions with Mr. Watkins, was Ms. Sweitzer your only other source of information about him?"

"That is correct."

Fine draws Rey out further. It is his recollection that Jack went to Atlantic City by himself, and that he somehow managed to make it back to Maryland on his own. Rey admits that Jack seemed coherent, even pleasant in his interviews with him—it was just that Jack had the persistent delusion that he was going to marry Nancy. Nancy told him, Rey says, that she was Jack's "former landlord."

"*Former* landlord?" Fine doesn't want the jury to miss this one—the implication is that on April 16, 1996, the date on one of Rey's talks with Nancy, Nancy has already, in her mind at least, gotten rid of Jack.

When it's his turn, Saunders gets Rey to acknowledge that he talked to Jack and Nancy separately, that she was never in the room whenever he talked to Jack.

"Okay," Saunders says. "And how did he describe what he experienced?"

"He didn't describe a lot of what he experienced. It's basically what was written: that he had felt dizzy, that he knows that he had to have the DT's, and that he had a problem with alcohol. He was in AA. He didn't give an elaborate description of what happened to him."

"He said he had been in AA?"

"Yes."

"Okay. Now, did you have several interactions with him over the course of his stay, that is one-on-one, sitting down, just with him?"

"Yes."

"Did he ever say to you, I need some help to contact the police or authorities?"

"No."

"Did he ever say that Nancy was spending money without his permission?"

"No."

"Did he ever say that Nancy was compromising any of his credit?"

"No."

# 32
# NORMAL

Now Fine has two final witnesses, Social Security investigator Sean Stephenson, and the social worker from the hospital. It's Stephenson who has assembled all the account information on Nancy's "scheme." He's prepared a spreadsheet that lists the twenty-six credit accounts opened in Jack's name. Between December of 1983 and July of 1992, Jack had only five credit accounts, all of them with minimal balances.

Then, from November of 1994, all the way to January of 2000, twenty-one more accounts were opened in Jack's name, including two after he was dead. Some of the accounts were paid off with the proceeds of the August 1995 mortgage, but many of the rest were charged off by the banks as uncollectible—at least $30,000 worth. This didn't include the $44,000 ripped out of the house during the August mortgage grift, or the unpaid balance on the BMW lease, over $22,000 by the time the car was recovered in 1998.

Fine takes Stephenson through a plethora of documents—Social Security checks for Jack, endorsed by "Jack Watkins" and Nancy after his death, an extract of all the Social Security payments that had been made to Jack since 1996, New York Life insurance annuity checks, BMW paperwork, his spreadsheet on the twenty-six credit accounts, documents on the accounts themselves—all very tedious, but essential to document the Jack Watkins portion of Nancy's "scheme." This takes most of the rest of the afternoon, and another hour the following morning, March 15, 2009. At one point, Fine cues up the videotape of the surveillance of Nancy, driving into the Ellicott City post office parking lot on February 4, 2003, entering the post office, then exiting a few minutes later, her baseball cap pulled low over her distinctive blond hair.

She turns her witness Stephenson over to the defense for cross-examination.

Saunders quickly zeroes in on the weak link in the government's case against Nancy, the five predicate credit card bank fraud counts.

"Who applied for the credit card?"

"We do not have the application," Stephenson says.

For each four of the first five predicate cards, Saunders asks the same question, and gets the same response. The government, Stephenson admits, doesn't have the actual applications. It's impossible to say *who* applied for the credit from the crucial banks. On Count 12, in which Nancy was charged with fraudulently changing the mailing address to one of Jack's pre-existing accounts, Saunders asks Stephenson if the government had ever recovered the original request for an address change.

No, Stephenson admits.

"So in all this material that you accumulated, through searches and seizures and subpoenas, you didn't find *anything* that shows that Nancy Siegel, Nancy Sweitzer, was the person who initiated these?"

That's true, Stephenson confirms.

"There was never a concession by Ms. Siegel that she murdered Jack Watkins?"

"No, sir, there was not."

Saunders tells Davis he's finished with Stephenson.

Fine wants to plug these possible holes in her case. She asks Stephenson more questions on redirect examination.

The government's investigation was thorough, was it not? she asks.

"We issued hundreds of subpoenas for all kinds of records," Stephenson says. "The retention period for a lot of these records had expired and a lot of these records were destroyed." Fine's point is that it isn't that the records never existed, it's only because Nancy has been so successful in her "scheme" that time has erased some of her tracks. The records might have been destroyed, Fine's point is, but that doesn't mean they never existed.

Fine calls one last witness, Julia Lubis, the social worker who met with Jack and Nancy in April of 1996, when Jack had become so agitated upon learning Nancy was trying to place him in a group home. Jack insisted that he and Nancy were going to be married, Nancy had denied it, and shortly thereafter, Jack was placed under psychiatric observation. No one at the hospital had believed him at the time.

"I want to go back to Howard County General [Exhibit] Ninety-four, the second note that you wrote," Fine tells Lubis, referring again to the Howard County General Hospital records of their treatment of Jack in April of 1996. "This is a note where you discussed helping Ms. Sweitzer tell Mr. Watkins that he was going to a group home. I think you said that the patient [Jack] became upset and agitated, is that right?"

"Right."

"And that, based upon his response and Ms. Sweitzer's statements, he appeared delusional?"

"Right."

"If this patient had indeed been told for months or for years that he was going to marry Nancy Sweitzer and had in the previous few days gone to Atlantic City with her to celebrate that marriage, how would you characterize his reaction to what he was told?"

"Normal," Lubis says.

"Thank you," Fine says. "I have nothing further of this witness."

Saunders asks Lubis the same question he's posed to Doctors Vellanki and Rey, before.

"Did he ever complain to you that Nancy Sweitzer was using his credit, stealing from him, or in any way defrauding him?"

"I don't recall. And it wasn't in the documents. So I don't know."

"Well, let me phrase it this way. If he made those statements, would you have recorded them?"

"Yes, I would have."

"Right. And, had he made those statements, would you have referred it to some authorities in the hospital to take further action?"

"Yes."

"And you didn't do that?"

"Right."

"I have no other questions, Your Honor," Saunders says. He's trying to show that even up to a month before he died, while in the hospital, Jack *still* wasn't complaining about Nancy, eighteen months after he'd first met her. If he'd thought Nancy was trying to cook him, why hadn't he told Lubis, the hospital's social worker?

And if not—if Jack *hadn't* told Lubis in April of 1996 that Nancy was abusing him and his house and finances—how in the world could Nancy have had any "intent" to prevent Jack from informing on her then, at least in April, as to her supposed "federal crimes," which, according the government's theory, had by then already been perpetrated—the supposed bogus credit card applications?

The only way that could make any sense was if Jack hadn't known about the credit cards, and even Stephenson's just-completed testimony seemed to indicate that Jack knew all about the credit cards—he'd signed off on the payoffs after the August 1995 mortgage, hadn't he? It was a major contradiction in the government's case against Nancy. But Fine was like Potter Stewart—she knew bad stuff when she saw it. There were still two questions, though: what exactly was the bad stuff, and more important, how to prove it?

If Jack, in the hospital in April of 1996—after having been seemingly thrown over by his "new gal," meaning Nancy's shocking, to Jack, collaboration with Lubis that he should go to a "group home"—*still* had not complained to the hospital people, or the police, or his step-daughters, or his sister, or Ralph Hodge or anyone in the "breakfast club," of Nancy's supposed depredations (and there wasn't a shred of evidence that he had), where was the proof of Nancy's intent to tamper with a federal witness? Why, in April of 1996, almost eighteen months after Nancy had tried to sell Jack the crypt, after taking him to the hospital on April 11, where he could have easily exposed her, would she suddenly decide, a month later, to strangle him? On paper, it made very little sense. On the other hand, it was possibly typical of Nancy—more seat-of-the-pants decision-making, more gambling, yet more evidence of poor impulse control so often associated with bi-polar disorder.

All of this begged another question, something missing from the evidentiary equation. What, if anything, happened between Jack and Nancy between April and May of 1996 that caused Nancy to decide to get rid of Jack? In April, she was concerned about his health—she'd taken him to the hospital, and eventually agreed to take him back. Why? She could easily have walked away from him at that point. But by May, if the government was correct, she'd decided he had to go. This was the reality, not necessarily what's probative in a court of law.

The facts seem to show, Saunders and Levy are thinking, that such an intent by Nancy never existed. No intent, no tampering. In other words, no harm, no foul. They hope the jury understands what they're trying to say. It's subtle, but still legally real: to Saunders and Levy, the evidence seems to say that Jack allowed Nancy to do what she did, with his credit—if indeed, he hadn't helped her do it, for whatever reason.

The government asks no more questions of Lubis, and then rests its case.

# 33
# RULE 29

With the government case complete, the defense now moves to accomplish by a new motion what it failed to achieve with the partial plea offer some years before. Realizing that the Social Security theft counts and the post-death fraud counts can't be defeated—Nancy had been willing to admit them in 2007—they've gone straight for the throat of the case, the witness-tampering-by-murder charge, Count 22, and the five predicate "federal offenses" Jack theoretically could have reported to law enforcement, the bank card frauds, Counts 8 through 12. Without Nancy's conviction on the frauds that allegedly occurred while he was still alive, Jack can't be deemed a possible witness of "federal offenses." No federal offenses, no witness-tampering. They want the judge to acquit Nancy of these core charges under a federal rule of criminal procedure, Rule 29, on the grounds that the evidence is insufficient to sustain a conviction on those six counts. It's like asking the judge to dismiss the guts of the indictment for failure to prove the required facts beyond a reasonable doubt. This discussion, of course, is conducted out of the presence of the jury.

The government in its just-rested case failed to prove any

of the five predicate frauds, Saunders tells Davis. There is simply no way to show who had opened or altered the five critical, pre-death credit accounts—it *could* have been Jack himself, trying to woo Nancy. And if Jack indeed had opened or altered the five accounts, he wouldn't have been a witness subject to "tampering," because there was then no "federal offense"—no bank fraud. Bankruptcy, maybe, for Jack, but not fraud. Therefore, Judge Davis should find Nancy not guilty on Counts 8 through 12, and 22, even before the case is given to the jury. It is technical, but it is also real, under the law.

"Your Honor will note that, in . . . the facts put out by the government, according to their theory of the case, Ms. Siegel presented herself to Jack Watkins as a paramour, fiancée, however you want to phrase it, a romantic relationship, and as a result took advantage of him, obtained information, et cetera, and . . . resulting in him turning over assets, money, et cetera. What we know through the facts is that clearly is where they have gone with that.

"Now, at best, the government has shown that, *if*, in fact, those facts are true . . . Ms. Siegel defrauded Jack Watkins. That is, you know, a finagled story of an older man being infatuated with a younger woman and making a fool of himself, spending money on her freely. People described him as happy, delighted at the idea that he had this younger woman who cared for him, wanted him, and with whom he'd have an ongoing relationship as he aged." That was all the government had proved, Saunders says—that Nancy had taken Jack for a ride.

"And so, at best, what we have is, Ms. Siegel pretending that she actually cared for him in that way, and would stay with him as he aged. And he spent money that a prudent man should not have spent on her."

But even if what people said about Nancy and Jack was true, Saunders continues, it wasn't a "federal offense" subject to the witness-tampering statute. It might have been a con, a grift, a scam, but lying to someone about intending to marry them wasn't a federal offense, and probably not even a crime.

The government had attempted to plug this critical gap in their evidence by using all the "prior bad acts" to make the inference that, because she'd done it before, she was the person who applied for or altered the five predicate frauds, Sanders argues.

"That is, her prior conduct with her husbands, et cetera, of acquiring information without their knowledge and opening the accounts. That's not *proof* of what she did with Jack Watkins. It's merely . . . an *m.o.*, so that [unless] she denies she has any ability or knowledge of how to do these things, it's not substantively available to the jury . . . [it's] not available to the government to say, *Because she did this in the past, we* know *she obtained Jack Watkins's information and opened these accounts without his knowledge or permission.*" A *modus operandi* is far short of proving, legally, that she had done the same thing with Jack, Saunders says. Unless Nancy took the stand to deny she'd ever done anything like that, the government couldn't use her past against her. [Although it already had, thanks to the fourth Circuit Court of Appeals.]

"In fact, we don't even know if she opened them or Jack Watkins did. We only know that on dates after she met him, the accounts were opened—period—in his name." All the government had offered, Saunders tells Davis, was the "propensity evidence"—she'd done it before, so she had probably done it again with Jack.

Here it is again, all the old 404(b) controversy, the "surplusage." The defense is essentially inviting Judge Davis to stick his tongue out at the Fourth Circuit Court of Appeals, and say, *I'm right, you're still wrong.*

Davis invites Fine to respond to Saunders.

"Your Honor, we believe that in this case . . . there's more than sufficient evidence to establish that, in fact, Ms.

Sweitzer, Ms. Siegel, opened those accounts and that she did so without Mr. Watkins' knowledge," Fine says. "And I don't believe that we can ignore, and I don't believe that the Fourth Circuit has *instructed* us to ignore, the 404(b) evidence on that, because it goes directly to *modus operandi*, in the way in which she has defrauded each and every one of the husbands and her children in the same fashion and manner."

Fine lays a slight emphasis on the words "Fourth Circuit" in order to remind Davis that they've been there, done that. The use of *modus operandi* as evidence, she now claims, has been legitimized by the higher court's decision. So has the use of *m.o.* to prove "identity" of the perpetrator—if the *m.o.* has been used again and again, that tends to show who did it.

"Your Honor," she continues, "it seems to me that that is *exactly* appropriate [evidence], from which to draw an inference, particularly in a case where this victim has been killed, has been murdered, and is not available to testify as to whether or not those accounts were opened by Ms. Siegel."

(Every time the defense has raised the 404(b) rule, Fine has been quick to wave the bloody shirt—to point to the corpse of Jack in the trunk. She wants to keep Davis focused on the reality, not the vagaries of the law. Perhaps she has in mind Davis' ambitions for a higher court. By this point in the trial of Nancy Siegel, all of the players know that Davis is on the fast track to the Fourth Circuit Court of Appeals. If he acquits a woman for murdering a senior citizen, a veteran of World War II, on technical grounds, it won't play well with the U.S. Senate, which will have to confirm Davis for the higher court. All's fair in love and litigation.)

Fine now strives to provide Davis a reason to rule in her favor.

"The absence of an application [for credit, the destroyed records] is not the issue . . . And the United States believes that the documentation that is reflected [in Stephenson's and others' testimony], the documentation that reflects that these accounts weren't going to Mr. Watkins, [proves] they were going to Ms. Sweitzer's [benefit]. The telephone number on these accounts which would be called by creditors to alert, and could alert, Mr. Watkins, that an account had been opened [in his name], they weren't Mr. Watkins' telephone numbers, they were Ms. Sweitzer's at the time, now Ms. Siegel's telephone number.

"It seems to me, Your Honor," Fine continues, "that there is literally a *mountain* of evidence that reflects that these accounts were opened without Mr. Watkins' knowledge and consent."

"Okay," Davis says. "Well, I certainly now understand far better than I did before why the government was so anxious to make this a twenty-year scheme. Mr. Saunders, isn't Ms. Fine right, that Judge Traxler has already decided this issue for me?"

Saunders says she isn't—she's wrong, he says.

"Tell me why."

Saunders fumbles a bit for his argument. After a false start, he tells Davis the appellate court didn't address the issue of the *lack* of evidence, the missing proof of who applied for the credit, only Nancy's prior "tendency to scheme." Identity of who opened the pre-death credit accounts wasn't the issue in the higher court. But Davis is skeptical.

"And the Fourth Circuit has said [because] she did it to three [sic] prior husbands, the government's entitled to argue to the jury [that] because she did it to three prior husbands, she probably did it to Mr. Watkins," Davis tells Saunders. Well, of course, Nancy had only *two* prior husbands before meeting Jack—Eric Siegel being post Jack—but Davis has made his point. The higher court recognized Nancy's *m.o.* as an indicium of her identity. It was, in the higher court's appreciation, indicative of a "scheme." If she'd done it to Charles, and she'd done it to Ted, and she'd later done it to Eric, she probably did it to Jack.

"Well, you know, 'probably' is not the legal standard," Saunders says.

"Well, yeah. Of course." The standard, of course, is "beyond a reasonable doubt," not "probably."

"And *if* the Fourth Circuit said that she [Fine] could argue 'probably,'" Saunders continues, "you know, I can't believe they would say quite that. But they *did* say [it could] come in as 404(b), but 404(b) is limited. And you've repeatedly told them [the government], *You're hearing this evidence,* [but] *you cannot use it to convict her.* It's [for a] limited purpose." The government wanted to use the inference, not hard proof, Saunders was saying. They shouldn't be allowed to do that. It was Levy's 404(b) argument all over again.

"But of course, I don't really believe that," Davis says. "I mean, let's be honest. That's why I made the tentative ruling that I did [in 2007], and that's why the government appealed it, and that's why Judge Traxler reversed me. The government and Judge Traxler believe that, but I don't believe it for one second. But, you know, I'm operating under the law as it's given to me." He might agree with Saunders, but he was reversed by the higher court, and that's just the way it was. That is what Davis is saying, now.

"We have to assume the jury will follow the law," Saunders says, perhaps now trying to induce Davis to tell the jury they can't draw any inferences from Nancy's "prior bad acts" as to who initiated the disputed credit cards, either she or Jack. The jury can decide the question for themselves, no matter what the higher court has said, Saunders implies. All Davis has to do is tell them what the 404(b) rules are, and if the jury adheres to the rules, it won't matter what the Fourth Circuit has ruled.

"It's clearly, well, it's clearly bad-act evidence intended to show that Ms. Siegel's a bad person and will defraud anybody any time she gets a chance," Davis says. He seems to be wavering in Saunders' direction.

Saunders tries to shove Davis over the line. He argues that the inference that Nancy would defraud "anybody any time she gets a chance" was refuted by the fact that Jack willingly signed over the proceeds of the August 1995 mortgage on his house to pay off Nancy's previous credit card debts, those she had rung up in his name. That was evidence that she had no intent to defraud the banks. Jack Watkins maybe, but not the banks. And even if Nancy scammed Jack, was that really fraud on the *bank*, rather than Jack? And if it was Jack who was defrauded, not the banks, where was there a "federal offense"?

Even if Nancy clipped Jack, Saunders says, there is still no way for the government to prove beyond a reasonable doubt that *Jack* didn't sign for the credit cards, and for the same reason he might have been wooing her—that he wanted Nancy to take care of him in his old age.

"But correct me on this," Davis says. "My understanding of the record, or at least one understanding of the record, would be that in November of 1994, when Mr. Watkins met Ms. Siegel, he didn't owe anybody anything."

"Absolutely."

"Essentially?" Davis asks.

"Absolutely," Saunders says.

"So it's passing strange," Davis responds, "for an argument to say that between November 1994 and—when was it, August of 1995?—Ms. Siegel, to use round numbers, runs up twenty-five thousand dollars, whatever it was, on his credit accounts, some of which, according to the government, he didn't even open himself, to say that now or in November of 1994 or at the closing, I guess, in April of 1996, for her to now take his equity out of the house and pay his bills, which she's run up, how's that in Mr. Watkins' interest?" Here Davis seems to have confused the sale of the house in April of 1996 with the first mortgage of August of 1995. Despite the misapprehension, he's only trying to cut to the chase—why would Jack agree to any of this?

"No. Very limited," Saunders admits.

"Okay."

"I've been very clear, Your Honor, that based on the government's evidence, Jack Watkins himself was defrauded."

"Right."

"Okay? He was promised he'd be married and taken care of, et cetera. Granted. And as a result, running up those bills, considering his income, was probably unconscionable. Okay. So I'm not going there."

"All right. Your point is the more narrow one," Davis says, "and I got it, and I was going to ask Ms. Fine about it, and I will ask Ms. Fine about it. Your point—let me state it and then you correct it. Your point is, and frankly, what I'm leaning towards is, this is a jury question [a matter of facts, not law], but your point, I think, is a very powerful one. How can you say beyond a reasonable doubt that what occurred in late 1994 and through early 1995, in respect to these accounts, now we're talking about Counts Eight through Eleven or Twelve?"

"Right."

"How can you say that that was without Mr. Watkins's permission?"

"Right."

"Or without his [permission], let alone his knowledge, when, in fact, in [August of 1995], as [was] . . . testified, he sat there in that closing and . . . [the] testimony was clear that he fully understood, and I think this is your point, he fully understood that these checks were being, going to be cut payable to these merchants jointly with him and that these accounts were going to be paid off as a result of that settlement. That's your point."

"Yes. And it is his equity that was being used to do that. Absolutely. He was fully cognizant of that."

"And there was no evidence that he was not fully cognizant."

"Right. And there's no evidence he complained that he didn't open the accounts or they weren't his."

"Whether he did or not, he didn't complain about them."

"Exactly."

"Right. So it's almost, again, not to venture too far afield, but it's almost like you're making a ratification argument. That whatever else may have happened between him and Ms. Siegel, whatever else Ms. Siegel did or didn't do, he effectively forgave her or ratified these accounts by paying them off?"

Saunders isn't sure he wants to go that far, but it's an intriguing idea—by paying the supposed fraudulent cards off in August of 1995, Jack was essentially adopting them as his own debts—authorizing them. No harm, no foul. Nancy might have defrauded Jack by lying about her promise to marry him, but she hadn't intended to defraud any *banks*, just Jack. No federal offense, no witness-tampering. Hearing this, Fine begins to get agitated.

"Just hold your seat, Ms. Fine," Davis cautions.

Now Davis embarks on a discourse with Saunders as to how the predicate credit cards were used. Saunders explains: the sales slips from 1994–1995 have been destroyed. The applications have been destroyed. The notification of the change of address on one of the predicate cards has also been destroyed. So: where's the proof beyond a reasonable doubt that Jack didn't use the cards himself, to buy pretty things for his "new gal"? That's Saunders' story, and he's sticking to it.

Soon Davis and Saunders are discussing whether the billing statements might have encompassed "men things" or "women things" as purchases. The issue is—who might have used the credit cards back in 1994–1996, before Jack died? There's no evidence of who bought anything—it's all been destroyed, so many years after the fact. Saunders argues that there is no evidence that Jack hadn't been with Nancy when some of the purchases were made, back in November of 1994 to May of 1996. There is no proof—that's the defense mantra.

Davis asks: "Why can't the jury infer that if she signed his accounts or she opened an account after he was dead that, in light of the Fourth Circuit's ruling, that that's probative evidence that she did it *before* he died?" Here was the rubber hitting the road again. This is what the government's case was all about.

"Well, what you have is evidence clearly that Jack Watkins was willing to spend extraordinary amounts of money on her, witness the BMW," Saunders says. "We have that. I mean, it's clear that he was aware that he was spending money an extravagant way. And if he's going to give her a forty-two-thousand-dollar automobile, why not give her thirty thousand dollars' worth of credit to buy nice things for her, because she's going to be his bride?" It seems as reasonable as it is irrational—it all depends on what was going on in Jack's mind at the time, and, of course, he isn't around to testify.

Davis asks Saunders what the total credit Nancy had allegedly obtained from using Jack's name and identification was.

"Whatever it was. A lot of money," Saunders tells Davis. "You know, obviously, he was a man who was infatuated . . . with Ms. Siegel at the time, and he made what I could only characterize as extremely bad choices about that. But what we don't know is the extent to which he, as a willing 'victim,' during this time period before he died, allowed her, willingly, to spend his money."

In fact, Saunders adds, there is no evidence to prove just *when* Jack moved in with Nancy at her Ellicott City condo. Jack could have applied for new credit cards while living with Nancy in her condo months before the house was actually sold. *He* could have been the one who filled out the missing applications using Nancy's telephone number. There simply wasn't proof beyond a reasonable doubt.

(The fact was, the government had never established exactly *when* Jack had left the Sungold Road house—a fairly critical piece of evidence—and the evidence that was available was equivocal: Ralph Hodge later said he thought it was perhaps in late 1995, and Jack's neighbors remembered grass in the yard growing very high in the months before the house was sold in April of 1996, which suggests a prolonged absence, given Jack's dedication to his yard. So, in fact, it was possible that Jack had moved in with Nancy weeks or months before the house was actually sold. It was therefore entirely possible that Jack himself could have applied for some or many of the credit cards between their first encounter in November of 1994 and Jack's death in April of 1996. Where was the proof of who dunnit? So maybe Nancy's "scheme" wasn't quite so coherent, after all. Maybe, for a while, she really *did* intend to marry Jack. Well, this is what reasonable doubt is all about.)

Fine ripostes: the government's only intention in bringing forth to the jury all of Nancy's "prior bad acts," her "wrongs," was to prove identity—it was circumstantial evidence, powerful circumstantial evidence, that it had been Nancy who obtained the new credit card applications, and who had altered the billing address of the 1983 card.

Fine advances other arguments, but soon plays her trump card, the Fourth Circuit Court of Appeals decision.

"Your Honor, the bottom line is that the probative value of the 404(b) evidence has already been resolved in favor of it being allowed in, allowed in to prove exactly what the government is seeking to prove with it. The standard is not whether or not the court believes that a conviction is appropriate. It's whether there's any evidence from which a jury could convict. [Here Fine is echoing the Fourth Circuit's decision, and in a way, throwing it in Davis' face.]

"And, Your Honor," she continues, "I believe that there is plenty of evidence that the government has put forth in its case from which a jury could convict Ms. Siegel appropriately on any of these pre-death fraud counts."

They could have brought in evidence against Nancy that would have been truly prejudicial, banned by 404(b), Fine suggests—doubtless she's thinking of the Mayberrys, or the wallet thefts—but they had previously agreed, under Davis' pressure, not to do this.

"And as we've already discussed," she adds, "despite the fact that the Fourth Circuit said that we could bring in all sorts of other crimes' evidence, we've actually very, very narrowly limited that to specific purposes. Again, precisely because it's *not* the government's intent to convict by [prior] bad act."

They weren't interested in convicting Nancy by character or propensity evidence, she says, but only by the circumstantial likelihood that if Nancy had cooked Charles, Ted and later Eric, not to mention her daughters and others, it lent considerable weight to the proposition that she did the same with Jack.

"It's the government's intent to use the 404(b) evidence for exactly the purpose that the Fourth Circuit said it could be used for," Fine says. "Your Honor, the bottom line is that the probative value of the 404(b) evidence has already been resolved in favor of it being allowed in, allowed in to prove exactly what the government is seeking to prove with it." One more reminder of the Fourth Circuit panel's decision, the one Davis has already said he disagrees with, but which he has to abide by—maybe.

Davis thinks all this over. One part of him says that Saunders is right, another part agrees with Fine. What to do?

There is a break, while Davis reads the relevant cases cited by both sides in the defense motion for acquittal.

"Well, I am constrained to deny the motion," Davis says, after re-reading the Fourth Circuit's decision on Nancy's case, along with other cases each side has cited on the issue of "prior bad acts."

"It's not often that a district judge gets instructions from a court of appeals as to how to try the case," Davis notes, with a sense of chagrin, tinged with doubt about the wisdom of those he was soon to join. "And that's exactly what's happened here. I'm looking, of course, at the Fourth Circuit's opinion in this case."

Despite the defense objections to any inferences from the "prior bad acts," the appellate decision has tied his hands, Davis says. "I mean, it's pretty clear that the [appellate] court believes that all of this evidence is admissible and highly probative."

The fact that the grand jury in its superseding indictment of Nancy had included all the bad old stuff meant that he had to glue it to the five predicates, Davis says. The way the indictment was written made it "intrinsic" to the charges— "including"—even if the earlier and later "wrongs" were not themselves criminal charges. He still worried whether Nancy's grifts against Charles and Ted and Eric were really "wrongs," as defined by 404(b). They had to some extent allowed them to go on—was that really a "wrong"? But the higher court had a different idea than he did, Davis admits.

"And thus the grand jury's inclusion of all of the earlier thefts and defalcations and fraudulent acts of Ms. Siegel, going back to the early 1980s, according to the government, turned that evidence into intrinsic evidence, because it was one huge fifteen- or twenty-year scheme. And the Fourth Circuit absolutely embraced that. Absolutely embraced it," Davis says. The repetition says volumes about Davis' disagreement with his future colleagues.

He wasn't sure they were right, Davis says. But the way it works, he has to follow the decision of the court that was above him.

"What that means," he says, "others will have to say. But certainly, the entire arc of Ms. Siegel's life provides context to the criminal charges." Nancy's entire adult life showed a capacity, if not a propensity, if not a *modus operandi*, to cheat men who had fallen in love with her. Saunders and Levy argued that the past couldn't be used as evidence to prove something that happened later, and Davis had once agreed. But the big boys in Richmond overruled him.

"She engaged in that pattern when defrauding each of her husbands, her daughters, the Mayberrys . . . and, of course, Jack Watkins," Davis says. "Because the other crime evidence [Davis meant the wallet thefts and the mailbox raids, and Eric Siegel's losses], established a *modus operandi*, it *is* admissible under Rule 404(b) . . .

"The fact that she victimized Siegel, Mr. Siegel, and/or her [previous] husbands and her daughters, quote, 'tends to show the hold that gambling had on Siegel, and tends to refute any suggestion that Watkins knew about the accounts she opened in his name.'" Davis is quoting from the Fourth Circuit decision.

"Well, of course," Davis says, "he clearly knew about the accounts, because he clearly arranged to have them paid off." But the Fourth Circuit had apparently skipped over that part of the facts, Davis' comment suggests. The higher court seemed to have bought the government's argument, hook, line and sinker.

"And then they refer again to the context," Davis says. He means the "complete the story" part of the opinion. "So it seems to me that the Fourth Circuit has signaled very clearly that this evidence can be used in the way that the government apparently intends to use it. And I have to confess, frankly, I admit that even in my clipped instructions to the jury during the trial about the purpose of the 'other crimes' evidence, the record will reflect that I stumbled over it both times I gave it."

Davis is referring to his attempts to tell the jury what the limits were on considering evidence that he had long before decided was too prejudicial, but which the higher court had said he should still allow the jury to hear. He thinks the appellate court was wrong in reversing him, and he was therefore flummoxed in trying to explain the law to the jury in his opening orientation.

"And I have to be perfectly honest and say, I really didn't know what to say to the jury. And I'm not sure I know what to say to the jury *now*. I mean, I suppose I could say to the jury, 'The other crimes evidence was admitted to prove *modus operandi*.' I don't know what in the world the jury will think of that. So that's where we are." The whole idea of allowing a jury to use uncharged "wrongs" to decide other allegations bothers him a lot, Davis admits.

Levy wants to make one thing clear for the record—that the Fourth Circuit's opinion on the "prior bad acts" did not encompass the defense position that not all the evidence was addressed by the government. He wants to make sure that the trial record recognizes that the defense has established that there was no overt, incontrovertible evidence that Nancy was the person who had opened or altered the predicate accounts, and that the use of the "prior bad acts" of Nancy was objectionable at trial, and grounds for an appeal.

"I acknowledge that, Mr. Levy," Davis says. "And again, as I say, I agree with you, except I've been instructed otherwise, to do otherwise."

Levy won't let it go.

"We don't think you have to. But we understand," Levy says. He still believes that Davis could have granted the acquittal under Rule 29.

Now Saunders speaks up again.

"Your Honor," he says, "I want to advise the Court that our client has advised us that she will not testify. We have no witnesses. So therefore, I'll do it again in front of the jury. But I would rest our case, I would renew—"

But Nancy isn't so sure about this. She wants to speak her piece in front of the jury in the worst way. She's jogged Levy's elbow to stop Saunders before he goes too far.

"I am informed," Levy tells Davis, "that we are going to need to have another discussion with our client over the lunch hour."

"I take all that back," Saunders says.

By this point in the trial, Larry Kaskel and his wife, Mary Jeanne, have had numerous discussions with Nancy. Nancy very much wants to get on the witness stand to tell her side of the story. Saunders and Levy are not only against this, they're aghast. Everything they've tried to do to establish reasonable doubt about the predicate bank card charges will be at risk if Nancy testifies. But once a grifter, always a grifter—Nancy has confidence that she can convince the twelve tried and true that she did not kill Jack Watkins. It's her whole way of being—she's too little, too cute. All her life she's been able to talk her way out of anything. And right now, this is her whole life—what does she have to lose?

A lot, Saunders and Levy tell her. If she gets on the stand, Tamera Fine will slice her to pieces. Isn't it true she lied to Charles? To Ted? To Eric? To her own children? If you were lying then, why should we believe you aren't lying now? And this is only the beginning. Fine will eviscerate her, leave her credibility bleeding all over the courtroom floor. And why should she do it? There was at least an outside chance that the jury would understand what the defense is trying to say— that there is no proof beyond a reasonable doubt that it was Nancy who applied for the critical credit cards.

Larry and Mary Jeanne talk this over with Nancy. By now Nancy has accepted her fate—she's going to be in prison for most of the rest of her life, no matter how the trial comes out. She's made friends in prison, and she has rediscovered her religious roots. But she insists—she did not kill Jack Watkins. This is why she wants to testify. Larry and Mary Jeanne urge her not to do it—there's a chance, they say, that Nancy can be found not guilty of the big one, the witness-tampering charge, Count 22. On the other hand, if she takes the witness stand, she's almost sure to be convicted, even if she didn't do it. Once Fine goes to work on her, there won't be a single juror who will have any pity for her. Nancy says she'll think it over.

Over the noon recess, Saunders and Levy meet with Nancy. They know that they can't prevent Nancy from testifying if she insists, but they urge her not to do it: this is not the time to gamble. Nancy wavers, then agrees—she'll rely on the advice of her lawyers.

When the court reconvenes, Saunders tells Davis, "We have no witnesses. The defense rests."

With that, Davis denies the Rule 29 motion for acquittal. Now all that's left is for the judge to instruct the jury on how to apply the law, and closing arguments. These will begin the next day, and on them will hinge Nancy's fate. If Saunders and Levy can't convince the jury to look past Nancy's "prior bad acts," she will probably be sent to federal prison for the rest of her life.

# 34
# UNTIL DEATH
# DO THEY PART

Richard Kay gives the first installment of the government's closing argument. It's his job to "complete the story," show how all the parts fit together. Then, after the defense tries to poke holes in the case, it will be up to Fine to close them again.

"On August fifth, 2003, the defendant in this case walked into the post office in Ellicott City," he begins. "It was just another day, picking up another couple of checks in the mail. But those checks were not payable to her, but to Jack Watkins."

Almost as soon as she was confronted by Greg Locke and Jon Moeller, Kay says, Nancy began lying.

"She said Jack was fine, that he was living in Pennsylvania. She said she cashed his checks for him, then gave him the money. But none of that was true. She wasn't giving him the money. He wasn't fine. He wasn't living in Pennsylvania. He wasn't living at all."

When the investigators showed her a photograph of the trunk, Nancy burst into tears, Kay tells the jury. She admitted taking the trunk to Virginia, the one that had Jack's body in it. "She blamed it all on gambling, her addiction to gambling."

Her whole life, Kay continues, whenever Nancy got into trouble from defrauding people—her former husbands, or afterward, people she didn't even know—Nancy retreated to the defense that she was a compulsive gambler.

"What did she tell Investigator Locke? 'You don't know what gambling will do to you. It will cause you to do things.'"

One of those things was murder, Kay says.

He goes back to Jack. "He was a quiet gentleman. He owned his own house, free and clear. He had no debt, no debt at all. And then he met the defendant, and everything changed. The next thing we know, he's buying a BMW—a forty-five-thousand-dollar car, not for himself, but for Nancy Siegel. He quits 'the breakfast club.' His friends there tell him, *You're being an idiot, you're being stupid. She'll take you for everything you've got.*

"Jack was upset. He left. And that was the last time anyone there saw Jack Watkins. Jack said he was getting married.

"'Getting married,'" Kay reiterates, so the jury understands the basis for all of Jack's subsequent behavior, while undercutting Nancy's later statements to the doctors at the hospital, when she denied any marriage plans. This is evidence that Nancy has been a liar, and used her lies to cook Jack Watkins.

Kay turns to the disputed bank credit card accounts, only five of which have been charged by the government. As Davis had said years earlier, this was a case in which the government had a surfeit of evidence—almost too much. Limiting the case to only five of the credit cards was a way of making it manageable, for purposes of a trial.

"You saw that Jack had twenty-one new accounts opened after November of 1994, the month he met the defendant," Kay says. "How do we know it was the defendant who opened these accounts? Several ways—there are the billing statements sent to the defendant's apartment, for one thing." And

Jack's neighbors saw Nancy remove mail from Jack's mailbox. Nancy had done this before, with other victims, Kay points out. "It's the exact same pattern with Jack Watkins."

The defense would try to raise the possibility that Jack himself had given Nancy permission to open the accounts in his name. "But this is where common sense becomes important."

Jack had only a small income, Kay points out. "Does it make any sense that he would tell Nancy, *Go ahead and open fifteen or twenty credit cards in my name*? It doesn't make any sense."

Opening credit cards in other people's names—Nancy had done that with her first two husbands, and then again with Rick. "It's the same pattern," Kay says.

And there were also the BMW payments, then the mortgage of August 1995, followed by the refinancing of November 1995, in which Nancy got $20,000, supposedly to buy the condo she lived in, and would share with Jack, but never bought—in fact, the place was never for sale. All the money and benefits went to Nancy, all the responsibility for payments went to Jack—more payments in total than his entire monthly income. Kay could quote Ralph Hodge's observation at this point, if he could remember it: "You could talk Jack into anything."

It simply made no sense that Jack would have given Nancy permission to open credit card accounts that would leave him destitute, Kay tells the jury. And then there was the sale of the house, for peanuts, in April of 1996—$90,000, when the place was resold for $110,000 only a few months later. Of course, by then, Nancy had Jack's power-of-attorney. Kay's implication is that Nancy was desperate for cash—she'd sold out Jack's only real asset cheap.

Nancy, Kay continues, had taken the $3,800 remnant from the sale of the house, and they went to Atlantic City, to celebrate their imminent wedding, as Jack soon claimed. Within a few days after that, Jack wound up in the psych ward, labeled as "delusional" because he kept insisting he and Nancy were going to be married, and suffering from "Korsakoff's syndrome." Kay doesn't explain—probably because he doesn't know—that Korsakoff's syndrome is all too frequently over-diagnosed, especially in public health hospitals like Howard County General. It's an easy way to move elderly patients through the system, to make time to go on to the next crisis.

"She said he was confused, wandering off, drinking too much. She was trying to get him into a group home. 'The patient remained delusional throughout his stay in the hospital.' You heard the doctors read from their notes. Where did that come from? Nancy Siegel. He said they were going to be married. Nancy said they weren't, that he was making it up. Dr. Rey said he had dementia." But there was no delusion on Jack's part, Kay adds. He points to the gasoline company credit card obtained at the same time as the BMW, in which Nancy Sweitzer was listed as an authorized user—Jack's "fiancée."

And there was Dr. Haber, whose notes from his conversation with Nancy about Jack in March of 1996 referred to "Nancy Sweitzer" as Jack's "girlfriend." Haber wouldn't have used that term unless Nancy had described herself that way in the conversation.

What was Nancy's plan at the time? Kay asks. "She wanted to get him committed to an institution so she wouldn't have to take him home. She wanted to be rid of him." But the plan failed.

"Where did he go? He went back to her apartment. He had nowhere else to go." Nancy told Locke and Moeller that she'd tried to get Jack's sister Doris to take him in. But Doris told the investigators that Nancy had never suggested any such thing. She told them Nancy had told her tried to get his step-daughters to help. "But she never made those calls," Kay says.

And why? "Because she could not let Jack go to his sister, or his step-daughters. Because they would ask the same questions: 'What happened to your house, what happened to your money?' He would tell.

"This woman took everything he had. She couldn't let him go—he would tell. Remember, she was on probation for ten years. She had a suspended sentence of three years. She would go to jail. She couldn't let him go. And something else: she was starting a relationship with Eric Siegel. She couldn't start a relationship with Eric with Jack still there. She had to do something to get rid of him.

"She began to scheme out of whatever, out of maybe, desperation. She made a plan. She would starve him. She made a plan. Jack would die. Jack would disappear." Nancy had tried to get Haber to prescribe sedatives for Jack, but Haber wouldn't do it. So Nancy bought over-the-counter sleep aids, and cold medicine. The toxicology report showed that Jack had been taking large doses over a long period of time, Kay points out.

"Then the defendant starved Jack. Sedated, malnourished, he must have known he was in trouble. He tried to leave. 'I'm out of here.' That's what the defendant said Jack told her, when he tried to leave the house. That was when, she said, he fell down and injured his head. 'I got him back inside,' is what she said."

Then Jack died.

"Someone cut off the blood supply to his head," Kay tells the jury. "Until he stopped breathing. The L-shaped mark on his neck—that could have been made by a heeled shoe."

Now here it was, at last—"the complete story." Kay has filled in the last piece of the puzzle, and the image he's conjured for the jury is very ugly indeed. There, on the floor of Nancy's condo lies Jack, weak, emaciated, sedated, struggling to get up and leave, and Nancy, standing over him, with her foot on his neck, until death do they part.

# 35
# "IT WOULD BE UNJUST"

Levy gives the closing argument for the defense.

"Your job is really just beginning," he tells the jurors. Not an auspicious start for Levy—what, is he saying they haven't been working for two weeks so far, hearing all that testimony?

He begins with the "suprlusage," the "prior bad acts."

"In this case, there's been an awful lot of bad stuff about Nancy Siegel," he says. "It would be silly to pretend otherwise. There are a lot of things she should be condemned for. The government did a good job of proving Nancy Siegel a chronic thief. They did a lousy job of proving she's a murderer."

The judge gave them an instruction of application of the law, Levy continues, that they should not consider evidence of bad character in determining whether Nancy is guilty of the charged crimes. The natural human impulse is to conclude that if someone has done something wrong once, there's a good chance they have done it again. "You're not allowed to do that . . . it's perfectly logical, but prohibited to you as jurors."

The government has thrown up so much character

evidence, Levy continues, that it's possible that they might be confused as to what actually is charged in the case. All the stuff about Charles and Ted, Nancy's daughters, the other "wrongs," isn't charged in the case they have to decide. The government isn't using the "prior bad acts" to prove that Nancy was a thief, "but to show a pattern."

But what the case really comes down to, Levy says, are Counts 8 through 12, and 22, the witness-tampering count. And there is no way for the jury to know for sure that such a "pattern," if indeed it existed, applies to those critical counts. "I submit to you that the government is making you guess." Without proof that Nancy was the applicant on the five credit cards, that it hadn't been Jack instead, it is impossible for the government to prove beyond a reasonable doubt that Nancy intended to defraud the banks. Without the intent to defraud the banks, there could be no intent to tamper with a witness.

"The nature of the relationship between Jack Watkins and Nancy Siegel" is the key, Levy continues. "From time immemorial, lonely old men have fallen in love with young women and made fools of themselves. We can perhaps say that about Jack Watkins' relationship with Nancy Siegel. The fact that a young woman convinced an old man that she was in love with him, and he should spend money on her, is not a crime. It is not charged in this case."

There was no evidence presented that Jack was ever unhappy with Nancy, Levy continues. His friends and neighbors all said how happy he was to have Nancy in his life. "If he wanted to spend money on Nancy, no matter how bad an idea we think it is, it was his right."

The government had just argued that Jack didn't know about the credit cards opened in 1994 and 1995, Levy says. "But the evidence shows he did." The testimony showed that Jack had willingly signed the mortgage documents, that he'd known where the money was going—to pay off the credit card balances in August of 1995. Jack had gone with Nancy to pick out the BMW, so he certainly knew about that, and he'd signed the lease papers. "It wasn't smart," Levy says, "but it wasn't illegal. It wasn't a crime. It doesn't warrant a finding that she's guilty of other acts."

And there was more, Levy said: there was no evidence that Nancy ever tried to stop Jack from complaining about the credit cards—to his neighbors, to his friends, to the people at the hospital.

The government had proved Counts 1 through 7, the Social Security check thefts, beyond a reasonable doubt, Levy concedes. "They had evidence fourteen ways from Sunday on those—videotapes, documents, photographs." But these were all post-death crimes, ones that Jack could not have been a witness to.

So that should give the jurors some idea of what "beyond a reasonable doubt" looks like, Levy says.

"Compare the proof on the post-death charges to the proof on the pre-death charges," Levy tells the jury. "It's non-existent on Eight through Twelve, and Twenty-two. Ladies and gentlemen, there's no comparison."

On Counts 8 through 12, the government failed to prove that Nancy had committed the fraud of any bank. They failed to provide any evidence that it was Nancy who'd obtained the credit lines, not Jack.

"Really, ladies and gentlemen, this is where the rubber meets the road. You cannot throw the book at Nancy Siegel because she's a thief, and took advantage of a lonely old man."

In asking the jurors to infer that it was Nancy who'd opened the accounts, based on her supposed "pattern," the government was really asking them to speculate, Levy argues. "To say, 'it wouldn't surprise me if,' well, that's speculation . . . in a courtroom in the United States of America, you cannot convict a defendant on that sort of speculation."

If the jury looks hard at the government's case on Counts 8 through 12 and 22, he says, they will see that it falls short of proof beyond a reasonable doubt.

"Given how terrible they have portrayed Nancy Siegel,

it's surprising how little evidence they had . . . Take Count Twenty-two, the allegation of witness-tampering. There are really two aspects to that for you. First, you need to decide how Jack Watkins died. Then, if you conclude that the defendant killed him, you need to decide the next aspect: why?

"In federal court, that's only half of it. The government contends she did it, at least in part, to stop him from reporting the bank fraud in Counts Eight through Twelve."

But that is piling assumption atop assumption, Levy argues.

"There is, first, no evidence that Nancy Siegel killed him. Then, second, there is no evidence that she had a motive to stop him from reporting."

Kay's image of Nancy's shoe on Jack's neck—"It's out of whole cloth," Levy says. There was no firm evidence that anything like that had taken place. "The medical examiner couldn't tell with any specificity where that bruise had come from. If Dr. Fields couldn't, you can't either." In fact, Fields couldn't rule out death by hanging, Levy says.

"We don't really know the details of the death of Jack Watkins," Levy says. "All we know is what happened afterward. There are a number of inferences we can draw from the way his body was found. Did she have a desire to keep the Social Security checks coming? It wouldn't surprise me. Did she have a panic response? It wouldn't surprise me. But it is not evidence of murder."

There is evidence, however, that Nancy never had an intent to prevent Jack from "reporting a federal offense." First, she took Jack to see Dr. Haber for the brainscan on March 18, 1996. "If you're so desperate to keep someone from a cry for help, you would do what you could to prevent him from contacting other people, particularly people in authority, like doctors or social workers."

Then, the following month, Nancy took Jack to the hospital. "Far from trying to stop Jack Watkins from contacting the outside world, she takes him to the hospital. At the hospital for a whole week, he never once complained that he had been stolen from, victimized."

That alone should put the lie to the government's contention that Nancy had to kill Jack to prevent him from ratting her out. "You have to use your common sense," Levy says, echoing Kay.

"They have *beau coup* evidence of what happened after Jack Watkins died, but no evidence beyond a reasonable doubt of what happened *before* he died, or *how* he died. All you've got is a defendant who does foolish, shocking, frequently dishonest things. Nancy Siegel has, shall we say, a checkered past. But you can't say that because of that, she's got what's coming to her for Jack Watkins' death. It's a natural, human emotion to have. But it would be unjust."

# 36
# "TICK-TOCK"

Now it's Tamera Fine's turn for the final closing argument. She's lived with this case for more than five years. She knows all of it, every piece of it. Nothing Levy argued to the jury has caught her by surprise. She will try to sew up the case, and rebut all of Levy's attempts to raise reasonable doubt.

She zeroes in on the predicates, the five bank card frauds. After all that's happened over the past half-decade, she knows as well as Levy and Saunders that these are the linchpin of her case, the charges that must be sustained.

"The defense says that the evidence is consistent with the idea that those bank cards were known to, or even obtained by Jack Watkins," Fine tells the jury. "This is the 'Jack did it' defense. 'She did it with her own relatives, yes, but she didn't do it with Jack Watkins.'

"There are a lot of problems with that approach," Fine advises the jury. For one thing, she says, Nancy's "hijacking" of Jack's identity resulted in a false representation to the banks—the implication that the money would be repaid by Jack, not Nancy. And the banks would never have agreed to extend the credit to Jack if they had known that it was really Nancy who had applied, using Jack's identification.

When the defense argued that it was Jack who was defrauded, not the banks, they were trying to bamboozle the jurors, she suggested.

"The defendant took the *banks'* money, not Jack's money," she says. The fruits of the scam were enjoyed by Nancy, not Jack. Ergo, it was Nancy who had engineered the scam, the grift.

All the jury had to do was look at the "prior bad acts" evidence to know who did it, Fine says. "She was convicted of fraud four times in the year or so before she met Jack Watkins."

The argument over who actually applied for the credit cards is "a red herring," Fine says. "They're trying to distract you from the mountain of evidence that tells you who did it." All the argument about Jack's willingness to lease the BMW, about signing the mortgage, about paying off the credit card bills that had been rung up since Nancy met Jack, was just more obfuscation, defense dust in the eyes of the jurors. All the defense arguments about Jack's willingness to sign the August 1995 mortgage papers, the money from which was used to pay off credit card balances Nancy had rung up in Jack's name, didn't obscure the fact that Nancy was the one who had abused Jack's credit. The jury had to know that, based on Jack's credit history before his ill-fated meeting with Nancy in November of 1994.

"You don't get a do-over because you committed another fraud to pay off your old fraud," Fine tells the jury—the only difference between Nancy's fraud of Jack and her fraud of the banks was that the banks could afford to cover the losses. "But Jack Watkins was destitute." That made all the difference, Fine suggests. That's why Nancy had to kill him.

Jack's sudden poverty made him very likely to tell someone, sooner or later, what had happened to him—all about the "new gal." And when he did, once the authorities got involved, Nancy would go to jail for a long time. That's why she killed him—to shut him up, Fine argues.

"We would like it even more if we could call Jack Watkins as a witness," Fine says. "But of course, we can't." When Nancy concealed Jack's identity, she did it to cover up her crimes.

One of those crimes was murder—tampering with a witness, forbidden by federal law. And the evidence showed, Fine says, that Nancy did it with premeditation and malice aforethought: Jack had lost 18 pounds in the weeks before his death, based on Haber's records of his usual weight. By April 11, he weighed only 116, according to the hospital records. By the time he was dead, his body weighed only 111 pounds.

"Nancy Siegel was responsible for that," Fine argues. "She knew that man was starving to death in her bedroom."

And there is one more thing, Fine adds. She brings up the image of Nancy standing on the struggling Jack's neck. Not just momentarily, either. The medical examiner testified that it had taken at least two minutes for Jack to pass out, then more time for him to die.

"Two minutes or more, she put pressure on his neck," Fine argues. "One hundred twenty seconds. Tick-tock. Tick-tock. Think about that, and ask yourself if she didn't *intend* to kill him." Fine leaves the image burned in the jurors' minds— Nancy, all 105 pounds of her, standing with her hard-soled shoe across a gasping, struggling, emaciated 76-year-old man's throat, leaving the L-shaped mark on his neck, from the junction of sole and heel. In the picture, he weakly tries to push her foot off his neck. He can't do it. At the last seconds of his life, he realizes she's actually trying to kill him. In the next instant he grasps his fatal mistake—he'd fallen in love with a predator—someone he thought was a house cat, who later took off her mask to show she was really a leopard with very large claws and teeth. She was seriously going to kill him.

He begins to lose consciousness, his hands become even weaker, he can't get her shoe off his throat, she's glaring at him, he knows he's going to die. He also knows that she has taken him for a fool. And at the last instant before he can no longer think coherently, he remembers his friend Ralph— "She's going to take you for everything you've got," Ralph told him. But not even Jack thought that meant his very life. He tries to get her off him, but he can't do it.

But Nancy is stronger, younger than Jack is, and determined to kill him. A few minutes go by, and Jack stops breathing. It is all over, finally, for both Jack and Nancy.

It is a picture to die for, or maybe *of*, in a manner of speaking.

This is what the government has left in the minds of the jurors. It is very, very ugly, and it has nothing to do with any claim by Nancy that she was afflicted by compulsive gambling. There are no moral ambiguities when the government decides to go after someone. As the lawyers say, you don't mess with the G.

The arguments are over. It's late Thursday afternoon, March 12, 2009. Davis has dismissed the jury for the rest of the day. They are to return on Friday to begin their deliberations. Now, as Levy so un-adroitly suggested—however accurately—their hardest work is just about to begin.

That next day, of course, is Friday the Thirteenth. Is this an omen? If so, what could it mean? Is it bad luck for Nancy? Or the government? Or is it just another number on the calendar? Of course, no one really knows—it's like punching the button on a video poker machine. The numbers might have meaning, or maybe it's random—it depends on your particular illusion, or if you even have any. Those without illusions would say that anyone would be a fool to bet their life on triskaidekaphobia, fear of the number thirteen. Or even vice-versa—*not* to bet their life. It isn't "Incense and Peppermints," and it's not the "Fun, Fun, Fun" of the Beach Boys—any way you see it, or even hear it, it's still "She's Not There," where no one told them about her, the way she smiled.

Well, that was the ambiguity that made the 1960s and 1970s—Nancy's generation—what they were.

The jury comes to court that day and begins to deliberate. Larry Kaskel and his wife Mary Jeanne wait for word. So does Nancy in a nearby holding cell. Amanda and Jennifer are close by. Davis and the lawyers clean up several loose ends. Everyone waits. Late in the afternoon, the jury sends a note out. They're ready to break for the weekend. They want to come back on Monday morning and resume their deliberations. Davis lets them go.

On Monday, the jury returns. Again they shut themselves in the jury room. At one point they ask for a transcript of Levy's argument about the lack of specificity of Jack's asphyxiation. Davis doesn't give it to them—argument isn't evidence.

At quarter to 5 on Monday afternoon, the jury sends another note out—they have reached a unanimous verdict. Levy calls Larry and Mary Jeanne, as well as Amanda and Jennifer. About half an hour later, everyone is in the courtroom. The jury is brought in.

How say you, the jury?

Guilty. Guilty on nineteen of the twenty remaining counts, including tampering with a witness by way of second-degree murder. As for the second-degree murder, rather than first-degree, the jury concluded that Nancy must have strangled Jack on the spur of the moment, in a panic, rather than with premeditation. It's small comfort to Nancy, though—she's still looking at more than 30 years in prison, when it's time for Davis to sentence her. The jury has found Nancy not guilty on Count 12, one of the bank fraud counts.

As for Nancy, she has known almost from the start that this was going to happen. Once she'd seen the picture of the trunk—Amanda's one-time trunk—she had known. Still, she weeps. It's hard to fully accept what it really means—she'll be behind prison walls for the rest of her life. She will never again get to give another grandchild juice and graham crackers. She will never again be allowed to make Rick Siegel laugh the way she used to. She will never again be able to hold her own daughters in her arms—probably the only other human beings she's really loved. The upside: at least there are no video poker machines where's she's going.

# 37
# "YOU ARE A MURDERER"

A little over a month later, Nancy is back before Judge Davis to receive her sentence. According to her cousin Larry, she's feeling a little better. She's just glad it's all finally over, except for this part. She still insists that she didn't kill Jack. This may not be a case of simple denial for purposes of appeal, but in fact evidence of something much more complex going on in Nancy's mind. She may well have done it—the jury said she did—but simply can't *remember* doing it. Otherwise, at this point, why not say so? As Saunders has repeatedly argued, it isn't whether Nancy murdered anyone, but if she murdered someone who could be a witness against her— possibly Jack, but maybe not. That's what the real issue is.

So why doesn't Nancy now cough it up—tell what really happened to Jack Watkins? But she doesn't. Perhaps she can't, even if it would be something that would give her peace in the remaining years of her life. Perhaps she's erased the memory and replaced it with one she can live with. Sometimes it's better to live with an illusion than the reality. Sometimes, though, it's not. Certainly her old illusions of winning the big electronic pot have done her no good at all.

Jack himself would probably forgive her—he loved her

enough to not want her to torture herself with lies as to what really happened.

Nancy's sentence is strictly determined by a complicated formula involving the severity of the crimes, the amounts she stole, her previous criminal history, her age, and a wide variety of other factors, including her cooperation or lack of it with the government's investigation. When it's all added up, it comes out to be over 33 years. Nancy and her family have hopes that she will be incarcerated close to Maryland. At least then she might have some contact with Larry, Mary Jeanne, Amanda, Jennifer and Eric.

As the sentencing hearing unfolds, much of the argument has to do with the amount of restitution. In court, it's ridiculous—the chance that Nancy will ever see the light of day long enough to pay "restitution" to her victims is absurd. There is no way in this universe that Nancy will ever make enough money to pay off her victims. But the number counts in the sentencing matrix—the higher the amount of court-ordered "restitution," the more months or years behind bars. As far as Fine can calculate—even she admits the numbers are extremely hard to figure out—Nancy had bilked between $400,000 and $1 million in her career as a grifter. This would put Nancy into the higher end of the determinate sentencing range. With something like this in her prison jacket, Nancy would probably have to live to be 102 before she ever got out of prison. In fact, the government wants Davis to sentence her to life in prison.

Saunders thinks this is extreme. He and Fine fence over the way the government has tried to calculate its recommendation for Nancy's sentence. Fine asserts that Jack, being elderly, was especially vulnerable. That requires the court to find an "enhancement" on the sentence—more months, if not years. Saunders disagrees—Jack wasn't any more "vulnerable" than anyone else. The two lawyers go on sparring, splitting legal hairs to the very end. Some of us may cavil about all this—like Shakespeare, we say, first, let's kill all the lawyers. But it's not so simple. Without them, we have no way of knowing what's in, or what's out of bounds. The law is something that really lives—it evolves. This is what we pay them for—trying to define and defend the Constitution. It's really the living, beating heart of American freedom.

After Fine concludes her argument for an enhanced sentence, it's Saunders' turn to argue for mitigation—a lesser sentence. He begins by saying that over the years, he's come to know Nancy well.

"Nothing that I say, obviously, could take away from the seriousness of this, the grief of the family, just the string of frauds and pain, et cetera, that she has brought to her loved ones, people around her, and people she's exploited. But she's a much more complex person than that, because she's been painted in strictly black and white, evil or good terms. And she's much more complex."

Saunders sketches in some of Nancy's background, beginning with the fact that her mother left her in the care of her father when she was very small.

"Her mother chose not to have her. Her mother chose her sister and raised her. She was abandoned by her mother from the very outset. Her father, who she loved and adored, in order to work, had to leave her with a relative who ran a bar, who had alcohol problems, . . . [she] may have done the best . . . But it was a dysfunctional situation. And she grew up her entire life, knowing that her mother didn't want her.

"She was charming, pretty, witty. All of the cousins and family that we interviewed describe her as bubbly, charming, always doing things for people, always concerned with them.

"She married Charles Kucharski. And for seventeen years, before their marriage broke up, she lived a relatively normal life. She gave birth to two children. She raised them, cared for them, loved them. And then something happened and her life spiraled downward. She started stealing. I can't put it any other way. She developed an addiction, which in no way justifies what she did. But as we all know, addictions are very powerful things.

"And to a certain extent, it plays out like a traditional tragedy. The main character, who has some very positive things and various powerful strengths, but an underlying flaw which, once activated or exploded, exploited, brings death and havoc to those around him. And something in her was broken.

"Now, I can say this, too, because what you see is, there are probably close to fifteen members of Ms. Siegel's family and friends present here in court. And to each of them, the person who did this is not the person they knew. It's baffling, confusing, and very painful."

Saunders says it was remarkable that Nancy, despite her propensity for grifting, still managed to raise "two wonderful children, young adults who are not involved in crime, not involved in theft, not involved in this criminal world that she put herself into. I don't know how she did it. I rarely meet someone with this kind of criminal history who has not poisoned the well of her own family. She raised two children to be decent, middle-class, law-abiding, you know, members of our society, raising families, who find what she did as abhorrent as any of us.

"Which leads to that utterly confusing thing where you look at Ms. Siegel and say, *Who are you?* Like a Dr. Jekyll and Mr. Hyde. How can you, on one hand, raise your children in such a positive way and give them a rich, emotional life, and then turn around and exploit individuals to have money so you can gamble? Because that was her addiction, gambling.

"I also think it's more than that, too. It was things. And forgive me for the pop psychology, but going back to the void in her life about never knowing why her mother didn't love her enough to want her, to want to spend time with her, to raise her, care for her, hold her. And she's been filling that with her compulsion to gamble, her compulsion to buy, sort of decorating her life, with the interior somewhat hollow.

"What I wanted to do today is to tell the Court that she's more complex than that one-sided picture of what she is convicted of here, and the history that you've heard of her long trail of victims. I don't know why she did it. She's been treated for her compulsive gambling, but she's always returned to it. And like every other addict who fails to go with the program, [to] reach down into themselves and stop, she now faces the full reality of what she's done.

"I ask Your Honor to, in making a final judgment, just to be aware that she is more complex than what you've heard about, the terrible actions that she's been convicted of here in this court. She's a multifaceted individual who's given love, who's got a niece who considers her a second mother, two children, despite their sense of shock at what their mother did, still love her, still willing to see her, still want their children to know her as his grandmother.

"I would also point out, Your Honor, that the father that she had left was essentially murdered when she was sixteen. He was beaten very badly in a mugging and died sometime shortly after that. And then at sixteen she went to the family that had been caring for her while her father worked, and they finished raising her until she left home. So her life has been full of those losses, which she's tried to fill in the wrong ways. And I would ask Your Honor, to whatever degree, despite the severity of what she's done, that you be compassionate in forming an appropriate sentence under all the circumstances."

Davis thanks Saunders for his presentation, then advises Nancy that she has the right to make a statement on her own behalf. Nancy indicates that she does want to speak. She has a little trouble getting to her feet. Her health is still somewhat fragile. She makes it, though, and Saunders puts the microphone in front of her.

"Your Honor, first, I would like to say for the pain, for any pain that I've ever caused, my actions have ever caused, it was never my intention to ever, ever hurt anyone in my life, ever. I know that some of my actions have been despicable, and I made many mistakes and have tons of regrets in the last years. I know I've been convicted of murder and I have to accept that, for right now. If the prosecution's theory were true, nothing could have made me kill, take another human being's life. I would have taken my own, I would have killed myself before I'd kill someone else." Nancy is still denying that she killed Jack.

"And I want to apologize to my beautiful daughters that I love so much, more than life, for causing disgrace," she continues, now weeping. She pauses to try to get control of herself, then goes on.

"And I stand before you totally ashamed of a lot of my actions, and totally disgraced and humiliated. And I know that your mind's already made up, and I know I can't change it. And I wish today, because there is a victim here—I did care for Jack. I loved him. I loved him as a fellow human being and as a person. And not a day has gone by in the thirteen years that I've not thought and been saddened that he died, and I have to live with that forever.

"And just to my family, to anyone I've not mentioned in this trial that I've hurt, I've already asked for forgiveness, and I know that—that's all, Your Honor. I— The many in my family that have supported me, that know me, I'm grateful. And for my actions, the throes of addiction, gambling addiction is not an excuse. I have to take and I do take responsibility, of course. That's all, Your Honor."

"You may be seated," Davis tells her. Nancy sits. "You are convicted of murder, Ms. Siegel," Davis goes on. "You're convicted of murder by a jury that was fair, followed the court's instructions, listened to the evidence, evaluated the evidence as it was tested by your excellent counsel. You are a murderer."

Davis goes on to congratulate all the people who worked to solve Jack's murder. "I would be remiss if I did not express the court's regard for the work done by the Virginia authorities. I know that it was a real effort all around. But I hope that their work, diligent work, shown by their determination to identify Mr. Watkins, is some solace to his remaining family members.

"The government has asked the court to give you a life sentence, Ms. Siegel, not at all without justification. The court will not sentence you to life, but it's the court's expectation that, given your age, that it is highly unlikely that you will come back to the community. And there is justice in that."

Davis then hands down the sentence—10 years for the theft of the Social Security checks; 30 years for all the bank, mail and wire frauds, 15 years for the identity thefts, and 33 years, 4 months on the witness-tampering-by-way-of-murder count. All the sentences are to be served concurrently, Davis says, and she would be credited with the time she's already spent in jail from August of 2003—altogether, so far, more than 6 years. That makes for a total prison term to come of 27 years. Nancy will probably have to serve at least two-thirds of that before she can be released. That would make her about 80 years old before seeing the light of day once more. She is appealing her conviction.

# AFTERWORD

So, sun is set, day is done. An honor guard of seven dress-uniformed U.S. Army soldiers with their ceremonial M-1 Garand rifles, salutes from some distance away on the grass, their faces utterly stoic, their formation perfectly aligned as they present arms. In the distance behind them, one can see the Washington Monument, a stone obelisk 555 feet, $5\frac{1}{8}$ of an inch tall, dominating the nation's capital. Overhead, the roar of passenger jets accelerating on takeoff from nearby Ronald Reagan Washington International Airport is ever-present, the engines an echo of conflicts past, present and future.

We've come to Arlington National Cemetery today, Friday, August 14, 2009, to bury Jack Watkins. Or what's left of him: Jack-in-the-box is now reduced to a small square container, covered in red velvet. After all has been done and said—to him, and later, about him—Jack has gotten his wish: at least they won't throw dirt over his face. Instead, the last mortal remains of Jack are to be interred in an above-ground crypt at Arlington National Cemetery.

The riflemen wait in the distance, rigidly at attention, arms in salute. Seven other soldiers, all in full dress blue uniforms of the United States Army, remove the small urn from the vehicle that has transported it to the cemetery's columbarium. In perfect, measured step, they carry it to the place of honor. The rest of us follow: Cheryl, Anita, and Connie, Tamera Fine, Bobbie Ochsman, Greg Locke, Mark Carr, Sean Stephenson, other family members and friends, altogether more than two dozen people. The family takes seats in two rows in front of the bier where the small, red-covered urn has been placed; the rest of us stand to the rear. The flag detail, on crisp commands from a sergeant, unfolds an American flag over the urn. Each movement is sharp, precise, intense—the large flag is unfolded, and covers the bier, with the small, pathetic box beneath it. Every soldier does his duty. This is the most solemn obligation they have—the ceremonial end of a fellow soldier's life.

The Army chaplain, a captain, who has only just learned the details of Jack Watkins' sad ending, sums up: Jack had joined the U.S. Army in 1941, a month before Pearl Harbor, and he had served for a little over four years, most of them in India and the Asiatic Theatre of War. He had been an Army Air Force teletype operator who surpassed 35 words per minute, and had qualified as an expert with the M-1. He'd spent over three years in an exotic war zone, where peril from enemy attack or disease was always present. He was a young man who had defended his country, who had done what was necessary in a time of great crisis. Like many people, he didn't think all that much about it at the time. And like many people, he was wrong—because Jack Watkins was a hero: he gave up more than four years of the most important time of his life, simply because his country needed those years more than he did. Which, when you think about it, is saying a lot, about Jack as well as the country.

In the distance, the armed honor guard stands ready with their Garands, the basic infantry weapon of World War II. Some, perhaps all of them, have been in harm's way—in Iraq or Afghanistan, armed with far more sophisticated weapons. The M-1 for them is an antique—something only for use on ceremonial occasions like this. The idea of fighting a war with such a limited weapon probably seems bizarre to them, but then, they already know more about sacrifice than you or I can tell them. They are heroes, too.

The chaplain reaches the end of his valedictory to Jack's military sacrifice.

"As he honored the flag with his service," the chaplain says, "the flag now honors him." A soldier in a hidden alcove some distance away raises a trumpet to his lips. The haunting strains of Taps wash over the columbarium, then fade away. With that, the flag guard with precision movements re-folds the red-white-and-blue precisely, passes it to the detail's sergeant, who passes it to the chaplain, who kneels and presents it to Cheryl and Anita. Everyone stands up.

Thirty seconds later, a volley of seven shots sounds in the distance. Seven more. Then, seven more.

With that, in the ensuing silence, the flag guard departs, cadenced footsteps marching into the distance—echoing an Army on the march, one of old soldiers, the sound of their rhythmic footfalls fading away, ghost-like. Those who were once here, vital, alive, willing to take on the whole world for what was right and just, are gone. One's hair rises on one's scalp.

Jack is finally back among those who loved him. It was all he ever really wanted.

# ACKNOWLEDGMENTS

It is always difficult to reconstruct many years of different peoples' lives. The paper records can only go so far, even when they haven't been destroyed as an unintended consequence of our society's focus on *now*. In the case of Jack Watkins, though, the effort by the Federal Bureau of Investigation to automate old, historical records of the fingerprints of enlisted men from a very old war was crucial to solving a contemporary crime. This should be a lesson to all of us: we shouldn't be so quick to dismiss the past as irrelevant—one never knows when the old might illuminate the new.

In the preparation of this book, I was very fortunate to have had the counsel and advice of many individuals who knew far more about these matters than I did. Many had spent well over six years of their lives trying to sort out the very complicated factual, legal and psychological issues involved. Their insights, while not always in agreement, were nevertheless vital in reaching some sort understanding of what happened with Nancy Jean Siegel and Jack Watkins.

Foremost among these was Bobbie Ochsman, who had kept Jack Watkins' death photograph on her desk for many years. Investigator Ochsman patiently answered many questions that arose during my attempts to understand what had happened between Nancy Siegel and Jack Watkins. Without her generous assistance, this book could not possibly have been written.

Special thanks is also due to Capital District Information and its affiliates, the representatives of which assisted in collecting many pages of court documents on the case of *United States* vs. *Nancy Jean Siegel*, which provided a foundation for understanding the issues. At the same time, the court clerks of the United States District Court For the District of Maryland, and Howard County Circuit Court, provided invaluable assistance. So too did Mary Zajac, a certified court reporter for the United States District Court, who provided many vital transcripts of various proceedings. U.S. District Court Judge Andre M. Davis also demonstrated a judicious appreciation of the public's right of access to criminal proceedings under the First Amendment. Toni Thompkins of Judge Davis's staff was also very helpful.

Assistant United States Attorney Tamera Fine was of great assistance in explaining some of the more arcane legal points involved in the prosecution of Nancy Siegel, as was defense lawyer Thomas Saunders. Nancy's former defense attorney Robert Feinberg was particularly helpful.

And last but hardly least, were the various family members who later had to pick up the pieces from the tragedy: Cheryl, her sisters Anita and Carol, and on the other side, Larry Kaskel and his wife, Mary Jeanne. Each has their own memories of Jack and Nancy; and each now has the task, probably a life-long endeavor, of trying to understand what, if anything, it really meant, and of trying to make sense of what was essentially senseless.

It's what humans do—at least, those who have consciences. It's what makes us different from any other creature on the face of the earth.

*Selah*.